# THE ORIGIN OF RELIGIONS

## An Open-eyed Journey through a Mystic World

B.K. Karkra

GYAN

The Origin of Religions:
An Open-eyed Journey through a Mystic World



ISBN : 978-81-212-1167-3



First Edition: 2013
1st Reprint: 2013
2nd Reprint: 2014
2nd Edition: 2014 in India by
Gyan Publishing House
23, Main Ansari Road, Daryaganj,
New Delhi - 110002
Phones : 23282060, 23261060
Fax : (011) 23285914
E-mail: books@gyanbooks.com
website: gyanbooks.com

*Laser Type Setting :* Rajender Vashist, Delhi
*Printed at :* Chawla Offset Printers, Delhi

*Dedication*

Dedicated to the memory of my late ancestor, Diwan Munshi Ram, at whose feet I learnt to welcome light, from whatever source it happened to shoot.

# Contents

# Contents

# Preface

As animal, for definite, have no religions and intelligence is the dividing line between man and animal, the religions have clearly risen out of the intelligence of man. They started germinating as soon as the first spark of intelligence got ignited in the human brain. A conscious being is always keen to know about his past and his future. It is thus the curiosity about the Creator and the fear of future that have brought the religions in to being. These are about God alright, but not from God.

The book traces the story of religions from the earliest times. The existential anxieties first kept the man tied to his present for quite a while. As the things started getting somewhat under his control, he began thinking about his future and the next life. This was the stage at which religious ideas started blipping on his mental radar. At first the animal and the elements of nature that overawed him or to whom he felt beholden for meeting his needs, got deified. Then it was the turn of some royalties to be seen in the image of gods— for instance, the Egyptian Pharaohs (rulers) got installed as gods after their death and the Chinese emperors were considered just next to the Spirit of Heavens, their highest deity. The belief in after-life also resulted in development of the art of preservation of mummies. The climatic conditions of Egypt helped in the matter.

Ultimately, around four millennia back, man became conscious that there was some supreme power managing the affairs of the universe from behind the scenes. Thus, the humankind progressed from gods to God. God remains undiscovered and would remain so. However, the concept of God, as we know today, got first mooted by the Jewish Prophet Abraham (AC 1900). He named God as 'El Shaddai'. This got changed to Yahweh during the time of Prophet Moses in around BC 1500. Near about the same time, the Aryans identified Him as 'Om' on the basis of the primordial humming sound that the galaxies produce during their motion at an unimaginably long distance from us. Accordingly, it was the Jews and the Aryans who must be given credit for introducing God to us. Who went past the post first, could be a matter for an interesting research.

Judaism and Hinduism, are, thus, the parent faiths. Two major religions, Christianity and Islam, have their origin in Judaism. These three Semitic religions together command the faith of over half the humanity today. The major off-shoots of Hinduism are the Buddhism, Jainism and Sikhism. Confucianism and Taoism are the indigenous faiths of China and Shinto that of Japan. Interestingly, all these religions are of Asiatic origin. There are numerous smaller religions like Zoroastrianism, Baha'ism and various tribal faiths. Besides, all religions stand divided in to a number of cults.

All these belief systems have been discussed in the book in a brutally objective manner, but with a deeply reverent attitude. There is neither an attempt to flatter nor to malign any faith. After all, behind all the religions stands the faith and wisdom of man. An attempt has been made to get to the inner core of every religion and present what they really stand for in essence. It is true that the religions turn in to business-like ventures in no time. Still they keep on getting periodic course corrections to maintain their majesty. Their sacredness and high station in mind of man can never be denied. Moreover, their 'Sufi' strains greatly help them to stay spiritually relevant.

The negativity about the religions; in the form of close-mindedness, intolerance, a frequent cry for crusade, attempts at conversion through questionable means, woeful attitude towards women and meaningless conflict with science and lure to mix in the mud of politics etc., has also been appropriately touched upon. After all, they are meant to meet the spiritual needs of people and not to bloody the pages of history. In the concluding chapters an attempt has been made to draw a balance-sheet of religions to assess their overall contribution to mankind. An effort has also been made to have a peep into their future.

There is a mountain of literature about the religions already and a lot more is being regularly written. It is impossible to delve into all that has been said about the religions over the ages. However, if we remove repetitions, fuzzy philosophies and excessive fantasising about the cosmos and creation, we shall be left with a manageable mound where man would be seen sitting in class before God to learn how life is to be lived. This book thus presents a sort of macro view of religions. A purely rational view would have blanked out the essential area of faith. I have, therefore, chosen instead to have a realistic look at religions. I think the book would be of interest to the readers who are curious to know how man's mind has worked in this mystic area over the ages.

**B.K. Karkra**

# Acknowledgements

Ever since I started working on this book years back, help has been pouring generously for me to do justice to my work. So deep is my feeling of indebtedness to the institutions and individuals who helped me in my mission that I have more difficulty in choosing my words of gratitude for them than I had in writing this book.

First and foremost, I am grateful to various archival institutions and libraries for allowing me access to the material on their shelves. I particularly thank my niece, Dr. Deepti Loroia whose whole-hearted cooperation and membership of the Panjab University came extremely handy to me.

I landed in the Officers' Messes of the Central Reserve Police Force at Chandigarh and Pinjore in search of solitude to concentrate hard on my work. I feel deeply indebted to the officers there, particularly my erstwhile colleagues, I's. G.P. R.K. Saxena and A.S. Sidhu, who allowed me to spend some time there and thus, helped me greatly in my mission.

My grateful thanks also go to Prof. Rakesh Kumar of the Jawahar Lal Nehru University who took the trouble of explaining some Chinese classical texts to me. I have also gainfully used the inputs received from the discussions with a congregation of some Islamic scholars from Pakistan at Tabouk in Saudi Arabia. They gave me a good glimpse into the core values of Islam. Similarly my interaction with a Christian Bishop in Andhra Pradesh (India) gave me a peep into Christianity and my tenure in Sikkim (India) helped me in understanding Buddhism, as it is practised on the ground. My prolonged stay in N.E.F.A. (now Arunachal Pradesh, India) enabled me to form a view on the belief systems of the tribal in the area.

A lot many inputs that I picked up during my animated discussions on the subject with highly learned people like M/S P.S. Verma, Bijoy Premi, A.K. Bandopadhyay, Harish Sood, Surinder Gosain and others, have also found their way in this work.

In the end, my appreciation and applause also goes to Mr. Muhammad Mahdi Karim, Mr. Nick Leslie (bangers), other copyright holders and the managers of the Wikipedia for their kind permission to use their wonderful photographs for my work.

**B.K. Karkra**

# 1

# Man's Initial Engagement with the Divine

Initial engagement with the Divine began when a brainy creature, called man, evolved. Otherwise, there were no religions when the world was born billions of years back. As animal, for definite, have no religions and the dividing line between man and animal is intelligence, it should be absolutely obvious that all religions have risen out of intelligence. Religions deal with the Divine alright, but these are essentially the product of the thinking faculty of man. The men of faith, however, believe that their religion is the God's message to man and it is something that would smoothen the things for them in their next life. However, all religions, for sure, are only the man's message to man. These, of course, streamed from the minds that had remained deeply engaged with the Divine or the mysteries of life and nature over long periods of time. At some stage in their meditation, they might have also felt themselves to be in communion with God.

In fact, the intellectuals generate ideologies and the masses deify these into religions. The basic fact is that an ordinary man is too innocent to understand the intricacies of the religious philosophies. However, man seems to be born to worship. He is always keen to worship anybody and anything for slightest of reasons that remotely appeal to him. If all of us were equally intelligent, there would be no religions or as many religions as the number of people. It is the common man and his ready willingness to follow the intellectual lead that brings religions in to being and lift these to dizzy heights.

Thus, man's faith itself is something sacred and it deserves to be respected or at least viewed with sensitivity. Besides, there are vast areas beyond our brain. Faith has relevance in these spaces.

Religions should, however, keep vacating the regions that are getting known. For instance, there is no point in holding on now to the earlier formulations like that sun revolves round our earth, that there are habitations on sun and moon and, as Aristotle believed over two millennia back, that male seed causes coagulation of the menstrual blood and it is this coagulum that develops in to an embryo. Human life, coming out of the caves, has already charted its course to the Moon and Mars and it surely would develop reach to many other parts of the cosmos also by and by. Religions would have to realign themselves often with the ever changing realities, as more and more areas of the cosmos are laid bare. Only the God element at their core would stay constant.

We may now proceed to examine how the religious spark got initially ignited in human brain. Genetic studies indicate that humans and chimpanzees have a common ancestry. They split from each other some six million years ago. The genes that separated them permanently hold the key to what really made the animal human. The break between the two is so complete now that there is no doubt whatever who is a Chimpanzee and who is human. Nature, however, is never in a hurry. The evolutionary processes always move at a leisurely pace. The Sub-men, like the Pithecanthropus, thus appeared on earth about half a million years back or somewhat earlier and proper man has been around for some one hundred and sixty thousand years only. We can safely presume that curiosity about the Creator started making inroads into his mind as soon as intelligence sprouted in his brain. It is the relentless search for his roots that has given birth to the religions. Unmistakably, there is some mysterious high urge in man that draws him to his roots and consequently to religions.

Religions certainly predate the recorded history of the world. We have some hazy ideas about the human civilisation that existed some seven thousand years back. In fact, a specimen of the oldest writing known as the Hoffman tablet is preserved in the General Theological Seminary in New York. It is dated to the period around BC 5000. An image of this writing is reproduced below:

Though we do not know much about the pre-historic religions it could still be safely surmised that some sort of theological thought had already germinated in human mind right in the beginning.

However, the existential issues always take precedence over everything else. The first focus of our earliest generations was surely on security and survival, as proper social systems took time to evolve. Manifestly, the primitive man lived on edge in an essentially hostile environment for which he was inadequately equipped. He was then all the time afraid of the beasts with sharp claws and powerful jaws, the reptiles with venomous stings and even his own fellow beings, besides, of course, the forces of nature. The darkness disturbed him. The storms shook him. Today man can dam the rivers, seed the clouds and, to a degree, control the climate and even protect his buildings against earthquakes. He was then totally powerless in face of the fury of nature.

Besides, he had to hunt to take care of his hunger and when unable to lay hands on his prey, he had to sleep on empty stomach. Thus, the primitive religions had something to do with enabling man to deal with the elements of nature, ancestral spirits, wild beasts and the need to hunt for food skillfully and the like. He was to later learn to read these immediate concerns of his in the overall setting of nature. That is when the religious thought entered its next phase.

Some isolated aboriginal communities scattered in various parts of the globe in Australia, America, Andaman, Africa, Japan, Malaysia etc. are still living their lives, more or less, at the Stone Age level. Modernity has just brushed by them. They are where they were millennia back. Centuries have just tiptoed past them unnoticed. They are thus in a position to provide us a glimpse into the distant past. Some western thinkers have therefore considered it worthwhile to supplement their anthropological information by interviewing them about their perceptions and beliefs. The following lines from an Eskimo from the icy Arctic region of the earth in one of such interviews sum up their situation rather lucidly:-

"We fear!

We fear the elements with which we have to fight in their fury to wrest

Our food from land and sea.

We fear cold and famine in our snow huts.

We fear the sickness that is to be daily seen among us.

Not death, but

The suffering.

We fear the souls of the dead, of human and animal alike.

We fear the spirits of earth and air."[1]

This describes the existential setting which the early man found himself in. Faced with the fury of nature he must have often felt something like this:-

"As flies to wanton boys are we to the gods:

They kill us for their sport."

— Shakespeare

Being thus overwhelmingly occupied with his very survival, man did not have much time and inclination to think of the higher things in life. Yet, 'all people are spontaneously religious in crises'. A thought must have thus continually crossed his mind if the various unpredictable forces of nature that troubled him a lot at times could be propitiated in some way and whether there was anybody in control of these elements. Often in his hour of agony and grief, the primitive man must have instinctively raised his hands heavenward hoping for help of the Unknown. Otherwise, he was too deeply engrossed with the chores and anxieties of this very life to think of the next one. Thus, the religions must have been in their very nascent stage at this period of human history.

Once some sort of administrations came in to existence to ensure a semblance of order in societies and man felt somewhat secure both on the life and food front, he started craving for immortality or thinking about the life after the present one. The quest for eternity brought supernatural and metaphysical trends in its wake. This was a big leap forward for religions. Once the idea of after-life entered human mind, the religions that were earlier founded primarily on the fear of elements and animal, got a big booster dose. Man was henceforth to carry the concerns of two lives on his mind instead of one. He was now equally anxious about the life to follow the existing one. Religions reminded him that he was merely a tourist on earth; otherwise his real home was somewhere up in the heavens. They claimed to know about what happened to man after his death. Future is often more important to man than his present and the religions, in a way, implied bartering some of his present for his future. He thus felt irresistibly drawn to religions and was often prepared to make sacrifices for his faith. Interestingly, the worry for the next world, about which nobody has any idea, rules supreme in human psyche.

Belief in after-life is clearly reflected in the manner the dead have been dealt with since the times immemorial. Artifacts and flowers buried in the fifty thousand years old Neanderthal graves (this man existed from around 100000 to 25000 years back) make it evident that idea of continuity of life after death in some form had already homed in the human mind at that early stage and it continues to be safely lodged there. Things considered as basic necessities or ornamental or otherwise dear to the dead continued to be placed by their bodies even after the proper civilisations dawned in some parts of the world many millennia later. The Hindus still hold regular 'sharadh' ceremonies for their deceased ancestors. These are not in the nature of mere remembrance. The ritual is wrapped in the belief that the sumptuous food served and the gifts given to the priests on the occasion would eventually make their way to the departed souls.

The Egyptians believed that an animating soul (Ba), conceived as a human-headed bird, escaped from the body of a dying man with his last breath. However, it always yearned to come back to its former lodging. So, it was necessary to preserve the body for the soul to return to it and also to make available the necessities of life by its side. In fact, a duct was left in the burial cabin for the 'Ba' to make its way to the body. This led to development of skills for mummification of the bodies. The soil and climatic conditions of the land helped in this preservation effort.

In ancient China, the burial chamber of the dead was luxuriously furnished with silks, works of art, precious stones, gold, silver, weapons, armour, musical instruments, vases, mirrors, parasols and fans etc. Sometimes, in case of the deceased emperors and persons of rank, even horses, men and women were entombed alive by their side to serve them in their after-life. In BC 619, 170 persons, including three ministers, followed their dead master, Mu, the ruler of Ts'in, to his grave. However, this happened sporadically and there was no settled custom in this regard.

Side by side, a negative belief also prevailed that the dead would come back to haunt and oppress the living. So, some societies trussed up their dead, bandaged them and buried them under heavy stones so that they did not return in their midst to cause upheavals in their lives. Even in medieval England, the arch-criminals were quartered (cut in to four pieces) after their execution and the pieces were buried in four corners of the city separately. This was done under the fear that if their bodies were left one piece they would be reborn with the traits malignant to the society. The notorious Guy Fawkes who was caught in his attempt to blast the British parliament in session in the early hours of the 5th of November, 1605, was stretched on rack, tortured in variety of other ways, hanged and finally quartered.

The meaning behind such practices can hardly be missed. Obviously, the people close to the buried men believed that the dead would come alive after a period of time and then need what had been placed by their side or offered in their name. A belief had also settled in human mind that the dead had tremendous capacity to obstruct or assist as higher beings. A faith had thus been kindled in human mind that life flowed in an eternal stream and death was really not the end of existence. The concerns of next life made religions all the more relevant for man. After-life now is an essential ingredient of the faiths flourishing around us. In the absence of this belief, common man would lose bulk of his zeal that binds him to his religion. In any case, the mystic content of the religions has always taken precedence over the moral one.

Life was, however, yet lived largely at instinct rather than idea level. The man had no doubt put his thinking cap on as soon as he came into being. That is how some artifacts, implements and weapons began to be developed and some elementary technologies came to be acquired. During the Neolithic period (12000 to 5000 years back) polishing of stone implements, early forms of agriculture, domestication of animals, pottery, plaiting, weaving, building of rudimentary shelters and boats and even some sort of surgeries etc. had come in to vogue. Burial rites had become a little more sophisticated and in some regions cremations also came to be practised. Megalithic monuments like dolmens, menhirs, cromlechs and alignments ( heavy stones arranged in series) like the well known Stone Henge built by them somehow connect with their religion. These were perhaps regarded as the sacred spots for worship and sacrifice. By the way, animal sacrifice has been a time-honoured tradition with most of the religions of the world. The practice has its origin in the fact that the primitive man mainly lived on meat. The idea was to offer meat of the freshly slaughtered animal to please the gods. The sacrifice was often followed by ceremonial feasting by the community. The religious rites for the purpose became increasingly sophisticated with the passage of time.

On occasions, when man escaped death or injury in the face of some starkly imminent danger fortuitously or recovered from an illness unexpectedly or something unthinkable occurred coincidently, he was drawn to the belief in some occult power around him. This way, a plethora of superstitions started entering his mind—many of these still survive despite all the progress man has made over the millennia. Some people of ambition and comparatively higher intelligence who had acquired some knowledge of the processes and the herbs that healed, techniques to tame and render safe the reptiles and also to influence the psyche of their fellowmen, encouraged this trend. They, known in ancient history as medicine-men or magicians, were often able to push their ideas about the supernatural down the credulous throats and never failed to take credit for the things that might have happened just accidently. For instance, if a sick man recovered with the help of his own body resistance rather the charms applied to him, they would attribute it to their own occult powers. They posed as if they were the only ones in communication with the supernatural. Centuries later, this intellectual aristocracy and attempt to tag semi-divinity to humans gave birth to the institution of priesthood.

Thus, many features of religion like recognition of the sacred, mana (belief in the supernatural or occult force), magic/miracles, taboo, purification rites, animism, sacrifice, mystic attitude towards the dead, mythology and totemism (identifying relationships with other orders of being, including inanimate ones) had already started making inroads into human consciousness and behavioural patterns.

Religions, undoubtedly, had taken roots, but there were no meaningful religious philosophies yet. The concept of God was also not clear to the people at the time, though it must have got lodged somewhere in the back of their brain. Man just looked in awe at the elements of nature that made their presence felt to him and governed his life. He was also in awe of the animal that could tear him apart or bite him to death. These elements and animal came to be venerated and were deified in to various gods and goddesses in course of time. The fear and veneration thus turned into worship.

As Petronius rightly wrote in the first century AD, "It is fear that brought gods into the world." These gods obviously feed on faith. In an interview, a Maori tribal put it rather succinctly in the form of conversation among gods as if he had overheard it: "When men no longer believe in us, we (deities) are dead." That really is the truth in essence. This actually applies to all the earth-related Gods also. If something happens to man and the earth where he lives or he otherwise loses his faith, the man-made Gods would cease to exist. Only the One who has made man and all else would always be there. Since we do not know who or what God is, it is impossible to assign Him a correct name. Yet, we have to think of Him as someone or something so as to be able to focus our thoughts on Him. So, the plethora of names that He has got from us does serve a purpose. This enables us to fix our mind on Him. Any particular name given to Him would really be as good as any other. However, this aspect of the matter deserves to be taken up at the concluding stage of our discussion. So, we leave it here for the time being.

Simultaneously, man felt beholden to some animal that catered to his hunger, clothed him and sheltered him (in tents made out of their skins). They also found place in his mind as the venerable beings. Thus, he came to worship anything that frightened or fed him.

The human beings are rather generously equipped in the matter of fecundity. However, high mortality rates then seemed to have ensured that they did not multiply exactly in geometric progression. Man rather remained concerned in the matter of procreation. Goddess of fertility was thus among the first to be invented. Images of the fecund women have represented fertility since Paleolithic times. Venus figurines, with exaggerated bust, belly and buttocks, indicating bountiful fertility, lie buried by the dead in the Neolithic graves. Fertility, of course, was not related to procreation alone; it also meant fertility of soil and abundance of animal for food. Many more gods and goddesses soon started making appearance on earth in human consciousness.

Egyptian civilisation flourished around five millennia back for around three thousand years. Incidentally, the present day inhabitants of the land have nothing much to do with this ancient civilisation that just vanished in thin air, leaving behind the great pyramids and mummies. Their religion was originally animistic. The nomadic tribes of Nile worshipped various local gods in animal form. As they moved to the cities their deities started getting demi-humanised. These often assumed the appearance of hybrid human animals. The typical example of this is the world famous sphinx at Giza, with the head of a pharaoh (Egyptian monarchs of the age) and the body of lion. There is really nothing very unusual about these depictions. Endlessly, fertile human imagination has created many such gods even in the Hindu mythology— just think of Lord Ganesha, Narsimha and Hanuman to name just a few. In fact, Lord Vishnu is believed to have put up as many as nine appearances on this earth— three of these in animal form (as fish, boar and turtle), one in hybrid form (half man and half lion i.e. Narsimha) and he has incarnated himself five times as a human being.

The elements and animal dominated the Egyptian consciousness while devising their deities, the most important among these being Osiris (the king and judge of the dead), his wife, Isis (the most powerful Egyptian goddess) and Re (the sun god). In fact one of the pharaohs assumed the title of the Son of Re. The pharaohs acted as mediators between the mortals and the gods and eventually, on their death, they were themselves deified as gods. Their temples were the preserves of the pharaohs and priests and were not accessible for community worship. The ancient Egyptians wore amulets in the belief that these would provide them protection against evil spirits. They also often kept small charms in the coffins to see the departed souls safely to their new abode in the next world. Recently, a red granite door has been discovered close to the Karnak temple in Luxor that was considered to be the doorway to the next life in ancient Egypt.

The gods started being increasingly depicted in human form as the caravan of our civilisation moved forward. Unlike the Egyptians, the Greco-Roman civilisation that followed presented most of their gods as supernatural human beings. The Greek gods like Zeus (the paramount god), Apollo (son of Zeus and Juno, linked with eternal youth, beauty, music, poetry and fertility), Poseidon (god of sea), Ares (god of war), Nike

Temple at Karnak — The ruins of the ancient temple at Karnak near Luxor in Egypt Attribution: Cornell University Library—Retrieved from the Wikipedia site.

(goddess of victory), Cynthia (goddess of moon) and Aphrodite (goddess of love and beauty), Athena (the patron goddess of Athens) are mostly divinised humans and they have inspired plethora of sculptures, paintings and poetry over the ages. The Romans did not take the trouble of inventing their own gods and readily adopted the Greek gods as their own for the reasons given below:-

> "The Romans believed that every culture worshipped the same gods under different names, so they transferred supreme Greek gods who lived on Mount Olympus to the centre of their own belief system"
>
> — Judith Millege (Sacred Imagery)

They, however, did not fail to rename them to gel well with their own language. Zeus thus became Jupiter; Poseidon was adopted as Neptune, Ares as Mars, Cynthia as Diana, Aphrodite as Venus and so on. The status of the gods besides, of course, the depth of faith in them, depended on the clout that their adherents commanded. Venus was a relatively minor goddess before the great Julius Caesar claimed descent from

Aeneas, the son of Mars and Venus. Similarly, with the Thebes emerging as the Egyptian rulers sometimes around 2000 BC, their local god Amon (fused with the highly revered god, Re, of Egypt) emerged as the national deity, with Mut (the vulture-headed Theve goddess) as his wife and Khonsu (the moon god) as his son.

Now, the gods needed a place to stay and get worshipped. So a number of temples started sprouting where the faiths had taken firm roots and a situation of adequate prosperity prevailed. These shrines are a decent source of historical information for inquiry in to religions. There stood a temple of Enki at Eridu, 14 miles from Ur in Iraq. Its ruins and other evidence suggest that it could be as old as six thousand years. The temples started getting more majestic and gorgeous as the mankind advanced. The Greek temple of the time of King Minos (BC 1700) still exists at Knossos in fair state of preservation. The temples of Apollo at Delphi and that of Athena (built between 447 and 432 BC) at Parthenon in Athens also hold lot of history in their womb. Unlike the Egyptian shrines the Greek temples were open to the common man for community worship.

The Chinese and the Indus Valley Civilisations are nearly contemporaneous to the one in Egypt. It would be interesting to understand how the religions shaped in their part of the world. The Chinese have a long history of monarchical rule running deep in to the third millennium before Christ. There were a number of emperors from BC 2852 to BC 2197, including, the Great Yu. They were followed by the Hsia, Shang and Chou dynasties. What then occupied the mass mindscape in China were the nature and life i.e. the fecundity of earth and blessings of the heavenly forces for happy life. They conceived the cosmos as earth (Yin) with a canopy of heaven (yang) on top, with numerous natural elements operating in between. They tried to understand the interplay of these elements with the fortunes of man. This led first to 'The Five Elements Theory' in the reign of Emperor Yu around BC 2200 and then the 'Yin-Yang' thesis a little later.

The first of these doctrines had a rural setting. The five elements finding mention in it were wood, water, fire, metal and earth. All these materials were of direct relevance to the predominantly agrarian society. It was believed that there was a pattern to these and each one of these elements had ascendency during different seasons. The understanding of this arrangement could lead to good crops and prosperity. Similarly, Yang (standing for male or father) and Yin (conceived as female or mother) had a deep bearing on the fortunes of people. Their fusing or coming together accounted for procreation, production and many other things like water, wood, wind, thunder, mountains, marshes and all things in nature. Lot many divinations were thus woven around these formulations. These theories, whatever their worth, were possibly well- understood by the intellectuals of the period, but had to wait for around a millennium and a half to get properly explained and elaborated in writing.

What other religious beliefs and practices were followed during those times is not clear. However, the Chinese never believed in idols, gods and temples till Buddhism arrived in the land for permanent settlement around two thousand years back. This is a unique phenomenon of the religious history of the world. The Far-east is perhaps the only region free from prophetic proclamations and revelatory claims. The Chinese, rather than delving into the mysteries of the Divine have concentrated instead on the philosophies and precepts of life. Their emphasis has been on living this very life well.

The Indus Valley civilisation that was predominantly urban in its content and character is believed to have dawned some times during 3250 to 2750 BC. It was centered round Harappa in Punjab and Mohenjo-Daro in Sindh. It flourished in full glory for about a millennium and a half and then vanished with the arrival of the Aryans. Its astonishingly well-planned cities and towns remained buried under silt with their seals, pottery, copper tablets, bangles and history for over three millennia. Bulk of the credit for bringing this epoch of the Asian sub-continental history to light goes to R.D. Banerji who discovered its ruins in AD 1922 and Sir John Marshall who followed up the great discovery. It has not been possible to decipher the pictographic script of the period. Still, the artifacts unearthed from its mounds tell us a good part of its story.

The population of the region had many strains of ethnicity. Discovery of objects like seal amulets and talisman of stone and pottery make it quite clear that the people of the time believed in superstitions. Most often they cremated their dead. However, burials also took place occasionally. With more excavations newer facts are progressively coming to light.

Though the documentary evidence relating to its religious beliefs and practices is lacking there are reasons to believe that the religious thought had developed to a fair degree of sophistication in the period. One stone image recovered from the site is clothed in a robe carried over left shoulder and under right arm. It bears a trefoil pattern, obviously a sacred symbol. Its half shut eyes are suggestive of its yogic posture. Several pottery figurines indicate towards worship of female deities and some stone objects speak of phallic veneration. Quite a few Clay figurines wearing horn point to the practice of animal worship. Some deities standing in 'koyotasarga' posture would remind one of Jain yogis. A bronze figure of a dancing girl is suggestive of ritual dancing.

The available evidence indicates that many features of the modern Indian cult may have been derived from the belief contours of this period. The Indus valley religions could well be the forerunners of Shaivism and Jainism in our country. John B. Noss has expressed similar views in the passage reproduced below from his book, Man's Religions:-

> "—— on the Indus before 2500 BC, a people of mixed origin and diverse ethnic composition combined to produce a bronze age civilisation with a well-developed art and architecture (brought to light by excavations at Harappa in Punjab and Mohenjo-Daro in Sind), probably an equally advanced religion, containing at least in germ the ideas now in the Hindu doctrine of the law of Karma and the transmigration of souls. Unfortunately, no writings have come down from this civilisation and we are still much in ignorance."[2]

There is a clear indication in the following conversation excerpted from the Rig Veda (Dasham Mandlam, Sukta-108) that the Aryans settlements to the south-east of Hindukush soon came in clash with the Indus Valley people who have been referred to here as Panees (Words 'Pania' and later 'Bania' related to the trading communities of North India seem to have been derived from this very word):

इमा गाव: सरमे या ऐच्छ: परि दिवो अन्तान् सुभगे पतन्ती।
कस्त एना अब सृजादयुध्वयुतास्माकमायुधा सन्ति तिग्मा।५।५
असेन्या व: पणयो वचांस्यनिषव्यास्तन्व: सन्तु पापी:।
अधृष्टो व एतवा अस्तु पन्था बृहस्पतिर्व उभया न मृलात्।६

"O' Sarma (the Aryan ambassador), you have come all the way from the Aryan borders. On this consideration, you can point out to us some of our cows that you are interested in. We shall hand over these to you peacefully. Otherwise who agrees to part with such wealth without war? (Cows, incidentally, were considered to be the primary wealth of the people in those times and most of the wars were fought over their possession. In fact, till around half a century back most of the tribal transactions in our Arunachal Pradesh were also carried out in terms of 'mithuns', a sort of flat-faced cow.) — Shloka-5.

"O' Panees, You are devoid of any strength worth being reckoned by the brave. You carry sin within. You better be careful that your bodies may not get pierced by Indra`s arrows. If you do not part with your cows you would have to face an Aryan attack and get in to trouble at the hands of Brihaspati. — Shloka-6.

अयं निधि: सरमे अद्रिवुघ्नो गाभिरश्वेभिवंसुभिन्यृंष्ट:।
रक्षन्ति तं पणयो ये सुगोपा रेकु पदमलकमा जगन्ध।७

"O' Sarma, we are surrounded by mountains that secure us. We abound in horses, cows and other wealth. Our brave soldiers are quite capable of defending our land. Your adventure into our cow-rich land is not going to serve much purpose." —Saloka-5

एह गमन्नृषय: सोमशिता अयास्यो अङ्गिरसो नवग्वा:।
त एतमुर्वं भजन्त गोनामथैतद्वच: पणयो वमन्नित।८

"O' Panees, our great leaders like Angras would descend on you after invigorating themselves with Som Rasa and carry away all your cows. You would then find your ego totally crushed." — Shloka-8.

एवा च त्वं सरम आजगन्थ प्रवाधिता सहसा दैव्येन।
स्वसारं त्वा कृणवै मा पुनर्गा अप ते गवां सुभगे भजाम।९

"O' Sarma, You have been sent here by your fear-stricken people. At personal level, we take you as our sister and are prepared to offer you a part of our wealth i.e. some cows. After this you may like to settle among us and drop the idea of going back to your people." —— Shloka-9.

नाहं वेद भ्रातृत्वं नो स्वसृत्वमिन्द्रो विदुरङ्गिरसश्च घोरा:।
गोकामा मे अच्छदयन् यदायमपात इत पणयो वरीय:।१०

"O' Panees. I am not interested in this brother-sister contrivance. I have been sent here fully protected by Indra and Angras with the object of taking possession of your cows. I, therefore, suggest that you better vacate this land and find shelter somewhere far away from here." — Shloka-10.

The Indus people appear to be negotiating here from a much weaker position. It is obvious that the Aryans had the better of the exchanges with them. They may, in fact, be one of the causes of the eclipse of this glorious civilisation. Possibly, the Panees merged with the Aryans to eventually form the backbone of their mercantile class.

Babylon is another area that has been intellectually active in the distant past. Many of the Biblical episodes like, the Great Deluge and the mythological account of the early life of Moses, in all probability, are of Babylonian origin.

Thus the primitive phase of the human understanding was coming to a close. An effort had been initiated to lift the veil of nature to see if some hidden hands were at work there.

It was becoming increasingly clear to man that some power was managing the things from behind the scenes. Thus, the human faith took a critical step forward— from gods to God.

## Notes

1. 'Primitive Religion— Its nature and origin' by Paul Radin, Dover Publications Inc., New York, 1957, pp. 54-55. Permission obtained from the publishers to use this quotation vide their letter dated May 5, 2011.)
2. Man's History by John B. Noss, McMillan Company, New York, p. 114)

# 2

# From gods to God

God, as one perceives, is the soul of nature. It is easier to understand body than the soul. Man's attention, therefore, went first to what was immediately evident before him. Thus, the gods that reflect various forces and creatures of nature came first — well before God came to be formally mentioned. However, it could be presumed without running much risk of going wrong that the curiosity about his Creator must have entered the mind of man as soon as he rose above the instinct level and acquired some capacity to think. After all, there is an instinctive urge in man to know about his origin. Spirituality flows when a man's mind tries to understand the reality of the divine creation. It is nothing but the human intellect in relentless search of his roots. This overpowering impulse has, in fact, been the theme round which numerous fictions have been written and many feature films shot all over the world. We often come across the scripts in which a character shown in ignorance about the identity of his father strives like a man possessed to solve the riddle. Nobody would really like to remain rootless. Even 'etymologically, the word religion means that which binds one to the origin'.

However, this incipient urge could not find an outlet because of the primitive man's existential anxieties related to security of life and food. Even when these concerns got addressed to a fair degree, he was still in awe of the forces of nature which could upturn his apple cart at will. His attention therefore first went to the elements of immediate concern around him rather than to the power behind the scene. Such forces were duly deified in the course of time with the purpose of placating these to keep these in good humour and seeking their favour. As the thinking capacity of man got augmented with the passage of time he began going to the bottom of things. He felt that the elements of nature might not be operating by the will of their own. Some hidden hands might be pulling strings from behind the scenes. They might be following some dictates unnoticed by man and there could be a Divine control-room of sort to manage the universal affairs. He was thus now on the lookout of the supreme commanding authority of the universe. He began being increasingly aware about the four dimensions of divinity—time, space, matter and energy. A single word for these could be— 'Boundlessness'. The gods created by man still survive. But, with the awareness about the Supreme Being, their importance has diminished and they have been reduced to the status of the divine agents. Thus the mankind has decisively moved from gods to God.

God surely is still undiscovered and shall remain so, in the sense that man would never exactly know who or what He is, where He resides and how He operates. He shall thus have to be content with the philosophical descriptions of Him like that He is omnipresent, omniscient and omnipotent. Nevertheless, the credit for marking His presence or discovering Him in the form of a concept goes to Judaism and Hinduism. Between the two, we do not precisely know who went past the divine post first. Possibly, the Hebrew God, Yahweh and the Aryan God, 'Om' (believed to be based on the primordial sound of the cosmos on move) or 'the Unknown One', were born in man's consciousness more or less around the same time. However, the Jews thought of Yahweh as a sort of regional God with whom they had a private convent. If they worshipped Him and obeyed His commandments, He would keep them out of the harm's way at the hands of the other communities. The early Hindus, on the other hand, always visualised Him as the universal God who belonged to everybody in equal measure. God was, thus, already well-entrenched in human psyche when the other major religions appeared in the world millennia afterwards. So, they cannot be credited with His discovery in any way. They certainly built their edifice of belief on the foundation laid centuries earlier.

Jews have a heritage of nearly four thousand years behind them. They are, however, the singularly unlucky people of the world. Throughout their history they have lived on edge in hostile environs. There is, in fact, no end to their agony even today. They have been persecuted to the extreme by the Egyptians, the Romans, the Germans and many others during at least the last three millennia— just imagine, six million Jews, almost equivalent of the entire population of Israel, being exterminated in the German gas chambers during the Second World War. They have borne their destiny with an unparalleled degree of fortitude. All this happened because they could never bring themselves round to amalgamate their identity with the more powerful majority groupings that developed in their neighbourhood from time to time. They have really paid a heavy price for their exclusiveness.

Their prophets and ideologies have been accepted and adopted by the two biggest religions of the world. Yet they themselves remain in wilderness, engulfed in hate and hostility. They have, ındeed, been the thinking people. It has been aptly said about India that she let the legions thunder past and plunged in thought again. This observation seems to apply equally well to the Jews also.

At long last, with the courtesy of the western powers, they have got a land that they can call their own and to which they have been historically connected. Unfortunately, this has proved to be a case of a country being vacated of a nation to accommodate another. This situation naturally contains all the seeds of conflict right within itself. The dispossessed Palestinians cannot be expected to reconcile to it. Israel thus finds itself living dangerously yet again in a most unfriendly neighbourhood. Jews can hope to survive there only till they are able to hold their own militarily. One problem with them is that they are too few in numbers and the territory that they hold is too small. The only depth they have is the Mediterranean Sea to their west. This is where they might end up, if and when they suffer defeat.

They admittedly hold copy right over the original phase of all the Semitic religions. Yet, not having been very adept at mergers and acquisitions all through their long history, they have remained a miniscule minority. Being bright and wonderful people of history they deserve to live in peace in their homeland, along with the uprooted Palestinians and other Arabic nations on their periphery. Despite being small in number and widely dispersed they have nonetheless always counted wherever they happened to be.

Originally, they were the Semites who wandered about the northern fringes of the Arabian Desert for centuries, camping in their camel and goat skin tents that they pitched close to the ground. They were divided in to tribes that remained in friendly huddle among themselves, but always fearful of the surrounding world. At this stage in their history they believed in dynamism and animism. They saw life in stones, streams, springs and trees etc and revered the wild beasts out of fear like any other primitive people.

While being constantly buffeted around in the general area to the west of the Mediterranean Sea from Iraq to Egypt, Abraham appeared in their midst some times in the nineteenth century BC. He, in course of time, introduced to his people what he called 'El-Shaddai' ('El' meaning a superhuman being and 'shaddai' standing for mountains). The name was possibly picked up from among the family gods. Abraham raised him to the position of the chief god and placed all his faith in him. This way, El-Shaddai emerged as a sort of prototype of the Hebrew God, Yahweh and Abraham wrote himself into the Semitic history as a highly revered prophet of God. On his death, the tribal leadership passed on to his son, Isaac and then to his grandson, Jacob.

A terrible famine is believed to have forced the descendents of Abraham to move south towards Egypt. They were, however, overtaken by a wave of Aryan immigrants from the north who captured the fertile lands of the Nile delta and settled down as the masters of the land. They were known to the ancient Egyptians as Hyksos (standing for the pastoral princes). The Jews were able to follow them to Egypt and make peace with them. They were taken in their service as officials and the things remained quiet for about two and a half centuries. The local Egyptians were thereafter able to overthrow the Hyksos rule and force them out of their land in later part of the sixteenth century BC. The Jews were, however, allowed to live there in peace for another century and a half.

A catastrophe befell them then. They were not unused to such misfortunes, but this one was really serious. Ramses II, the maverick pharaoh (ruler) of the land got a brain wave to go in for massive construction activity in his domains, for which he needed a huge labour force. He set his eyes on the Hebrew habitations in the northeastern part of his kingdom. The helpless Jews were, thus, ruthlessly rounded up for bonded labour. For considerable period of time they had to do back-breaking hard work with only the lashings for reward. Finally they were delivered of this plight by a messiah from the north who led them in an exodus to Sinai. This man, Moses, now holds a highly revered position among the Semitic prophets. The Egyptian army was either too late in the coming or was by then rendered too weak to interdict them in this great escape out of slavery.

Moses is a central figure in Semitic consciousness not only for relieving his race of the Egyptian tyranny but also introducing them to their God, Yahweh who was to eventually settle down in their psyche as the Creator of the universe and as a sacred symbol of righteousness and fair play. The monotheistic process initiated centuries back by Abraham was thus destined to reach its culmination through the medium of Moses. Let us go through the event in the words of Old Testament:-

> "God spoke to Moses and said to him, 'I am the Lord. I appeared to Abraham, Isaac and Jacob as El Shaddai, but I did not make myself known to them by my name. I also established my covenant with them, to give them the land of Canaan (Palestine), in which they lived as sojourn. I have now heard the moaning of the Israelites because the Egyptians are holding them in bondage, and I have remembered My covenant. Say, therefore, to the Israelite people: I am the Lord. I will free you from the labours of the Egyptians and deliver you from their bondage. I will redeem you with an outstretched arm and through extraordinary chastisements. And I will take you as my people, and I will be your God. And you shall know that I, the Lord, am your God who freed you from the labours of the Egyptians. I will

> bring you to the land which I swore to give to Abraham, Isaac and Jacob and I will give it to you for a possession, I the Lord."[1]
>
> (Exodus- 6:2 to 8)

It was, however, only the beginning. It took a few more centuries for Yahweh to establish Himself as the undisputed Jewish God in the Hebrew consciousness.

As per the Hebrew belief, Moses was born during the regime of an Egyptian pharaoh who thought that the Jews were getting too many in number and could pose a threat to the security of his kingdom in the foreseeable future. He, therefore, decreed that all male babies born to the Jews should be thrown in the Nile. Moses, however, escaped this fate due to the efforts of his mother and a pharaoh's daughter. He, in fact, gets his name from the fact that he was 'drawn out' of the Nile.

When he grew up in to a strapping young man, he was adopted as son by the Pharaoh's daughter. However, he once happened to kill an Egyptian who he found committing atrocity on a Hebrew. When this incident looked like leaking to the state authorities, Moses escaped to Median in the east to avoid the penal consequences of the homicide at his hands. In course of time, he settled down there as son-in-law of a Median priest. The faithful believe that it was here that he had an encounter with God who appeared to him as a flaming ball of fire and commanded him to go and deliver the Israelites held in bondage in Egypt. While accepting in all deference this divine duty entrusted to him Moses enquired of God as to by what name he should refer Him to his people. The reply given by God as below is of high significance:-

> "I am who I am —— Thus you shall say to the Israelites: 'Yahweh—— has sent me to you'."[2]

This conversation, of course, echoes the views of some knowledgeable man of the Mosaic era that could be placed around BC 3500. God appearing as a smoking ball of fire (rather than having any recognizable features) and refusing to give a direct answer to the query of Moses about His name makes it evident that He did not quite like the idea of getting identified by man. He wished to remain undiscovered for all time to come. We shall later see that Rig Veda of the Aryans (X-129-5 to 7) conceived around the same period of human history echoes more or less an identical view about the Divine Being. Incidentally, it is interesting to note that, as per the Western view, one branch of the Aryans in their exodus from the central Asian regions was moving about in this very area at the time.

The Hebrew escapees from Egypt finally congregated near the foot of the Horeb or Sinai Mountain. Moses was summoned atop by Yahweh and commanded to bring two stone slabs along. Tradition says that God inscribed the historic Ten Commandments on these slabs with His finger. These were to stand as an eternal covenant between Yahweh and his people. Moses read these out to his men collected at the base of the mountain and they solemnly agreed to abide by these. These now form part of 'Torah', the sacred law of Judaism. Many more such stipulations got added as time passed. The first five books of the Bible (Old Testament) mention about 613 clauses central to the Jewish life. The following observations of John B. Noss constitute quite an incisive account of their faith:-

> "The ancient Hebrews and their descendents have grown morally and religiously after the fashion of their own, and yet their experience has a universal value and pertinence. —— One great theme dominates the course of Jewish religion; this is the theme that a single righteous God is at work in the social and natural order."[3]

With this, the Jews began switching over from a primitive religion involving a plethora of weird practices, gods and amulets to monotheism that gradually emerged as the core ingredient of their faith. Some other religions were to follow in their footsteps centuries later, of course, with Gods of their own or rather with their own names for God. This revolutionary shift led to the usual resistance in the form of apostasies to begin with, then to refinement of the rituals and reforms in the Israelite religious order. We shall be going into all this in a separate chapter on Judaism. What deserves to be taken note at this stage is that man had by now developed some awareness about the Divine Power that governed the universe on the quiet unseen by anybody.

Around BC 2000 or a little earlier, people now known as Indo-Aryans, began pouring down the slopes of the Hindu-Kush range of mountains in droves from the regions to its north. The Indian peninsula was then largely inhabited by the Dravidians. To the west, right up to Punjab and Saurashtra, were settled the Indus valley people. The mountainous regions to the north and north-east were occupied by the Mongoloid tribes. The migrants first came in clash with the Indus Valley inhabitants who lived in urban conglomerations and were primarily engaged in trade with the coastal states right up to Mesopotamia. There is a hint in the Vedic literature that they had the better of exchanges in these skirmishes. In any case, it is a fact of history that the Indus valley civilisation finally vanished (and it took three millennia to recover some of its traces) while the Aryans were eventually able to extend their sway over the entire subcontinent and even beyond. The Indus valley survivors seem to have completely merged their identity with the Aryans.

However, some overzealous Indian scholars dispute this Western view and insist that the Aryans were the original inhabitants of the land. The question that arises here is that if they were not the migrants who exactly they were— the Dravidians, the multi-ethnic Indus valley inhabitants or the Mongoloid tribal. A good idea about them could be had from their Vedic literature. They were certainly semi-nomadic pastoral people, ever on the lookout for pastures for their herds of cows, goats, sheep, asses and horses etc. It took them considerable time to settle down to an agrarian way of life. As against this, the Indus valley civilisation had a well advanced urban ambiance about it. The Indus inhabitants were certainly different people with a different script that has not been deciphered yet. Similarly the light-coloured and sharp featured Aryans could not be Dravidians or Mongoloids either. When the Iranians and even Europeans themselves— the British, French, German and others — have no hesitation in admitting that they are the descendents of these very migrants from somewhere in central Asia why should the Indians shy away from this fact of history? After all, this did not happen yesterday. They have been here in the subcontinent for at least the last four thousand years and they have among them people with more than five millennia old history. Then, the bloods have been mixing since the times immemorial— rather, how much time does it really take for bloods to mix? The Aryan majority of India need not feel in any sort of discomfort at the fact that they were outsiders in the land in so distant a past. That way, the original inhabitants of the earth are really the amoebae.

Not much is known about the religious beliefs of the Dravidians and the Indus people in the absence of historical records of the pre-Aryan period. Aryans, however, are credited with Rig Veda, the oldest book of the world, composed around BC 1500 or earlier and reduced to writing in the eighth century BC or a little later. The Vedic literature does not mention about any local or tribal gods of the Aryans. If ever they had any such deities they had left these behind before migration. It would, however, be safer to assume that they thought that the natural gods that they worshipped were the gods of all regions. Similarly they thought that one God was everybody's God.

They, like the people everywhere on earth at that point of time, were both in awe and beholden to the elements of nature. They thus worshipped many natural gods like Indra, Varuna, Mitra, Rudra, Agni, Pushan, Vayu, Marut and goddesses like Sarasvati, Usha, Vac and consorts of various gods. They wanted to keep them pleased through praise, prayer and offerings so as to keep themselves out of the harm's way and also to express their gratefulness to them for meeting their multifarious needs of life.

What deserves to be noted here is that these gods were worshiped as a sort of the divine agencies and not God. No god among them was treated as the head god like the Greco-Roman god Zeus/Jupiter. There was even no concept of any god being the first among the equals. They had to take their patient turn in the Aryan worship. When one was propitiated, the others were just forgotten. Rig Veda consists of some one thousand hymns. The largest number of these is dedicated to the rain-god 'Indra' and over two hundred to the fire-god 'Agni'.

The Aryans believed that the hidden hands of the Divine Being worked through these gods for delivering prosperity and justice. This deification of elements cannot be taken to mean that these people did not believe in the oneness of God. They, along with the Hebrews, were the first to introduce the concept of God to the world. The Aryans are after all credited with the first book of the world, Rig Veda, which is highly regarded even today. This is what Prof. Max Muller writes about the Vedas:-

> "— And if I were to ask myself from what literature we, in Europe, we who have been nurtured almost exclusively on the thoughts of Greeks and Romans, and one Semitic race, the Jews, may draw that corrective which is most wanted to make our inner life, more perfect, more comprehensive, more universal, in fact more human a life, not for this life only, but a transfigured and eternal life— again I should point to India."[4]

It is little knon fact that Thomas Alva Edison invited the great Snskrit scholar of Germany, to record the first human message on his invention, the grammophone formally. The message that deservedly went on record was the first verse of Rig Veda, 'Agnee meele puruhitam'. Max Muller explained its importance in the following words:

> "In the most primordial times, when the people did not know even to cover their bodiews and lived by hunting and housed in caves, Indians had attained high civilisation and they gave the world universal philosophies in the form of Vedas.

Quite a few verses of the Rig Veda and Atharva Veda point to the unity of godhead. Just think of the 'Gayatri Mantra' from the Vedic literature that refers to God as the lord of all terrestrial, atmospheric and celestial regions of the universe. If still there are some lingering doubts on this count, one may call to mind the following hymn from the Rig Veda (X-129-6 and 7) that relates to the cosmogony of our universe:

को अद्धा वेद क इह प्र वोचत् कुत आजाता कुत इयं विसृष्टि:
अर्वाग्देवा अस्य विसर्जनेनाऽथा को वेद यत् आबभूव ।६

(Nobody really has any idea how the universe came in to being. How can then anybody be expected to explain its origin? Even the gods appeared on the scene after the universe had already been created. Who could then know where all this creation came from and what was the purpose behind this enterprise? (Shloka-6)

इयं विसृष्टिर्यत आबभूव यदि वा दधे यदि वा न।
यो अस्याध्यक्षः परमे व्योमन् त्सो अङ्ग वेद यदि वा न वेद।७।१७

(Who created this universe and in what way this was done is beyond human comprehension. The lord of the universe resides at some supernatural spot unknown to the mortals. He is the only One who can unfold this Divine mystery. There is, however, no way of knowing whether even He has the knowledge of this divine creation. (Shloka-7)

The western view about these verses is that the Aryan thinkers of the period were a little confused over the issue related to the cosmogony of the universe and its Creator. Just let us have a look at the following passage by George Foot Moore:-

"—— the poets and thinkers of the period are struggling to express mythologically, theologically, or metaphysically, after their ability, the idea that at the origin of all things, before heaven, air and earth, above the whole pantheon of the natural deities, there is one ground of being—one god, some would say, and call him creator; to others it is the nameless one. The antecedents of monotheism, pantheism, monism lie crossed and tangled in these early ventures at the riddle of the universe."[5]

This writer seems unable to come to terms with the last line of the 7th Shloka (verse) that says that even God may not know how and why the universe was created. Everything would fall in place if it is appreciated that we really have no way of knowing what God knows and what He does not. In fact, those who say that they know little about Him are the most knowledgeable.

It has, however, been made clear that if anybody has any knowledge of the origin of the universe, it could be none other than He. It is also not very difficult to imagine that there could be a time when all that we see today was not there. Even the Bible (the Old Testament) in its opening chapter of the Book of Genesis talks about nothingness, void and silence pervading the celestial space before the Creation. There is, therefore, an astonishing amount of depth in these Vedic verses conceived so far back in time. We have at least to acknowledge that this was said at least three millennia back when the human understanding of the universe and nature was so very little. Consider it in the light of the modern thinking as expressed below; the greatness of what was said millennia earlier would become self-evident:-

> "All of human intelligence and wisdom - from Aristotle to Aryabhata to the Vedas and Einstein – do not have an answer; however, to the third key question that has divided sages and philosophers over the centuries: why does the universe exist at all? As even scientists concede wryly, God alone knows."[6]

These are perhaps the first words of man about his God. Rig Veda was conceived near about the time of Abraham and reduced to writing around the Age of the Old Testament. This antiquity lends added significance, greatness and worth to what is disclosed in these words. These nearly three and a half millennia old findings of man should rather leave us wondering how he had reached these conclusions so early in human evolution. What these two couplets reveal is the following:-

(a) The clear concept of God had entered the human mind at least three and a half thousand years back.

(b) Who or what God is, where He resided and how He functioned was not known to man then. In fact, He continues to remain a nameless eternal even today.

(c) Various gods came in to existence after the universe had already come in to being.

(d) God is not a being of history— He is beyond all history and geography.

(e) Man had come to the correct conclusion at that early age that somebody was surely in control of the elements of nature.

(f) All the Gods that we know of are the man-made Gods. Nobody has any idea about the One who has created man and all else.

The idea of God had been blipping around on the mental radar of man as soon as he got blessed with intelligence. By around 2000 BC this idea had crystallised into reality and acquired a ring of surety around it. Man was hence forth to make a relentless effort to uncover the divine reality.

## Notes

1. It has also been mooted that the idea of monotheism was introduced in the Land of Nile by an Egyptian pharaoh, Akhenaten, the husband of the legendary queen, Nefertiti. It appears that Moses was one of his courtiers and they seem to have worked out the idea jointly. — devdutt.com.
2. 'Man's Religions' by John B. Noss, p. 471.
3. 'Man's Religions' by John B Noss, p. 463.
4. 'Glimpses of the Vedas' by Prof. Satyavrata Sidhanalankar—Millind Publications Private Ltd., New Delhi, 1980, p. 2)
5. 'History of Religions' by George Foot Moore, p. 271.
6. Minhaz Merchant in his article 'The Intelligent Universe'—*The Times of India*, 20.8.2010.

# 3

# The Areas Beyond Brain

Broadly speaking, if the second millennium B.C. was the era of celestial curiosity, the first was the age of quest for the Divine reality. Some vague concept of the Creator had already slipped into human consciousness with the advent of intelligence. However, it took considerable time to crystallize in to a tangible form and philosophy. Fantasies about Him were already there, the philosophies also now started making appearance in India, China, and Greece and of course, the Middle East. These philosophers saw a spirit clearly manifest in the laws of the universe. Man thus started becoming clearer and more coherent about the presence of God with the passing centuries.

He earlier thought that various elements of nature were just the instruments of awe about which nothing could be done, except possibly their propitiation. Once he was finally convinced that there was some controlling spirit behind these forces of nature, he began making relentless effort to get to it. He now sincerely wanted to search God out or at least have direct knowledge of Him. Thus, an over-powering urge developed to unveil the divine mystery. The quest became a sort of 'holy grail' with the humanity. So much so that some people started renouncing the world and making their way to the solitude of forests to be able to think really hard, as to who or what this Phenomenon could be and from where and how He managed the affairs of the universe. There is a large cosmic area that is clearly beyond the reach of our brain and God belongs to this domain. This is what man was to realize in course of time. We shall see that from then onwards he dropped the idea of demystifying divinity and turned his attention instead to unfold the mysteries of life and nature.

Among seekers of the cosmic truth, Prince Siddharth was the one who tried the hardest. He withdrew from the society of his young wife at the prime of his youth, tore himself away from his infant son and renounced all princely comforts to go in quest of the Divine and understand what really ailed the human kind. So great was the intensity of his search and so rigorous the regimen of his meditation that it reduced him nearly to a skeleton. Ultimately, he came to the conclusion that all this was not going to work and this sort of self persecution was not exactly the way to God and enlightenment. The scheme of nature was such that no mortal would ever be allowed a peep into the Divine portals. Nonetheless, the humankind is still not ready to spare any ordeal in its eternal quest to access divinity.

What needs to be noted at this stage is that even Buddha, after all his superhuman effort, failed to unravel the mystery that man has been after for so many millennia. He just ended up philosophising about life. Similarly Prophet Mohammed spent considerable time in deep meditation before he came up with, what his faithful believe to be the revelations from Allah. The Prophet, however, also chose not to tell us who or what Allah is. Even Emperor Akbar had considerable curiosity in the matters metaphysical and was often seen sitting alone for hours thinking about God and His creation. In fact, he formally ushered his own brand of religion, Deen-e-Ilahi. The new faith, however, could not take roots because, the land where and the time when, this was done, was intellectually too advanced to entertain his creed. Akbar, despite all his statesmanship and political acumen, could not project himself as a prophet. Rather a commoner of the period, Guru Nanak, was able to establish his spiritual credentials much more effectively and finally emerge as the founder of a new creed, Sikhism. The difference between the two can be easily understood. Akbar was only semi-spiritual (otherwise, he had hundreds of women in his harem) whereas Nanak was totally devoted to the Divine.

Before and after them many other mortals also went in meditation in the like manner to explore the supernatural phenomena of the creation. In fact, there was a time when quite a few men in the Indian sub-continent routinely renounced the world after they were over with the domestic phase of their life to go in for search of the mystic aspects of the cosmos. Those breaking with the world in this manner are now legally known as the civil death cases. They are thus deemed to be the breathing dead. Despite, however, putting their being in this unworldly state they could never get anywhere near the hidden hands that govern the universe and keep it going in an orderly routine. God thus remains undiscovered, all claims of man about the knowledge of the cosmic constellations, gravitation, divination, placement of zodiac signs, astrology, gemology, numerology, vastu and palmistry etc. notwithstanding. Belief in such assertions is, in fact, reflective of a common man's inborn weakness to allow himself to get easily influenced by superior intellects. This leads to a sort of herd mentality in him and his eventual exploitation. Otherwise, nobody can really understand the ways of God— not even the best of brains. Man could not even be sure whether God lived within him or he himself lived within God.

Faced with this scenario and having failed to find God, the thinkers lowered their lofty aims, returned to realism, cut back on their targets and diverted their effort instead to what was actually knowable i.e. the nature and life which after all at least bear His signatures. Understanding these could, in some way, take us closer to Him. Nature is an infinitely vast canvas and life also has numerous dimensions to it. These, thus, provide abundant scope for our intelligence to exercise itself. Two tools are available to man for the purpose— philosophy and fantasy. All this resulted in attempts to philosophize and fantasize about Him and His creation.

We come to the philosophy part of it first. The first thing to be understood was who possibly He could be and how to define Him. He happens to be too boundless a phenomenon to be anywhere within the grasp of our words. Our philosophers therefore continue to struggle with the lines which might give us some idea who or what this Creator and Sustainer is. Closest the human mind has come to in its attempt to catch on Him is that He is someone Omnipresent (all pervasive), Omniscient (having knowledge of everything) and Omnipotent (all powerful). Incidentally, this points towards His oneness also.

This, however, by no means is the all that is there to God. The definition does not even take care of the Hebrew doctrine of the basic demand of Yahweh (God) for justice, equity, righteousness and morality in the social order. Jesus Christ is believed to have spoken of God as "the sovereign moral personality ruling the universe, the moving spirit behind the course of history, a transcendent being, sternly righteous, who never departed from perfect justice in determining the course of events or the destiny of an individual. But God was also forgiving and merciful, primarily occupied with human redemption, in character and action paternal."[1]

Jesus was born a Jew and his description of God has a Jewish tinge about it. Many more things have also been mooted in elaboration of these descriptions of the Divine. We may perhaps sum up all this with the observation that quite a lot has already been said about Him and still, an infinite more remains to be said. Similarly, despite the plethora of functional names given to Him by man (a thousand as per the Hindu understanding alone) He still remains a Nameless One, as nobody really knows what his actual name is. We could be sure that the situation would stay so in perpetuity. In fact, various names of God, gods, elements, animal and objects are based on the phonetic sounds that caught our imagination or the languages that evolved in various regions of the world in course of time.

The cosmic philosophy seems to have touched its zenith in the Upanishad period in the Indian sub-continent. Just sample this:-

> "Many of the Upanishads insist that, contrary to the naïve popular belief in the absolute individuality of the human soul, there is actual identity between 'Brahmn' (the Divine) and the 'atman' (soul)— and this is true of any and every form of 'atman' whether it is found in man, beast, insect, flower, fish, or any other living thing.

"Yajnavalkya", cries an eager inquirer in the 'Brhadaranyaka' (one of the most important Upanishads), "explain to me who is the Brahmn present and not beyond our ken, he who is the soul of all things." "He is your soul", comes the answer.

"He who dwelling in the earth...... in the waters..... In the fire.... The atmosphere..... The wind..... The sky..... The sun..... The quarters of heaven..... The moon and stars..... Space..... Darkness..... Light.....He who dwelling in all things, yet is other than all things, whom all things do not know, whose body all things are, who controls all things from within—— He is your soul, the inner controller, the immortal....

"He who dwelling in breath..... In speech.....the eye .....the ear.....the mind..... The skin.....the understanding, yet is other than the understanding..... He is the unseen Seer, the unheard Hearer, the unthought Thinker, the ununderstood Understander. Other than He there is no hearer.....no thinker ..... No understander..... He is your soul, the inner Controller, the Immortal."[2]

This is the height that the philosophic thought had attained in this part of the world as early as around twenty seven hundred years back. What the Upanishads broadly say is that religion is a sort of journey in to self. All of us are the rays shooting from the same source. We are separated as individuals at the world end and joined at the God end. Yet, all this has unmistakably filtered from the human mind itself. It is just man talking about man and his Maker in these apparently unworldly compositions. You would have to wear very thick glasses of faith to discover anything revelatory in these otherwise wonderful volumes of literature. In fact, some of the ideologies that emerge from what the Upanishads say about God and man, may even appear to be self-contradictory. Also, at some places the thinking even turns mundane and meaningless. Let us have another sample from the upanishads:-

अथ यस्य जायायै जार: स्यात्तं चेदुद्विष्यात्, आम-पात्रेऽग्निमुपसमाधाय, प्रतिलोमं शरबर्हिस्तीर्त्वा, तस्मिन्नेता: शरभृष्टी: प्रतिलोमा: सर्पिषाक्ता जुहुयात्-मम समिद्धेऽहोषी:, प्राणापानो त आददे - असाविति ; मम समिद्धेऽहोषी:, पुत्रपशूंस्त आददे असाविति ; मम समिद्धेऽहोषी:, इष्टा-सुकृते त आददे - असाविति; मम समिद्धेऽहोषी:, आशा-पराकाशो त आददे - असाविति ; स वा एष निरिन्द्रियो विसुकृतोऽस्माल्लोकात्प्रैति, यमेवंविदुब्राह्मण: शपति; तस्मा-देवंविच्छोत्रियस्य दारेण नोपहासमिच्छेदुत, होवंवित्परो भवति।। १२।।

(*Brhadaranyaka Upanishad* — 6.4.12.)

(If a man wishes to settle scores with his wife's (illicit) lover, he should perform the rite of kindling fire in an unbaked earthen pot, arrange stalks of reed and 'kusa' grass in an inverse way, and offer the reed tips, soaked in clarified butter, in an inverse way saying, "Thou has sacrificed in my fire, I take away thy 'prana' and 'Apana'—such and such. Thou has sacrificed in my kindled fire, I take away your sons and animals—such and such—————— The man whom a Brahamana with knowledge of this ceremony curses in this manner departs from this world emasculated and relieved of his merits. Thus, one should not even dare to act funny with the wife of a person knowledgeable about this ceremony, much less making him an enemy by giving him a more serious offence.")

The suggested rituals sound strange, besides being naïve and weird. Yet, on balance, the way the thinkers of the Age have talked about soul and its connect with the Creator suggests, as if they were under some divine stimuli. Similarly, the other religions while brain-storming over the philosophies related to life, nature and the Divine have produced lot of chaff along with the grain. Priesthoods that feed on faith often have a tendency to involve God in such writings to lend an illusion of infallibility even to the extraneous stuff.

A couple of centuries later the Chinese thinkers, like Confucius and Lao-tse and host of others, produced quite a few gems of philosophy related to the need to flow with the nature, morality, respect for elders and family values and social conduct. The most appreciable thing about these philosophers is that they did not invoke revelations to reinforce their message. They enjoy the same amount of reverence for their work and contribution universally as any of the recognised prophets. Same is the case with the Greek Philosophers like Plato, Socrates and Aristotle etc. who followed them. However, the astonishing depth of their thought notwithstanding, all this and what happened elsewhere took us nowhere near understanding the cosmic mystery. When the analytical capacity of human brain thus hit against the wall in the matter of its quest of the Divine, its imaginative faculty took over.

When proper religions started taking root, human mobility on earth was strictly limited. So, the founders of the religions mostly talk in relation to their restricted territories. They did not have much idea about the rest of the world. Some great intercontinental human movements (from Africa to Asia and from Asia to Americas, for instance) are, indeed on record. These, however, were unidirectional movements that took place at a very slow pace over long periods of time. Nobody involved in these migrations could claim to be a well-travelled person.

When the men with religious ambitions found it difficult to say anything with confidence about the regions of earth unfamiliar to them, their imagination soared skyward and they started talking about the heavenly bodies that have fascinated one and all since times immemorial. They knew whatever they said would pass muster with the faithful, as people then knew very little about what they saw in the sky. They were in no position to verify what was fed to them. If some stray knowledgeable man ever arrived at some heavenly facts and tried to expose them, he could always be got out of the way as heretic.

Thus, they started making out as if they exactly knew what God was and where He dwelt. They just looked heavenward for the spaces where they could place Him. A concept of multi-layered heaven was thought of and the highest heaven was declared to be the home of God. Hell and heaven, the easily understandable instruments of pain and pleasure, were also created somewhere in the celestial recesses to deal justice to the vicious and the virtuous. These men of imagination, of course, saw God and nature in a strictly restricted human image. They wanted us to believe that sun (Surya Lok) and moon (Chandra Lok) were inhabited by people like us and sun revolved round earth.

A chief god was pronounced to be the lord of the paradise and a hard-hearted one among the gods—thickly built and densely mustached, answering to the image of our typical S.H.O.'s of the Police Stations— was handed over the charge of hell. The paradise was equipped with all conceivable things that man thought could provide bliss, comfort and pleasure to the faithful. The 'apsara's or 'houres' (heavenly damsels), eternal youth, immortality, all sort of culinary delights, drinks, entertainments, freedom from work and what have you, was declared to be freely available there. The hell was laid out with all the horrors that man could think of. The wicked and the nonbelievers were to get tortured here in variety of ways—by lashing, clubbing, stretching, goring, sawing, ripping open, burning and so on, but mercifully, not by electric shocks, as electricity was not then known to those who invented this all. The Holy Koran describes hell and heaven in some detail in the following words:-

إِنَّ جَهَنَّمَ كَانَتْ مِرْصَادًا ﴿٢١﴾

لِّلطَّاغِينَ مَآبًا ﴿٢٢﴾

لَّابِثِينَ فِيهَا أَحْقَابًا ﴿٢٣﴾

لَّا يَذُوقُونَ فِيهَا بَرْدًا وَلَا شَرَابًا ﴿٢٤﴾

إِلَّا حَمِيمًا وَغَسَّاقًا ﴿٢٥﴾

إِنَّ لِلْمُتَّقِينَ مَفَازًا ﴿٣١﴾

حَدَائِقَ وَأَعْنَابًا ﴿٣٢﴾

وَكَوَاعِبَ أَتْرَابًا ﴿٣٣﴾

وَكَأْسًا دِهَاقًا ﴿٣٤﴾

— Koran, Surah 78, Verses-21 to 25 & 31 to 34..

(Hell is a real place of ambush. It is the dwelling meant for 'Taghun' i.e. the transgressors like the polytheists, disbelievers, hypocrites, sinners and criminal. They would have to be here for ages. They would be given nothing cool to taste or drink. They would have only boiling water and puss to quench their thirst.———— The Muttaqun, the pious believers in Islamic monotheism who fear Allah and do not get involved in evil deeds, shall live in paradise having gardens, vineyards, full breasted ladies of their own age and shall have overflowing cups of wine to drink.)

The elaborative Koranic literature and the scriptures of some other religions give even more graphic account of the hell and heaven.

The rational intellects would rather feel that all this trouble of creating heaven and hell might have been taken by the religions to keep flocks of their faithful together. Enforcing morality is also, indeed, one of the aims of religions, but they seem to be more concerned that their adherents should not slip out of their control. Thus, those who had no idea about what was going on a few hundred miles away from their homes charted out the entire universe before us. In order to impart credibility to their celestial constructs, these architects often dragged divinity in to their imaginative projects.

There is otherwise really nothing wrong with this mythicising of the faiths. Those who did it were people of above average intelligence. Mythology, after all, has an appeal of its own and is of interest to most of us, because it delves into the areas that are otherwise out-of-bounds to the human intellect and also because it often comes loaded with moral messages. Besides, the association of the Divine in these fantasies promotes a sense of nearness to God among the devotees. His proximity makes man feel secure and comfortable. God, in any case, is a reality and there is no devil in the detail either, so long it drives home a meaningful idea or it otherwise caters constructively to the curiosity of individuals.

God and his goodness, curiosity about the unknown, fears about the future, uncertainties of present life, urge for continuity, ancestral respect, antiquity, force of habit and ego keep man permanently glued to religion. And then, believing is something much easier on the nerves than understanding.

Thus, common man is always more comfortable with the myths rather than the philosophies of a religion. Human spirit loves to explore the unknown and it would never mind even if this is done through the flights of imagination alone. Fully knowing that certain things cannot be true we nevertheless like to hear about them. So long fiction does not get intermixed with fact leading to practical implications, it would always have a place in human life. However, when faith is allowed to overflow its banks blindly, considerable confusion is caused in the civil societies. A Pope is then able to dispose of a cathedral to line his pockets, Catholic Church openly sells indulgences or admission tickets to heaven (15/16th centuries) and monarchs start asserting their divine rights and the clergy their priestly privileges at the cost of the common.

Hindu religion talked about 'Chandra Lok' and 'Surya Lok'. Moon has since been physically explored and we have considerable knowledge about sun also. We now know for definite that there were never any habitations over these heavenly bodies. A plethora of other celestial claims coming from many other religions have also been found to be equally absurd. Yet, this has not, in any way, shaken the faith of the devotees in their religions. In fact, religious myths have inspired countless volumes of literature, paintings, sculptures and musical compositions over the millennia. The wizards of pen, paint, chisel and sound have always reserved their best for mythology. After all, religions have God and goodness at their core and they also take care to keep their crust shining—there may though be a lot of mud flowing in their folds somewhere in between.

Mythology seems to have a separate corner for itself in human heart. It does not normally come in the way of his cerebral pursuits. Even intelligent people enjoy reading 'the Arabian Nights' stories. The worlds of faith and fact can thus coexist peacefully side by side. In fact, some high profile political leaders, bureaucrats, film-actors, artists, businessmen and even scientists are known to have run after all sorts of 'Baba's', 'Guru's', 'Swami's' and 'Mata's' in search of solace. Some of these so called god-men get periodically exposed as fraudulent individuals and, in any case, as mere mortals. Faith, however, continues to flow in all innocence, mindless of whatever happens around. In fact, our world of advertising also gets sustenance from the fact that it is always possible to manipulate a large mass of people to put faith in make-believe contraptions which to a rational mind would appear to be simply ridiculous.

The universe has been viewed as a colossal mass of matter bubbling with energy and it has also been recognised that there is some guiding spirit behind it all. Our soul is associated with this divine spirit and our body as part of this cosmic matter. The material aspects of the universe have been reserved for science and the spiritual issues have been left to be dealt by philosophers. The imagination of man is allowed access to both these areas. The result is a stream of scientific discoveries, inventions, philosophical ideas about God and His creation, mythology and also poetry, paintings, sculptures, architecture and writings etc., relating both to reality and fiction. Both nature and life offer infinite avenues to man to play with his intellectual faculty.

The farthest the human intellect has been able to penetrate in physical terms is a situation where some queer interaction between matter and anti-matter could have resulted in generation of a mass of gigantic proportions and release of infinite energy. This phenomenon is explained something like this. The particles of matter and anti-matter usually keep cancelling each other out and thus a state of nothingness is maintained in perpetuity. In a highly rare of the rarest coincidences a particle escaped annihilation. This atom, which is significantly called the 'God Particle', started multiplying at a furious pace. As a result, the void or nothingness eventually got converted in to a colossal mass of matter pregnant with energy. For some mysterious reasons this mass then burst in to what is now believed to be the 'Big Bang'. Huge splinters of it were cast far and wide— some of these billions of light years away from the parent lump. Astronomers Vesto Slipher and Edwin Hubble believe that this main gobbet or the birthplace of the universe is some fifteen billion light years away from us. These splinters that are now known as stars, planets, satellites, comets and asteroids etc. were mostly beaten in to spherical shape by God through its miraculous instrument known to us as gravity. After all, the protruding parts of these bodies that were then in gaseous form could not defy their respective centres of gravity and the pulls from their bigger neighbours. Their rough edges thus got rounded. Their gaseous matter, in some cases, finally solidified into soil, with liquid lava boiling below it. The huge clusters of these celestial bodies are known to us as galaxies.

In course of time they found their respective trajectories for orderly revolution and their own axes for smooth rotations. Their further destiny got decided by the situation they found themselves in. Our moon, for instance, is a lump that got released from earth where we now have the Pacific Ocean. But having strayed away in a different slot of space it has acquired a vastly different character. The science has now fair knowledge about the distances and mass of many of these heavenly bodies in our neighbourhood and this knowledge is expanding with every passing year. It is very much possible for the human brain to pry into some of the celestial recesses. Possibly, even the question of consciousness in our brains would also be solved with the passage of time.

However, the living beings are not the body and brain alone. They carry something infinitely more important inside—a soul. The secrets of soul seem impossible to understand. The writers of our 'Upanishads' and others tried their hand to solve the mysteries of this Self, but had to stop well short of the ultimate solution. In fact, the position remains frozen at what has been stated in Book X (Dasham Mandlam), Chapter 129 ( Sutra 129), stanzas 6 and 7 (Shlokas 6 and 7) of Rig Veda (reproduced in the last chapter). These extra-ordinary lines say that nobody has any idea how this universe came into being and we also have no means of knowing, if even the One who has created this all knows the 'when', 'why' and 'how' part of it.

Thus, when the human intellect failed to decipher the divine reality, it deflected in numerous directions, hoping that the relentless effort towards unveiling the secrets of life and nature one after the other, would one day take man in audience before God who holds complete sway over what we see and perceive. After giving vent to his imaginations and philosophies about God, the heavenly phenomena and the earthly elements, man turned to the theme of life.

The thinkers first tried to understand why man was sent to the world in first place and what he was required to do during his journey through life. After considerable racking of brain, the wise finally came to the conclusion that the ultimate aim of life was happiness. Happiness is, indeed, the primary biologic urge with all the living beings and it is, in fact, the pole round which life revolves. Once born, a being has an inherent right to happy life. Nobody can really stop man and other beings in their pursuit of happiness. It is precisely for this reason that no punishment and no enforcement machinery have ever been able to eradicate prostitution or thrust prohibition down the throat of man. There is a lesson for the states in it— they must not try to totally suppress the natural urges and restrict themselves only to regulating these in the interest of social discipline to a needed degree.

Thus, whatever a man does, even an act of sacrifice for others, is motivated towards his own happiness. This doctrine finds an excellent echo in the old Hindu scriptures in the following words:-

> न वा अरे पत्युः कामाय पतिः प्रियो भवति, आत्मनस्तु कामाय पतिः प्रियो भवति। न वा अरे जायायै कामाय जाया प्रिया भवति, आत्मनस्तु कामाय जाया प्रिया भवति। न वा अरे पुत्राणां कामाय पुत्रा प्रिया भवन्ति, आत्मनस्तु कामाय पुत्राः प्रिया भवन्ति।
>
> (Brhadaranyaka Upanishad— 4.5.6.)

> (It is not for the sake of the husband, my dear that he is loved, but wife loves him for her own sake. Wife is not loved for her own sake either; her husband does so because loving her pleases him. Likewise, sons are also not loved for their own sake, but because their parents feel happy doing that. —————).

Mundaka Upanishad says that ultimately it is truth alone that triumphs (Satyameva Jayate). Hindu scriptures further elaborate, "—truth is only that which benefits the people, not what is otherwise" ('Devi Bhagavatam': 3-11-36). It is again clarified in Kshemendra's 'Bharata Manjari' (Santi-402), "Truth is that which is for the welfare of all the people. The rest is something else". Thus, this reality related to the 'Pursuit of Happiness' has been articulated in a variety of ways in the earlier ages also, but it eventually found a formal recognition in the American constitution along with the other two values—'Life' and 'Liberty'. So long the kind of happiness sought is not at the cost of others, does no violence to the good order of the society and is not of self-destructive nature, nobody should come in its way, whatever way it is sought.

Thus, the real concern of the thinkers was how to make the world a happy home for man. More of man lives in his mind and soul than in his body. His first worry, indeed, relates to the existential needs. If these are not met the body and soul would not really stay together. Next to this, he is concerned with his future, including the life next. This is the stage where spirituality enters into his scheme of things. For his lasting happiness, it is necessary to make him believe that he is not alone in this universe. His God is always there with him. The belief in adjacency of God has been a source of supreme comfort to man in his adversities.

Religions, therefore, start with spirituality. The first thing that they teach man is to hold God on heart all the time and set apart some time for prayer, pilgrimage and charity in His name. Elaborate procedures have been laid down for the purpose for various religious practices at state, society and family levels. Brahmana's' and many other Hindu scriptures prescribe the precise mode for various private and socio-political ceremonies and functions related to birth, 'namkaran' (giving name to the newborn), 'mundan' (mopping up the first crop of baby hair), marriage, death, 'shudhikaran' (rendering clean and thus restoring touchablity), inaugurations, assuming office, 'Rajyabhishek' (Accession to throne), festivals, travel, wars, victories, sacrifice and so on. The Christian church also has well-established rites from baptism to burial and for numerous other functions and festivals. Jews have their 'Passovers' and host of other rituals. Muslims have their 'Hajj', fasting during the month of Ramazan, 'Eid', 'khatna' (circumcision) and numerous other ceremonies. The other religions also have their own ceremonies and practices. The idea behind all this is that man has some spiritual needs and these must be satisfied for him to feel secure, happy and comfortable.

Next on the agenda of the religions has been to drum some discipline in the psyche of the citizens through the fear of God, so that they may live in peace and orderliness as social animal. This meant laying down a moral code of conduct for their adherents in tune with the prevailing ethos in the societies. Rig Veda (Dasham Mandalam/Sukta-34) talks comprehensively about the obsessive psyche of a gambler and the misery that it entails for him and his family. The thirteenth verse advises the gamblers:

अक्षैर्मा दीव्य: कृषिमित् कृषस्व वित्ते रमस्व वहु मन्यमान:।
तत्र गाव: कितव तत्र जाय तन्मे वि चष्टे सवितायर्य:।।१३

(O' you the gambler, Instead of seeking to make quick buck through gambling, put your faith in farming. Be happy with whatever you thus earn with the sweat of your brows. This noble earning would bring you cows and a woman to marry. So says the Sun god)—Shloka-13.

Some religions, in their wisdom, have gone quite a few steps further and drafted formal penal, civil and marital codes for their people. The revelatory ring put around them converts the word of man in to the word of God. Hindu's thus have their 'Samriti's', 'Shruti's' and other works as their early legal literature. Koran is more elaborate in the matter of jurisprudence. It is, in fact, a sort of book of life in the sense that it lays down in great detail how life is to be lived. Some religions now face a real practical problem on this count as the radically conservative elements among them insist on being governed by the codes created to cater to the socio-political situations that obtained millennia earlier. Only education and enlightenment can solve this problem.

The western world, to a degree, has grasped this truth. That is why they are ahead of the others. Every U.S.A. currency note and coin declares, "In God we trust". Yet, they have all through asserted that the religions have a very respectable place for them in the shrines and they must stay there and must not come out to mix with the mud of politics. That is precisely how that they are the super power of the world at this point of time and those at the bottom are the countries entrapped in the past. They seem to believe that whatever was worth saying has already been said by God and He has no business to open His mouth again. Every word said in His name millennia back has to be believed and acted upon whatever are its implications and consequences for human welfare. They have brought themselves round to think that the time stopped ticking when somebody they believe in declared what exactly God wanted them to do. Some moral principles established by the religions have, no doubt, been found to be of lasting value. These have provided the much needed guidance to the societies and ensured orderliness in them. Certain amount of rigidity in the religious principles is quite in order as it ensures continuity and discipline. However, those who think that change is not the law of nature are certainly wrong. Time is an essential ingredient of the divine. It just cannot be overlooked by anyone.

The attempt at law making by religions has not been able to stand the test of times that keep changing. The laws stream from the needs of a society and these must always remain in tune with the prevailing ethos. That is how the west got rid of its inquisitions long time back. The Hindu laws have been getting progressively modified to meet the requirements of the modern era. Even most of the Islamic countries have appreciated that their polity cannot be governed on the premises that prevailed in Saudi Arabia some fifteen hundred years back. They have opted to follow the spirit rather than the letter of the 'shariat' laws. However, Saudi Arabia, as the role model of Islam, feels itself under some sort of compulsion to persist with the Islamic laws. Even this country takes considerable pain to ensure that implementation of the ancient codes does as little violence to the contemporary thinking of the world as possible.

Besides, the religions have also tried their hand at influencing many other spheres of life like politics, education, health care, entertainment, art, architecture, literature etc. For instance, at one point of time, Pope at Rome and the Emperor of the so called Holy Roman Empire under the Hapsburg house (which is aptly described as neither holy nor Roman nor empire) formally divided the spiritual and temporal functions of the world between themselves, as if God had willed it that way. The pompous arrangement understandably proved to be a non-starter, because the empire was surrounded by many powerful nation states that would not take any of this.

But, finally some workable understanding has been reached between various states and the religions to coexist in peace. Where this has not happened, there are problems.

## Notes

1. Man's Religions' by John B Noss, p. 568.
2. Man's Religions' by John B. Noss, pp. 130-131.

# 4

# The Two Faces of Religions

All religions have two very distinct aspects to themselves—the spiritual and the communal. At the spiritual level, all the religions appear to be the same. Oneness of God is a settled fact among all the religions—no religion says that there are two or more Gods of this universe. All religions talk about truth, peace, love, charity, righteousness, universal brotherhood and moral values. There are, thus, hardly any differences among the religions on the spiritual side. Viewed from this angle, the religions serve a magnificent purpose in man's life. The feeling of proximity to God generated through the religious faith gives meaning to our mundane lives and works to soothe our soul. It gives us strength to stand up to the multifarious adversities of our existence. Man would feel terribly alone without God by his side.

It is really the communal ingredient of the creeds that has kept the cauldrons boiling all through the ages. As rivers lead to people, religions lead to community formation. You follow the flow of a river you would invariably find habitations on its banks. Similarly the followers of various faiths instinctively get grouped in to communities. In fact, the bonds that the religions forge are so strong and enduring that these often transcend the regional, racial, ethnic, cultural, linguistic, national and even the worldly barriers.

This very point was strongly stressed by the Muslim League to justify creation of a separate homeland for the Indian Muslim. Their argument was that bulk of the Hindus and Muslim in the Indian subcontinent were admittedly from the same ethnic stock, spoke the same language, had similar culture and were, in fact, the closest kin, but still they were two distinctly different nations who just could not gel with each other, because of their irreconcilable faith profiles. Later, of course, Jinnah, the founder of Pakistan, clarified in the National Assembly of Pakistan that he did not mean his country to be a theocratic state and all religions were to be given an equal opportunity to grow. This left a legitimate question on many lips— if this really was the case why the pitch for Pakistan was raised to such a crescendo on purely religious grounds.

The answer to this is pretty clear. The great visionary had only one thing on his mind, the welfare of the Muslim community and he was not wrong. Because of some not easily understandable reasons when the Hindus and Muslim stay together, the Muslim, by and large, tend to get reduced to a menial status. They end up doing what the people from Bihar and eastern U.P. are doing today in various better developed states of India—- pulling rickshaws, selling milk and vegetables, working as domestic maids and doing manual labour. Jinnah had taken note of the stark reality that, in the pre-partition Punjab, the Muslim constituted a large chunk of the landed aristocracy, but they were rapidly losing their lands to the Hindu money lenders and the tables were unmistakably getting turned on them.

It had become a Muslim habit to lay the blame for all this on the 'wily Hindu money lender'. However, the more plausible reason behind this curious phenomenon could be what the former President of Pakistan, Gen. Parvez Musharraf, had once indicated rather forthrightly that the Muslim lag terribly behind in modern education. This is abundantly clear from the niggardly number of the Ph.D.'s that the Muslim Ummah produce every year. Similarly, a large chunk of the white-collar government jobs in the country were landing with the Hindus who had taken to the English language like the fish take to water. In any case, whatever be the reasons for this Muslim plight, the Quad-e-azam did not want the bulk of his community to end up as drawers of water and hoers of wood in the undivided India.

Nevertheless, the question that still stays in place is why religion had to be used for achieving this well-meant community objective, instead of pressing for an added stress on modern education among the Muslim. The plain reason for this is that religion is a profound force that works easily on human psyche. No patriotic war was fought as ferociously as the crusades in the early part of the last millennium. The religions have a very high potential for communal mobilisations and mischief. Every politician likes to have his hand on this lever of power. Well before the horrors of the Partition got unleashed, a hate campaign was already in full swing in west Punjab. It was obviously initiated to secure division of the country on communal lines. A Muslim fanatic came up with a vitriolic book titled, 'Sita ka sarha' (Rape of Sita). Unwilling to get outdone in stupidity, a Hindu writer replied with an equally obnoxious title, 'Rangila Rasool' and got stabbed to death for this.

Anyway, Jinnah had already disclosed his hand before Pakistan lost the benefit of his vision. Having used religion for achieving Pakistan, he would have proceeded towards his real goal of securing better quality of life for his community. His early demise robbed his country of all this. His successors then just flew off the tangent and vied with each other to push Pakistan towards a theological anarchy, rather than strengthening and stabilising its nascent democratic polity. Their pure and simple territorial ambitions in Kashmir were also given a neat religious coating. The Indian subcontinent, however, is not the only place where the communal element of the religions has played havoc. Many other regions of the world have been the far worse sufferers. The unfortunate fact is that people belonging to various religious groupings innocently believe that they alone are the chosen people of God and the others are in ignorance about the Divine reality and are groping in the dark. One can clearly see the human ego at work in the brains behind all this.

All of us are born to the world with a mission. Everybody has a task to perform and he has been provided the wherewithal for that. He has to identify and understand his capacity for the task assigned to him by nature and live up to it. The general scheme of nature is that everybody should strive to make the world a better and a happier place to live, till it is time for him to depart. He is a success if he discharges the duty by the nature well and is a failure if he wastes the talents vested in him. According to a Hassidic tale, Zusia, a seer, once appeared before his pupil in a highly perturbed state. On being implored to take them in to confidence about his plight, he revealed that God had appeared in his dream and said that He did not blame him for not being Moses and leading his people out of slavery (the way the Prophet did). But He would certainly blame him for not being Zusia, i.e., for failure to carry out the assignments of his own life as per the capacities vested in him. This also means that everybody could take pride in his uniqueness and the fact that he was not born without a purpose.

On the other hand, the insignificance of man at individual level is also a settled fact. Nobody, not even the memories, are meant to live forever. Despite this, the desire to count and dominate is present in every mind as a powerful private urge. Never in our history there was anything like a world government and thus, nobody was ever in a position to call himself as the ruler of this earth— though many of the monarchs assumed all sorts of ludicrous titles indicating that they were the lords of the world. Then, our good earth is no more than an insignificant speck in this universe. Thus, none of us counts for much.

Yet, even the humblest among us, would like to believe that he is different and is meant to be something. All of us live with an illusion of permanence. No one is really prepared to accept that he is destined to get obliterated without a trace. Immortality is just not meant for man or any other living being and craving for immortality is an exercise in futility. Even if we leave some memories behind these would also have a limited life span, running not beyond two or three generations in case of an ordinary man. Even the most extraordinary individuals cannot hope to live forever, even by their memory. Should something happen to our good earth today, all of us, including the presidents, prime ministers, priests, monarchs and even the numerous man-made Gods and prophets would get lost somewhere in the space as unidentifiable matter. Only the One who has created us and all else, would always be there— and none else, for sure.

Man's illusions, however, refuse to die till he is alive. The desire to count and dominate is, in fact, a sort of biological urge with all living beings. Only the situational pressures and his own wisdom can inject some humility in man's head. This is how it happens. Man first tries to dominate by himself. When this is not possible he goes for collecting some supporters around him for the purpose. In fact, some lesser beings in awe of his ability and prowess, rally around him in the natural course. When, however, he loses leadership of his group for some reason, he breaks away from the group along with his faction of supporters to keep his prominence intact. The power games thus continue in communities in perpetuity. Only the characters keep changing. The individual ego gets carried further to clans, communities and countries.

Religions come handy in all sorts of power struggles. So, the manipulators of all hues hardly ever hesitate to hook religion to their cause. They know that truth prevails in the soul rather than the mind of man. Minds, thus, can always be manoeuvred. A man of faith sees a glimpse of God in his religion and he can be easily aroused to die for it. There is, in fact, something hypnotic about the religions. This has, of course, a lot to do with man's desire for luck in this life and the mysterious anxiety for the next one. It is widely believed that religions alone can address such concerns. This fear of the unknown and hope for better life after the present one, makes religions a convenient tool for communal mobilisations. A steady stream of the faithful is often available for martyrdom in the name of their God. Thus, as the innocent blood spills, some hidden hands are busy collecting their gains greedily. This is the unseemly side of the religions.

The Crusades or the wars of Crescent (Islam) and Cross (Christianity) are too big an event to be discussed and disposed of within this chapter. A separate chapter would be needed to study various dimensions of this religious conflict— indeed, one of the bloodiest ones of human history.

In the Indian context, the Aryan migrants first came in clash with the Indus Valley inhabitants. But this had nothing to do with religion. In fact, the Aryans benefitted and borrowed from the native religious thought. While advancing deeper into the subcontinent they had skirmishes with the Dravidians. These were also territorial or at worst of ethnic nature. Later, Buddhism came in to being as an off-shoot of the Hindu religion—even now the Buddhists of India are legally deemed to be Hindus and are subject to the Hindu civil laws of the country. For some centuries Buddhism flourished in the country, but finally it got totally obliterated in the land of its birth because of several reasons.

There is a view that Shankeracharya, a great Hindu personality of the period, got them dislodged by violent means. There might have been some spontaneous reactionary violence in some pockets in the country on this count but there was nothing like a full-fledged communal conflict on this count. In fact there was never a communal divide between the Hindus and Buddhists. They were always deemed to be one community. Buddhism vanished from the land for entirely different reasons that would be gone in to afterwards.

Similarly there were no communal conflicts when Buddhism poured over the Indian subcontinent into the neighbouring lands. This speaks volumes about the level of tolerance and identity-related self-confidence in these countries. They never felt alarmed over the arrival of the new faith in their midst and seemed to welcome light from whatever source it came. China, Japan and host of other countries on their periphery never felt threatened about their identity with the penetration of the Buddhist thought in their soil. Confucianism and Taoism are quite in harmony with Buddhism even today, though occasionally there is a small patriotic surge in favour of the indigenous faiths. In fact, a common cross-thread of apparent Godlessness runs through them all. They instead believe in spirituality, salvation, moral values and respect for elders etc. The differences of their present regime with His holiness, the Dalai Lama are also not based on any sort of communal tension. Similar parameters define the relationship between Buddhism and the indigenous Japanese faith, Shinto. All these faiths have generally coexisted in peace for centuries. The only reason for this is that the spiritual and moral fibre of these faiths is far stronger than their communal impulse.

The Indian subcontinent experienced real communal confrontations with the advent of the Muslim invasions from the eighth century onwards. The earlier ethnic ingresses were smoothly absorbed. All outsiders dropping from the west of the Hindukush melted into the Hindu majority without much fuss.

The seventh century really belonged to Islam. The spiritual credentials of Prophet Mohammed had already met wide acceptance with his people. His successful defence of Medina and later a grand victory over Mecca, lent added strength to his message. Islam soon gathered so much steam in the sands of Arabia that it burst forth in all directions. Initially, these soldiers of God seemed to be under some sort of divine inspiration. That is how these tribal warriors, equipped with just rudimentary weapons, were able to overwhelm much better organised armies. However, the lure of loot and the promise of heavenly comforts in the life next also appear to have played their own part in putting them on the roll. Four-fifth share in the booty in case of victory and the prospect of luxurious life in paradise on death, made fighting a win-win adventure for the followers of the new faith. These soldiers of God were, thus, very much the soldiers of fortune as well. The weak and wealthy countries on their periphery were asking to be won. There could thus be no second thoughts in the situation. They launched themselves in to action spontaneously like the men possessed. Syria fell in AD 635, Iraq in 637, Jerusalem in 638, Palestine in 640, Egypt in 641 and Persia in 649. These countries were nothing short of 'earthly paradises' in themselves in the 'scarcity-bred' minds of the desert warriors.

After these sparkling victories in the Near East, the Islamic on rush headed towards the west further. The Muslim armies went right up to the northern edge of Africa and then crossed over the Mediterranean to hold sway over Spain for a few centuries. Entire Europe would have gone under the shadow of the Crescent, but for the close Muslim loss in the Battle of Tour in France in AD732 at the hands of the Christian forces led by Charles Martel. This communal trouble between Christianity and Islam, as we shall see, was destined to bloody many more pages of the world history in the centuries to come.

In the east, the Muslim spread their wings right up to Indonesia. They swelled to the north in central Asia, Mongolia and China. In the south, they penetrated deep into the dark continent of Africa. Finally, they found themselves settled in the shape of a crescent covering Africa, Europe and Asia.

India felt the first heat of the Islamic steam when Mohammad-bin- Qasim invaded in AD 712. King Dahir of Sindh was killed, his domains devastated, women and wealth plundered and men were enslaved. Some royal ladies had to perish in the fires of 'jauhar' and two young princesses got dispatched to the harem of the Caliph. The raid, thus, left blisters all over Sindh. Small sporadic raids continued in the north-west of the country over the next around three centuries till Mehmud Gaznavi struck repeatedly in the area in a big way and went back every time with his pockets bulging with the looted wealth and taking pride in breaking the idols in the Hindu shrines. The raids were in the nature of a wake- up call that sadly was not taken seriously. The kingdoms in the interior generally felt themselves to be safe and they thought that it was none of their job to defend the principalities in the frontier areas. Nobody ever thought that it could be his turn next. India, thus, kept its eyes closed to the dangers lurking in the west of Hindukush for nearly half a millennium.

Late in the 12[th] century, the Muslim secured permanent presence in India as the ruling elite. The coming together of the two vastly different cultural entities could not be expected to be a smooth affair. The resurgent Islamic community and the Hindu society with intense pride in their past, were bound to view each other with antipathy and suspicion. So, lot of bitterness and blood-letting followed. The victors, in their flush of victories, did demolish Hindu temples and heaped many indignities on the vanquished. There were times when a bigot among them would demand that a Hindu should open his mouth when a Muslim felt like spitting.

Nonetheless, the spiritual streams of the two religions have also been flowing side by side. During the reign of Ferozshah Tughlak, an enlightened soul tried to establish that Islam and Hinduism were, in fact, the same in essence. The pious man, however, had to lose his head for his views. Hindus were formally treated as second class citizens i.e. the 'Zimmi's' in their own land during the regime of Aurangzeb. The 'zimmi's' were meant to subsist on bare necessities of life, if at all they had any right to live. They were, in fact, supposed to buy back their lives by paying 'zazia'. The hated levy had to be paid personally in all humility. One could recall thousands of such bitter episodes from the Indian past. Nevertheless, equally numerous are the instances where the two communities rose to dizzy heights of humanity, leaving all communal hatred far behind. This really means that the soul-side of these religions prevailed over the communal urges at frequent intervals.

In any case, the two communities had realised fairly early that neither could wish the other away. If it is a fact that the divide between the two continued, it is equally true that the Muslim soon stopped looking westward and adopted the subcontinent as their home. As early as the 13th century, Amir Khusrao, the poet laureate of the Sultanate was singing praises of his adopted land so lavishly that he came to be referred as the 'Tuti-e-Hind' i.e. the Trumpeter of India. In his 'Nuh Sipihr' (written in Persian in AD 1318) he seems to have tried to build bridges of understanding between the two communities. He pleads in his work, "The Hindus are not atheists as they do believe in God's eternal phenomenon—— They, undoubtedly, worship stones, cows, the sun, and 'tulsi' (the Basil plant) ardently. But they do so because they see God in everything. The actual focus of their worship is none other than the Divine Being."

Thus, if there were some intolerant and bigoted rulers like Ferozshah Tughlak, Aurangzeb and the like, there were also a host of individuals in the Islamic fraternity like Amir Khusrao, Abdur Rahim Khan-e-khana, Zain-ul-Abidin (deservedly called the Akbar of Kashmir), Nusrat Shah of Bengal (He had the 'Mahabharata' rendered in to Bengali) and of course, Akbar the Great who did their best to heal the hurt psyches. The fact that the Hindu institutions, ideology and way of life survived through a long spell of Muslim rule speaks well of both the communities. In fact, even today the spirituality of the religions keeps coming to the fore occasionally to relieve the communities of some of their tension.

Bonded by their blood (Bulk of the Muslims in the subcontinent are the Hindu converts), cemented by the soil, but fragmented by their faith, the two communities have come this far in time, quarrelling through the centuries. The nadir in their relationship was reached during the partition of the subcontinent in 1947. Nobody really knows where the communal divide is destined to take them in future. It has been repeatedly pleaded that the *'Bharat Mata'* of the Hindus happens to be the *'Madr-e-Watan'* of the Muslim also, suggesting that they are, in fact, the real brothers. Sadly, however, the communally-inclined would have none of this.

Jews are perhaps the most wonderful people of the world. They are the ones who brought prophets to the planet and they, along with the Aryans, introduced the concept of God to man. Judaism is the parent faith among the Semitic religions. Their prophets and scriptures are recognised and revered by all the Semitic creeds. Yet, for some curious reason, they have remained in the eye of storm all through the ages. The religions, in fact, have scant regard for ancestry. Christians have long forgotten that their founder was himself a Jew. They have been at odds with the Jewish community all through. Same goes for the Muslim. Koran makes reverential references to about a dozen of the Jewish prophets. Yet the Muslims have never been at ease with the Hebrew community.

The Jews never had a country of their own, though they always had a historical claim over Palestine since the days of Moses. Thus, they were buffeted around from Egypt to Iraq for nearly three millennia and finally got scattered all over the world. They always prospered moneywise wherever they happened to be. Their statelessness and prosperity in the alien lands has worked to their disadvantage and they have often been viewed as parasites by the native societies. The Jews have usually been seen in the image of the Shakespearean Shylock and have suffered communal persecution for centuries. The Nazi Germany, in fact, tried to exterminate them off the earth. One can just imagine the solace and comfort they must have derived when they finally got a homeland in Israel.

What possibly could be the explanation for this sort of communal ostracism of the Jews? One reason that comes to mind is the attitude of exclusiveness on part of the Jews as a community. They are too jealous about their identity to be able to gel with the neighbouring communities and the countries where they live in. Often it appears that they themselves have chosen to remain confined in their own world. They feel that they are the different people, having a private God of their own with whom they are bound through a bipartite agreement. Just view this extract from their holy scriptures:-

> "For thou (the Jews) art an holy people unto the Lord thy God: the Lord thy God, hath chosen thee to be special people unto Himself, above all people that are upon the face of the earth."
>
> —Deuteronomy 7:6.

Most holy of their scriptures, The Old Testament, is revered by the Christian world, but they, in turn, do not recognize the New Testament part of the Bible that relates to Christ. Their Prophets are the prophets of Christianity as well as Islam, but the Jews do not recognise either Christ or Mohammad as prophets. They have, thus, been at odds with the rest of the world and more so with the followers of the other Semitic faiths. Otherwise the Jews stand out for their brilliance in the world. Israel had a number of skirmishes with the Muslim armies in its hostile neighbourhood. Despite being heavily outnumbered, the Jewish army made them lick dust. They captured the desolate Sinai Peninsula from Egypt and kept it for a few years. They made the desert bloom.

Christianity and Islam are not only the historical off-shoots of Judaism, but also the Jews and Muslims have a common ancestry. Both have descended from Abraham— the Jews through his son, Isaac and the Muslims through his other son, Ishmael. During the time of Prophet Mohammad, the Jews were settled all over Arabia and controlled the levers of its economy. Initially, the Prophet tried to take them along. But when they refused to convert to Islam, he decided to cleanse Arabia of their presence. In AD 624, the Jewish tribe of Banu Kainuka was besieged and made to surrender. First, it was decided to put them all to sword, but finally they were banished from Arabia along with the tribe of Banu Nadir. Jews of Chamber and Banu Quraiza tribe were, however, not so lucky and met a more cruel fate. When they did not respond to the invitation for conversion, they were attacked by surprise. Their wealth and women were grabbed as spoils of war and the men were massacred. All this happened in the name of religion and in glory of God!

The most incendiary spot on the earth, however, is the Balkans region where three religious entities— the Greek church, the Roman Catholic church and Islam— have remained in eye-ball to eye-ball confrontation. The area has triggered both the world wars of our history. If man is to live in peace and comfort on this planet something would have to be done about the communal aspect of the religions. God appears to be the most misused being in this universe. The solution to the problem lies in creating conditions for all religions to stay in their shrines in peace and glory. There should be no need ever for them to bolt out from there shouting that their faith is in danger.

# 5

# The Land of the Prophets

Significantly, all major religions of the world – Christianity, Islam, Judaism, Hinduism, Buddhism, Confucianism, Taoism, Shinto and Zoroastrianism etc. are of Asian origin. This incidentally points towards the historical fact that Asia, at this point of time, was far ahead of the rest of the world. Jerusalem and the lands around have cradled three great Semitic religions of the world—Judaism, Christianity and Islam. Together they command faith of more than half the humanity. There is really nothing very Semitic about Christianity and Islam though, as their ethnic profiles are now almost entirely different from that of Judaism and there is very little sprinkling of the Semites among them. Yet, these three religions have a meeting point in monotheism and common faith in the Semitic prophets. However, individuality among these is stronger than their affinity. Every one of them considers itself as the only true religion with finality. Christianity and Islam among them also see universality as their manifest destiny.

They are, indeed, in a complex relationship with each other. Bible of the Jews (The Old Testament) is a sacred scripture to the Christians. They also acknowledge the Law (of Moses) and Gospel as the divine revelations. The New Testament and Koran are, however, peculiar to the Christians and the Muslim alone. In fact, they appear to 'complete and partly supersede the former revelations'. For this reason, Judaism does not validate these and it also does not extend recognition to Jesus and Mohammad as prophets. To them, the prophets are the ones who find mention in their own scriptures and none outside these. Nevertheless, the Jewish prophets, Jesus Christ and Mohammad rule the Semitic world from their graves.

Jesus, himself a Jew, fell to the machinations of the Pharisees and Sadducees who were then in control of the Jewish law and religious affairs. This notwithstanding, when the infamous Gnostic doctrine tried to relegate Yahweh to a lower rung of divinity below the Christian God, this was resolutely resisted. The obvious purpose behind this contraption was to cut Christianity free from its Jewish roots. The idea did not find favour with the Christian clergy. So, it was speedily squashed before it could cause confusion. After all, Christianity could not allow anyone to dig away the foundation from under its feet. It just could not afford to delink from its past.

According to the Islamic belief some 124000 prophets have put up appearance on earth–Adam among them being the first and Mohammad the last in the line. Prophet Mohammad was full of reverence for his Semitic predecessors. Had the Jew held the hand of friendship extended by him, Jerusalem could have been the common 'kiblah' (the most sacred spot) of the Semitic faiths. After all, all the three religions are historically and soulfully connected with the place. So far as the Jews are concerned it has been settled deep in their psyche right from the beginning. Jesus had his Last Super here. Prophet Mohammad is also said to have once visited the city on Allah's command. The Jew were, however, too conscious of their high status as the special people of God to agree to assimilate with the Muslim. Centuries back, they had spurned a similar offer from the Christians also. The result has been their racial ostracism, confinement to ghettos, frequent expulsions and attempts at their genocide by the societies, getting often exasperated with and intolerant of them. The Jews, however, hang on to their faith and attitude of separateness with stoic tenacity even today.

Despite their common nucleus, there are vast doctrinal differences among the three religions. Firstly, they have all chosen to give different names to the Divine Being. Secondly, they view their relationship with Him in considerably different terms. Jews see themselves as His special people. Christians believe Jesus to be his son. There is, therefore, a definite element of incarnation in their belief which sounds strange to the other two. Muslims, on the other hand, hold that Allah does not share divinity with anybody and regard humanity to be in master-slave relationship with Him. They believe that Allah is all by Himself and does not have any consort. So, the question of Jesus being His son does not arise. They, however, are quick to admit that he was born to Mary (i.e. Miriam, the daughter of Imran and Hannah who belong to the lineage coming right down from Adam and Noah) through some divine intervention. Thirdly, they have earmarked a separate weekly holyday /holiday for themselves. Jews have their Sabbath on Saturdays. Christians and Muslims instead observe Sundays and Fridays respectively as their days devoted to prayer and rest. Fourthly, the synagogues of the Jew are oriented towards Jerusalem, Mosques of the Muslim towards Mecca and the Christian churches do not have any such orientation. Fifthly, their holy scriptures—Torah, Bible and Koran— do have a common cross-thread running through them, but the Jew do not recognize the New Testament part of the Bible and Koran is exclusive to the Muslim only. Sixthly, the Jews, Christians and Muslims have different principle ceremonies peculiar to their respective faiths. The Jews have their 'Passover' related to their escape from the Egyptian bondage, Christians have their 'Eucharist', a sort of thanks-giving function connected with the 'Last Super' of their Lord and Muslims have their 'Hajj'. Seventhly, their dietary stipulations are also different. Jews do not take enlivened bread during the Passovers, whereas alcoholic drinks and pork are 'haram' (prohibited) for the Muslim. Eighthly, human idols and images are a taboo with the Hebrews as well as the Muslim. Jews give expression to their artistic urges by making richly ornamented Torah mantles, seven-branched menorahs for candles and hexagonal Shield of David (called the 'Star of David') etc. for decorating the interiors of their synagogues. Christians merrily display the paintings and sculptures of Jesus, Mary, Greco-Roman gods and goddesses and the epical characters and incidents from their mythology in their churches and elsewhere. The Muslims display their artistry through religious architecture, calligraphic excellence, drawing pictures of their principal mosques, 'Kaaba' and crescent-studded ambiences etc.

Numerous other differences in their faith profiles are also noticeable. For instance, there is much added emphasis on equality in Islam. All are deemed to be equal in the eyes of Allah. Equality, undoubtedly, is difficult to live up to in nature. The Muslims, however, do try to implement it in their system. The looted wealth is supposed to be evenly distributed among the Islamic soldiery. In Saudi-Arabia, which is struggling to act as a role model of Islam, one would be surprised to find a lowly sepoy sitting on the chair of his commanding officer in his absence and not bothering to get up in a hurry when he returns. Elsewhere even his second-in command would not dare to do it. The kings on their demise are buried in sand without any structure being raised as their memorial. Aurangzeb who also tried to live up to this tradition left a will that no canopy would be raised over his resting place. His grave at Aurangabad accordingly bears just a plant that was dear to him in his life. All this is, however, symbolic. Otherwise, a large bulk of the powerful posts in Saudi-Arabian establishment are held by the profusely numerous members of the royalty. Such a show of literal equality is not attempted in other two religions, though equality in principle is the cornerstone of their constitutional law in many western democracies.

The three religions also have vastly different perspectives with regard to the criminal, civil and matrimonial laws. Islamic criminal code is based on retributive justice—life for life, eye for eye and tooth for tooth. So, were the Jewish and Christian legal systems till some centuries back— the British criminal laws provided for death penalty for hundreds of offences (just call to mind the hanging of Raja Nand Kumar for forgery by the ruling East India Company in as late as the eighteenth century). Add to this, the dreaded inquisitions of the medieval period. Subsequently, there was a realisation that life could not be lived as per the codes decided thousands of years back, though revelations might have been attributed to these to reinforce their permanence. Most of the Christian world, therefore, modified their codes to bring these in tune with the times. Their legal systems, as they stand today, are based on the principle of deterrence rather than retribution. The ancient Hindu laws, on the other hand, were reformative in nature.

Some Muslim countries have also moved away substantially from the 'Shariat' (Islamic) laws that provide for amputation of limbs and floggings for a number of minor crimes and capital punishment for religious offences like insult to Prophet Mohammad or Koran, proselytising from Islam and even petty crimes like fornication etc. Even the provisions like 'triple talaq' related to divorce have been dispensed with or made more stringent by some. Saudi-Arabia where the Islamic codes are still in vogue also applies these with good care and due diligence. Still, some basic differences of outlook on the issue persist among the Semitic faiths.

The other fundamental differences among these religions relate to the veiling of their females. The Muslim believe in covering their women from the strangers almost from top to toe, the opening being restricted to a small slit around their eyes. On the other hand, the western world seems to have happily limited its decency concerns to the last few square inches of the female flesh. In fact, many western nations are thinking in terms of outlawing the 'burqa' (Islamic veil) in their countries.

The three religions follow vastly varied practices in the matter of worship. The familiar sound around churches is the sounding of their gongs and around mosques, the shouting of 'azans' (call for prayer) from their minarets. The ambiance inside their shrines is, in essence, the same, but their mode of prayer, discourses and other ceremonies are different. Similarly, the three religions have a different outlook on circumcisions, laws of evidence, moral policing, pilgrimage, fasting, dress-code, marriage, divorce, music, method of slaughtering animal for meat and many other areas and activities of life.

In the final analysis, Jews consider themselves to be singularly blessed people. After all, they believe that God took the trouble of appearing among them and offering to protect them, if they agreed to abide by His commandments in the form of a moral code of conduct and allegiance to Him. They were thus extended the honour of entering in to a sort of bipartite covenant with the Divinity. No other race or religion on earth could claim this privilege. They are also proud of the fact that, though they are just about fifteen million in number, their prophets command the reverence of over three billion people in the world.

The Christians believe in God, the Father Almighty and His only begotten son, Jesus, born of the Holy Spirit and Mary, the virgin. The crucial aspect of it is that they hold belief in the theory of divine incarnation. Jesus was crucified by Pontius Pilate and died for deliverance of his people. He, however, rose from the dead on the third day and ascended to heaven to sit by the side of the Father. They further believe that he would come back to earth some day to judge the living and the dead. For them, the Law given to Moses stands modified by what their Lord said during his discourses.

The Muslims have the simplest doctrine of certitude to follow. This requires them to believe that only Allah is worthy of worship and Mohammad is His messenger.

It is time now to take a closer look at these religions in all reverence, but with an open mind, to form a view how far their belief systems could be appreciated by the communities outside their ambit.

# 6

# Judaism—The Parent Faith

Judaism is the parent Semitic faith and the place where it sprouted is the land of prophets. We already had a glimpse into the Jewish history, faith, psyche and belief systems up to around the Mosaic era. The Jew are not all that religious people in the matter of observance of rites, but they take intense pride in their past for some very good reasons. The most striking feature of their character is that they have never been afraid to walk alone. Following their faith and fate would, thus, be an interesting, if not a rewarding study.

They have produced a galaxy of prophets like Adam, Noah, Abraham, Moses, David, Solomon and host of others who are recognised and revered by at least half the humanity. Christianity formally accepts them as the forerunners of Jesus, the son of God, who incidentally was also a Jew. The Muslims, despite all their antipathy for the Jews today, take pride in the fact that they are the descendents of Abraham. 'Kaaba', their holiest spot, is deeply associated with this Prophet. Around a dozen of the Jewish prophets find reverential mention in the holy Koran— Noah as Nuh, Abraham as Ibrahim, Moses as Musa, David as Dawoud, Solomon as Suleiman, Joseph as Yusuf, Jacob as Yaqub and so on. The Old Testament, the biographic record of the Hebrew prophets, their believed encounter with the Divine and their views about the origin of the world etc, forms an essential adjunct of the Holy Bible.

The Jews claim credit for introducing God to the mankind, first as 'El Shaddai' during the Abraham era and finally as

'Yahweh' in the time of their most highly regarded prophet, Moses. Moses is believed to have entered in to a covenant with Yahweh at Mount Sinai. This covenant containing a set of the Ten Commandments from God is the cornerstone of Judaism. The Jews thus believe themselves to be the chosen people of God who had the privilege of entering in to a direct agreement about their inter-personal relationship with the Divine. The text of this covenant is the written law, Torah and the unwritten one, Halakah. 'Pentateuch' (i.e. The Five Books of Moses) stands incorporated in the Old Testament that is often referred to as 'The Jews' Bible'. This aspect of the matter would be looked into in a separate chapter devoted to Christianity.

Judaism is thus a revealed religion like many other faiths. Still, it is more moral than metaphysical in substance. It does talk about Yahweh inscribing His commandments on stone slabs with his fingers and also descending down the mountain as a ball of fire. Yet, His commandments carry a predominantly moral message for His people for living a clean and righteous life and also, of course, to keep Him in mind in all their travails and triumphs. The Jews believe that the private covenant with God entitles them to claim themselves as the original people. Accordingly, they assert their separateness and superiority wherever they may happen to be. Prof. Goldscheider writes in this context, "A detailed examination of family, marriage, childbearing, social class, residence, occupation and education among Jews and non-Jews leads to the unmistakable conclusion that Jews are different. Their distinctiveness as a community is further reinforced by religious and ethnic forms of cohesiveness." Jews have, indeed, made tremendous sacrifices and paid a heavy price to sustain this claim of distinctiveness, though it is a matter of debate whether all this was really necessary.

They are scattered all over the world and are too few in numbers, hardly about 15 million. Yet, they have always made their presence felt in the world in one way or the other. There would have been many more of them in the world today but for their sustained persecution over the centuries, particularly their wholesale slaughter in Eastern Europe by the Cossacks in the seventeenth century and the holocaust they suffered at the hands of Hitler in Nazi Germany during the Second World War. Their biggest present day concentrations are in America, Israel and Russia. These three countries hold 80% of the world Jewry. They live huddled together in big and small clusters in the cities, maintaining good distance with the neighbouring communities. They are allergic to mixing with others, so as not to get lost in the crowd. Yet, they have generally desired to be at peace with their surroundings. The people around them have somehow always felt challenged by their exclusiveness. The only area where they could heave a long sigh of relief in their history is America.

Nevertheless, wherever they are, they are the prosperous people and the neighbours' envy for their money power and business acumen. Prosperity and persecution have always kept company with them as the two sides of their palpable destiny. They believe their prosperity flows from a sort of the Divine Will. One can have some idea about this from the following passage extracted from their scriptures:-

> "The Lord shall open unto thee His good treasures—— and bless all the work of thine hand: and thou shall lend unto many nations, and thou shall not borrow."
>
> —Deutronomy-28:12.

Similarly an indication about what they have undergone through the ages can be had from the following words:-

> "— neither once nor twice nor three times was our destruction planned; in every generation they rise against us (Jews), and in every generation God delivers us from their hands into freedom, out of anguish into joy, out of mourning into festivity, out of darkness into light, out of bondage into redemption."[1]

Their festivity profiles have been undergoing some evolutionary changes with the passage of time. The Jews after all are very ancient people who were semi-nomadic to begin with. After many centuries had gone tumultuously past them raising dust in their face, they started settling down to agrarian life. Now, they are involved in multifarious urban occupations. The contours of their festivals have been getting slowly redrawn in line with their societal needs and history, but the core continues to be the same.

Their most important festival is the 'Passover (Pesakh)' or 'Seder Feast' that falls in March/ April every year. It was earlier a spring festival connected with the sprouting of grain. The great escape of the Jews under Moses from the Egyptian bondage i.e. the Biblical Exodus, gave an entirely new meaning to these spring festivities. It turned in to a sort of the 'anniversary of Israel's natal day' or a great leap of faith. It is since celebrated as a day of their undying faith in liberation and renewal. The function begins with recitals from 'Haggadah' and remembrance of the adversities faced during the bondage. This is followed by singing of psalms till the meal time. As per their solemn undertaking with Yahweh enlivened bread remains a taboo for them for one week. In the end, solemnity gives way to festivity when the rejoicing children take over the function.

The next on the calendar of the Hebrew festivals is the 'Pentecost'. It is the thanks-giving rite for being given the Law at Sinai. This is followed by the festivals of 'Rosh Hashanah' or New Year's Day in September/October, the 'Yom Kippur' (Day of Atonement), 'Succoth' (for expression of gratefulness to God for His help during their wanderings in wilderness for long periods of time), 'Hannukkah' (in commemoration of the rededication of the Temple at Jerusalem by Judas Maccabeus in BC 165) in December and 'Purim' (related to deliverance of Jews through the patriotic effort of Esther) in February/March. Besides, they are enjoined upon to observe a weekly holiday, Sabbath, on every Saturday. This is meant to be a day of rest and prayer for them. (Similarly, both Christians and the Muslim also observe weekly rest days devoted to visits to their respective shrines for prayer. Since Saturdays already stood booked, the Christians have their holidays/holydays on Sundays and the Muslim on Fridays). These functions go a long way in keeping the Jews, sprinkled all over the western world, together.

The Jews worship in their synagogues guided by their rabbi's (priests). The synagogues are oriented towards Jerusalem and a cupboard in the east wall contains the scroll of Law, known as Ark. Before it hangs a lamp to indicate the eternal presence of Yahweh and this recalls the 'Ner Tamid', the candle-stick that burned perpetually at the Temple at Jerusalem, originally built by Solomon. Its fragrant smoke represents the prayers rising to Him all the time. The other symbol at the shrines is the hexagonal Shield of David which is now proudly displayed on the flag of Israel also.

As already explained, the Jews are not overly religious people. Not many of them are the regulars to the synagogues and a majority of them finds it difficult to observe Sabbath, their mandatory holiday or their dietary stipulations. The observant Jews or the orthodox among them do try to live by the Torah. But it is impossible to live up to the conditions settled three and a half millennia back, howsoever liberal you might get in your interpretation to fit these in to modern lifestyles. Some old ideas, whatever be the sentiment or sanctity behind these, have to make way for the newer ones with the passage of time.

It is, however, doubtful that the Jews, or for that matter the faithful from the other religions, would ever be able to reconcile to the truth that no text has directly descended from God — God does not talk in Hebrew, Greek, Latin, Sanskrit or Arabic. He converses in the language of soul through the channel of one's consciousness. The faithful should, however, be free to believe in whatever they like to. To the credit of the Jews, they have been adamant about their faith alright, but generally not violent about it. The worlds of faith and fact are perhaps meant to live side by side. Life, after all, is not logic alone. Specially, in a situation where literacy is lacking, logic carries very little meaning. The view that man needs faith to get to God does carry weight. After all, he, with his 'finite and fallible reason' cannot comprehend the phenomenon of revelation. Also, it seems to be the will of God that man must reserve a corner in his heart for faith also.

What have held the Jewish community together over the ages is their belief and value systems, literature, traditions, practices and festivals. Lost to us are the two stone slabs on which Yahweh is believed to have inscribed his initial commandments with his fingers and also the 'Ark' in the temple at Jerusalem that bore this Hebrew Law. Nonetheless, the will of God seems to be impressed permanently on every Hebrew heart that still beats. Their Prophets, rabbis and saintly personalities have left a comprehensive account of their traditions, practices, history, social regulations and moral precepts behind in the form of sacred literature, specially the 'Old Testament', 'Mishnah' and 'Talmud' to guide their activities in all spheres of their life.

The Mishnah compiled in AD 220 is based on materials of the last six centuries and takes in its sweep all the unwritten laws of Judaism. Talmud that was completed by the 5th century is an authoritative and exhaustive compendium, covering the Jewish beliefs, oral traditions, history, fasts, festivals, civil and criminal laws, moral codes, rites, rituals, mode of repentances, offerings, sacrifices etc. Generally speaking, it lays down how the Jewish life is to be lived. It is a sort of practical and elaborated version of Torah that has to be followed by the faithful, without raising any excuse relating to confusion and lack of clarity about their scriptures. Periodically, some 'Back to Torah' voices have arisen and some find the Talmudic way of life too inflexible, but the general acceptability and sanctity of Talmud still remains undiminished. Hebrew had, more or less, become a dead language long time back. Thus, the Jewish scriptures came to be translated in to Arabic. These were later rendered into Greek, Latin and many other languages of the world.

Yet, whether at all or to what degree, they should change with the times has caused some superficial divisions in the Jewish community. Four of these, the 'Orthodox', 'Conservative', 'Reform' and 'Reconstructionist' are easily identifiable. The state of Israel patronizes 'orthodox' Judaism only, though just around 10 to 15 % Jews identify themselves with this brand of their faith. The orthodox believe in a literal way that Torah was settled with Yahweh both in the oral as well as the written form. Being the God-given law, it could not be tinkered with at all. The conservatives also believe that Torah is of divine origin, but they think that it can accommodate change. Reform Judaism views Torah as a statement of eternal principles in historic context, but it recognizes the necessity of keeping it in tune with the times. The reconstructionist approach to Judaism is that their faith is a 'historical religious civilisation' and it identifies God in naturalist, rather than supernatural form. They are for creative adjustments in line with the needs of modern life. All forms of Judaism, thus, revolve around the Torah. The differences are just superficial and relate only to the degree of flexibility about the Torah.

'Orthodox' and 'Conservative' streams of Judaism define the Jew as a person born to a Jewish mother. 'Reform' Judaism extends this recognition to any individual born to a Jewish father also. Conversions to Orthodox Judaism are permissible if carried out by the Orthodox rabbis. In case of conversions to other formulations of Judaism, their validity is seriously questioned in Israel, though it does not pose any problems in the U.S.A. Because of the fact that the Jews are hardly enthusiastic and are rather choosy about inductions into their community, they have all through remained a miniscule minority, while their off-shoots, i.e. the Islam and Christianity, who pulled all stops for conversions when the going was good, have gone galloping far ahead of them.

Judaism differs from Christianity as it does not recognize the New Testament, though the Christians reverently accept the Old Testament as integral part of their holy Bible. Similarly, it differs from the Islam as it holds Moses as unique among the Prophets. In fact, it does not recognize any prophecy, including that of Mohammad, outside the ambit of their scriptural literature. This has been the historic cause of hatred against them among the sister Semitic faiths. They respect their ancestry, but hate them for their audaciously exclusive claim over their antiquity. We, in fact, need going a little deeper to explore this aspect and may wait a while for it.

After the great escape from slavery in Egypt under Moses, the Jews started collecting at the foot of Mount Sinai. There they had an encounter with their God, Yahweh and entered in to a covenant with Him. This agreement originally consisted of the Ten Commandments from God which relate to His demand for exclusive obeisance to Him and also some moral precepts and practices that the Jews were required to follow in their social life. Later a lot many more instructions were added and finally the first five books of Moses (Genesis, Exodus, Leviticus, Numbers and Deuteronomy, collectively known as Pentateuch) of the Bible refer to as many as 613 commandments. These commandments carry a clear imprint of the Age when these were pronounced, both with respect to the time and locale. Reason would, therefore, suggest that these could only be the words of man and not anything in the nature of an eternal message from the Divine. The faithful, however, believe that the commandments constitute a revelation from God, though they themselves find it hard to live by many of these in today's context.

The Jews on their escape from Egypt did not have a very smooth passage to the promised land of Palestine. They had to struggle hard for years to dislodge the native Canaanites and finally establish themselves in the area. This was the time when they started switching over from a semi-nomadic life to an agrarian culture. Since agriculture depends heavily on the mood of the natural forces and the Canaanite agrarian ceremonies (Baalism), connected with nature worship, were found to be more relevant, exciting and colourful, a trend developed among the Jews towards a sort of 'Baalisation' of Yahweh. Some of them seemed developing a tendency to see Yahweh as the chief Baal i.e. the primary agrarian god or the first among the many equals. This naturally clashed head on with the basic tenets of Judaism that recognised no god other than Yahweh. Thus, a number of illustrious prophets had to make appearance on the scene to pull the wayward Jews back on the track of monotheism. The most prominent among them are Elijah, Elisha, Amos, Hosea, Isaiah, Mica and Jeremiah who appeared in the later part of first millennium B.C. The ideas of Jeremiah out of them appear to be quite ahead of his times. He made out that man was in one-to-one relationship with God and individually responsible for his actions:-

> "Jeremiah brought men face to face with God as individuals who were responsible to Him for their conduct; they could no longer say that He dealt with men only through their group relationships. This was a preposition of great importance; for its logical corollary was: if human relationship to God is a direct and personal relationship, then the approach to God through Temple sacrifice may not be all-important, may even be no longer requisite to highest spiritual living of the individual."[2]

Also, the Near-East near about this time was abounding in Prophets. It became fashionable for the men of ambition to proclaim that they were carrying some message or the other from God for the masses. Such men duly invited the wrath of Jeremiah. He pronounces a severe judgement on them:-

> "Thus says the Lord of hosts:
> 'Listen not to the words of the prophets who prophecy to you!
> They fill you with vain hopes;
> They speak a vision from their own minds,
> Not from the mouth of the Lord..."[3]

The Hebrew national sovereignty in Palestine was, however, not destined to stay in peace for long and there was to be no end to the agony of the Jews. In B.C. 597, they were attacked by the Babylonian King Nebuchadnezzar over their refusal to pay tribute. They had to sue for peace and surrender unconditionally. Their temple at Jerusalem was looted and the Judean king and around ten thousand elite citizens, consisting of nobles, renowned warriors, craftsmen and smiths etc., were carried away to Babylon to be settled as colonists on the bank of River Chebar. In B.C. 586, the Hebrew felt strong enough to rebel against the Babylonian empire. This time they had their domains completely devastated and the temple destroyed.

In fact, nothing was heard about the Holy Ark kept there after this raid. All the surviving citizens of Jerusalem who in some way mattered were taken away and the country was virtually vacated of the Judean nation. Jews were no strangers to such misfortunes. Earlier, during the Assyrian deportation, a bigger tragedy had struck them as a result of which ten of their tribes just vanished into thin air, not to be heard of again in history. Only Yahweh knows what really happened to them. They were perhaps largely annihilated and a few of their members who survived melted into various other communities settled far and wide.

The exiles to Babylon were treated well in the alien land and were also allowed to return to Palestine during the regime of King Cyrus in B.C. 538 and rebuild their temple at Jerusalem. This was their third home-coming in history, the first two being historically connected with their Prophets, Abraham and Moses. Not all the exiles chose to return to Palestine. Those who did decide to come home organised themselves in to a priestly state. Judaism assumed its set contours in this period and it also came in contact with the Greek ideas and the Persian beliefs. These alien influences do not seem to have left any significant impact on the Judean faith. By and large, the Jews were able to keep both Hellenism and Zoroastrianism out of their creedal system.

The next round of misfortune descended on them when the Romans under Titus, the son of Emperor Vespasian, over-ran their land and destroyed their country so completely that it was virtually depopulated of the Jewish community and they got sprinkled over various places in the western hemisphere. Of their most sacred shrine at Jerusalem, only a portion of the western wall stands today for the Jews to lean against and cry their hearts out over their destruction and complete dispersal from their national home. They had to wait for nearly two thousand years to be back here. This holy relic from the distant past aptly goes by the name of 'The Wailing Wall'. This, of course, was not part of the temple and only a breast wall to support the filling that was done on a side of the mound to support the constructions thereon. Today its crevices get tucked in with petitions of the faithful addressed to the Divine Being.

After this great dispersal from Palestine, the Jews had to spend their time in Europe mostly as stateless people. Their attempts at seclusion and secrecy to maintain their identity as superior people did not go well with the neighbouring communities. They were often seen as conspiratorial people, with little sense of belonging to the place where they lived. They somehow survived as second-class citizens for centuries in various countries of Europe like England, France, Spain, Germany, Austria and Poland etc. Yet, they often had torrid time living there. When they were not being slaughtered, they were being expelled. When not being expelled, they were confined to ghettoes and subjected to all sorts of indignities. Ultimately, their destiny turned a full circle and they were forced to look eastwards again. Though they now had no home there, they could settle down in the neighbouring lands. Finally, after nearly nineteen centuries, they had a place, Israel, which they could call their home and where they could live as first class citizens.

Before destruction of Jerusalem in AD 70, the Romans had happened to crucify the most important Jew of history, Jesus. After this, the things were never to be the same again. His innocent blood was to change the course of human history. Some fellow Jews had a hand in his crucifixion and the Jews as a community had to pay a heavy price for this sin. Over his ashes was to arise the biggest religious community of the world—the Christianity.

The sprouting of the new faith was not a very spectacular affair to begin with. It was just the branching off of Judaism in a new direction with Jesus standing tall at the junction point, while the vintage Judaism went along its old ways. For good about three centuries,. the followers of Jesus tried to convince the Jews that Jesus was the Christ i.e. a Messiah in the long line of their own prophets, but their stiff-necked would have none of this. They stubbornly refused to accept any prophecy outside the ambit of their scriptures. This, however, could not stop the rapid spread of the new religion, particularly in the north-westerly direction. St. Paul carried the Christian gospel into Europe and the Greek with their flair for philosophy placed the figure of Jesus in a cosmological setting and developed a proper theology around it. In the year AD 312, Emperor Constantine embraced Christianity. This was a big leap forward for the new faith. Soon it rose to the status of a state religion. Now it did not have to look to the Jewish rabbis for credibility. The reluctance of the Jews to extend recognition to their faith left a bitter taste in Christian mouths. The Jews were to suffer heavily for this during the coming centuries.

The history repeated itself in the seventh century when the sands of Arabia came alive with the advent of Prophet Mohammad. The new prophet had a reverential regard for the Hebrew ideology and prophets and seemed to have picked up many of his ideas from this older creed. The intense reluctance of the Jews to share their divine legacy with others and accept a two-way religious relationship with other communities again came in the way of harmonious tie-up with Prophet Mohammad. They just would not accept him as a prophet. As a result of this they had to suffer massacres and migrations from Arabia. They, however, had much better time under the Muslim dispensations in Babylonia, Palestine and Syria till the Turks appeared on the scene.

It would make a study of great interest to visualize the shape of the world if the three great Semitic religions— Judaism, Christianity and Islam— would have been one, but for the monopolistic attitude of the Jews towards their religious legacy. Christianity and Islam were initially ready to go with them, but the Jew would not allow them to walk in their way. If one of the oldest religions of the world remained in a state of miniscule minority all the time there have to be reasons for it. It is really the intense pride of the Jews in their past and their stubborn belief in being the special people of God that seems to have deprived them of the glory that was theirs for the asking.

They are the chosen people alright, but not chosen to receive His special favours, 'but to serve mankind as bearers of light' bestowed on them. Thus, they appear to have missed the real part of their brief. It did not occur to them that God belongs to the entire universe. If Yahweh really was God, He could not be their God alone— He had to belong to all and in equal measure. They could take credit for introducing Him to the human kind, but not insist that they were His exclusive concern. A sort of attitude that nobody could be what they are, could naturally never be acceptable to anybody outside their fraternity. With the correct thinking on their part, the religious scenarios of the world would perhaps been quite different today. There would have then been just one religion of the Semitic world— Judaism, with half the humanity turning its head for prayer towards Jerusalem as its undisputed 'kiblah'. A magnificent temple would have stood at the place rather than just a wall to wail against. There is perhaps a lesson for the humanity in all this— religions must not divide, but rather endeavour to bring the God's family together.

## Notes

1. 'Haggadah of Passover' translated by Maurice Samuel p. 26, Hebrew Publishing Co., New York, 1942.
2. 'Man's Religions' by John B. Noss, p. 503.
3. 'Man's Religions' by John B. Noss, p. 501.

# 7

# Christianity—Born of Holy Blood

When a pious and innocent man is hanged, some sort of a shiver passes through the God's universe. Thousands were hung on the cross during the Roman reign of Palestine some two thousand years back. History hardly took any notice of these executions, though some of those executed might have been innocent. Such innocents are deemed to be the martyrs in the cause of justice, meaning thereby that justice just cannot be administered without some innocents also getting occasionally punished in the process. However, when Jesus was strung on the cross at Golgotha, the blood spilling from his wounds made the hideous wood holy, for he was not an ordinary innocent. His blood and pain was to give an incredible push to his message and an added meaning to his ideas after he was gone. Today more than one third of the humanity holds him in heart and wears the replica of his cross reverently round its neck.

However, as Rome was not built in a day, all this also did not happen overnight. Rather, those who had gathered to witness his execution, mostly women, withdrew quickly in awe as darkness descended, leaving him alone in his agony. It, in fact, took years for the followers of Jesus to have him recognised as 'Christ' i.e. a Messiah. Those who resisted the idea were primarily the people of his own fraternity—the Jews. Their clergy made out that the revelations part of their creed had already been long concluded and whatever was worth revealing to mankind had already been revealed by Yahweh to Moses and the other Prophets who found mention in their scriptures. So, there could be no more prophets to receive His messages for their community. This, unfortunately, is the problem with most of the religions. They attribute finality to something settled centuries back and thus, virtually make man a prisoner of the past. In fact, all this also does not speak well of the human intelligence. It often gets overclouded by religious traditions and inscrutable next-life concerns rather too easily.

God is not a being of history— He is an eternal phenomenon beyond all history. Jesus, believed to be His son, however, is very much a historic persona who lived among us in flesh and blood. His is the only case in the entire Semitic spectrum where incarnation has been mooted. Otherwise, the idea of divine incarnations belongs exclusively to the Hindu belief system. (Just call to mind the nine incarnations ('Avatar's') of Lord Vishnu, as already referred to.)

For the reasons indicated above, the account of Jesus that has come to us over the last two millennia is 'a mixture of historical judgement, religious and cultural tradition, and personal faith.' The historical part of it is that he was born at Bethlehem, south of Jerusalem, in to a family domiciled at Nazareth of Galilee. Palestine had then come under the Roman rule recently. The Roman, unlike the Greek who also held sway over the land in the past, did not believe in fraternising with the native populations or appreciating their sensitivities. They made no attempt to build bridges of understanding with the Jews and just went about administering the captured territory in a mechanical manner, devoid of any human touch. Their hard- hearted rule was felt like a yoke round their neck by the natives. Jesus was thus born in a bitter world.

He grew up in a large family of four brothers— James, Joses, Simon and Jude—and at least two sisters. His was a deeply religious family and he himself was a contemplative person. Nobody, except the staunch devotees, is clear about the date or even the year of his birth. He was probably born a few years before what the calendar attributed to his birth suggests. In any case, this Roman calendar was launched sometimes in the middle of the sixth century AD. His worldly father, Joseph, was in the profession of carpentry and Jesus also was trained as a carpenter. On his father's death, Jesus, as the eldest son, seems to have taken over the family business and his brothers helped him in running it. History is, however, silent about how he did as a carpenter. He may have made many a ploughshares, yokes and carts etc. for the Galilean farmers. He did not believe in asceticism and rather, enjoyed wedding feasts and banquets.

Right from the age of twelve, Jesus gave some glimpse of being predisposed towards a prophetic role in his life. All this, however, lay largely dormant within him. His baptism by John, a prophetic soul with a large following, around the age of thirty gave an entirely new direction to his life. Gone were the quiet years of his earlier life and he got filled with a mystic vision. He felt consecrated and commissioned by God to guide the humanity. He disappeared for a while in the sandy wilderness beyond river Jordan to meditate and decide about his next course of action. Here, it is said that the Satan tried to tempt him out of the mission that he had in mind. What it means historically is that he was yet undecided and felt like returning to his old ways of mundane life as a carpenter or to go for some other such worldly option.

Finally, he made up his mind that he would not walk the way of the rebellious Zealots, nor the close-minded legalists, the Pharisees and nor the Sadducees wrapped in religious rigidities. He did not want to retire into monastic seclusion either. Being a plain person himself, he wanted to stay and work among the plain people. He started with preaching in synagogues where he spoke in a heart-to-heart manner, with homely illustrations drawn from nature and native life. People felt quite at ease with his preaching as he never suggested that body was inherently corrupting and defiling or that 'soul was foully imprisoned in the flesh'. This meant that one could take life easy and there was no real need to put body in any sort of pain to cleanse it. Though he kept reminding his people that they should purge themselves of their sin as it would not be tolerated in the new dawn that was waiting to break, yet his discourses generally had a nerve-soothing effect. Soon the people started getting convinced about his divine calling and he began collecting quite a few disciples around him. The first to move under his spiritual umbrella were Simon Peter, Andrews, James and John.

Sustained oppression and adversity had nearly disoriented the Jews. They always seemed looking skyward for appearance of a Messiah to deliver them. An expectation was in the air that the day of deliverance was not very far off, as the limits of their endurance had already been breached. This was somewhat akin to the Hindu belief articulated in Bhagavad Gita. Let us have a look at some verses from this work to understand what was then churning in the Semitic mind:

यदा यदा ही धर्मस्य ग्लानिर्भवति भारत।
अभ्युत्थानमधर्मस्य तदात्मानं सृजाम्यहम्।।
परित्राणाय साधूनां विनाशाय च दुष्कृताम्।
धर्मसंस्थापनार्थाय सम्भावामि युगे युगे।।

— Bhagavad Gita Chapter- IV, Verses 7&8.

(O, Bharat, whenever righteousness comes to be trampled and inappropriateness gets in to a position of ascendency, I incarnate myself in the world age to age to bring succour to the pious, to destroy sinful propensities and to re-establish faith of the peop'e in righteousness.)

Jesus also believed that the prayers of his people were going to get answered soon and the 'Kingdom of Heaven' was just round the corner. People must make themselves worthy of His kingdom. They must be oriented towards Him as sons and towards each other as brothers. No man was to be excluded from God's grace and man's fellowship. There were to be no exceptions to the 'law of love'. Thus, Jesus, in a way, converted Yahweh of the Jews in to the universal God. Earlier, God was perceived to be in master-slave relationship with man. Jesus raised it to the far more agreeable filial level. Nobody, not even the angels, could time the day of deliverance exactly, but it was not very far off. This belief brought him close to his people and sent a flutter through the expectant hearts. The thrill of this expectancy is simply impossible to fathom today. He and the common people were thus on the same page in their predicament and hope for imminent deliverance.

Every society tends to develop a creamy layer in course of time. These vested interests are naturally eager to maintain their hold on the masses by means both fair and foul. They try to convince the people that they belonged to the chosen race alright but their deliverance depended on following a correct course under their guidance. Their religious leadership had thus convinced the Jews that they were, indeed, special to Yahweh and the others could never hope to have this privilege. Jesus, however, preached that God belonged to all in equal measure. His sun shone and rain fell on everybody— good or bad, high or low. He was 'Love' personified and hated only sin and not the sinner. Jesus fondly referred to Him as Father to all. He thus universalised Him and made Him in to an inter-racial and international Being. This was naturally not to the liking of the privileged ones who did not want to stand in the queue and share Him. Earlier also some Jewish thinkers had tried to lend universality to Yahweh. However, this was done to enhance His position for their own racial aggrandisement. They otherwise stubbornly believed that they were racially more equal than others in His eyes. Jesus simply upturned this claim on its head and eventually came to be seen as a rebel, trying to outreach the Jewish establishment. He was, in fact, a reformer, rather than a rebel. He did have the intention to selectively challenge and change the existing order, but entirely through a peaceful effort.

Miracles attract minds like a magnet because people see a glimpse God in these. Miracles are nothing but unexpected occurrences that many of us may have encountered at one time or the other in our lives. It is, however, doubtful if anybody, other than the Divine Being, has ever been capable of miracles at will. Common man, undoubtedly, expects miracles from his prophets and saints. Even Vatican does not like to raise persons to sainthood without somehow attributing miracles to them. This is how the case of Mother Teresa is held up, though her entire life itself has been nothing short of a miracle.

The Jewish society in the Age of Jesus was full of spiritual and nervous tensions and all the ailments that go with these. There were cases where some persons were thought to be possessed of evil spirits. Mental troubles can lead to some physical and functional disorders also. Jesus was seen to be having spiritual authority and thus, a healing touch. Sometimes the very contact with him might have worked wonders and the alarming symptoms of some patients' disease might have vanished miraculously. On some other occasions the body resistance of the patients might have healed them before they appeared before him for relief. Yet in other cases where healing effect was not in evidence, the patients might have brought themselves round to believe that they could not be cured because of their sinful background, undeserving of relief. Whatever might be the case, Jesus got established as a great faith-healer with the people and they thronged to him for cure in droves. Many of them felt cured, but Jesus was humble enough to tell his patients that it was their own faith that had healed them.

Jesus believed himself to have been 'sent ahead' to establish the 'Kingdom of God'. His authority seemed to be coming from within him. Once he told the gathering before him that there was nothing more important for them than to listen to him because through him, God spoke. He could thus preach, teach and heal with authority and confidence. He also had the privilege of choosing twelve men to follow him. He could even propound a law superseding that of Moses that no Jew had dared to do till then. Just sample this:-

> "You have heard that (the men of old) were told, 'An eye for an eye and a tooth for a tooth'. But I tell you not to resist injury, but if any one strikes you on your right cheek, turn the other to him too; if anyone wants to sue you for your shirt, let him have your coat too."
>
> —Mathew 5: 38-40.

The principal points of departure from the traditional law were that he saw no room for vengefulness and violence in the 'Kingdom of God'— Here even the enemies were to be loved— and he placed higher premium on the spirit rather than the letter of the Law. He stressed on inner morality and not just on the observance of law. This clarifies what he in fact meant:-

> "—— anyone who looks at a woman with desire has already committed adultery with her in his heart."
>
> —Mathew 5:28.

He had a very correct and clear perspective of the greatness of life that came directly from the Divine and believed that the laws were meant for life and not life for the laws. Once when some distracters tried to needle him with the accusation that his men were violating the tradition of Sabbath, he is said to have retorted — "The Sabbath was made for man, not man for the Sabbath"

— Mark. 2:27-28.

Besides the Romans who were hardly concerned whether the people they ruled lived or died, there were then three more power centres in Palestine— the Pharisees who interpreted and administered the Jewish law, the Sadducees who controlled the Temple and the religious affairs and the Zealots who as rebels against the Roman rule, though badly crushed, still wielded some power as an underground force. Jesus had scant regard for any of them. He felt that the Pharisees were like the 'white-washed tombs having bodies and bones inside', the Sadducees were more concerned with the religious rites and practices rather than the inner ethics and the Zealots had brought only death and destruction to their community by putting faith in the sword. He rather pointed out that those who live by the sword, died by the sword.

Jesus was himself seen emerging as yet another power centre with thousands of people thronging to him for his discourses as well as faith-healing ability. He appeared to be assuming all the trappings of a Messiah. He was openly criticising the established authority and reinterpreting and even superseding some Mosaic laws. His universalising the Jewish faith was also not to the liking of the vested interests as it meant stripping their community of their special status with God. They finally decided to take on his challenge.

The Pharisees and Sadducees of Jerusalem therefore sent teams to report on him and heckle him before the people. The Zealots also turned against him. Under the weight of this combined opposition and the sustained propaganda against him people started getting disenchanted with him and ultimately he was forced to retire towards the regions north-west to Tyre, Sidon and south Syria. Jesus, however, could not reconcile with this escapist solution. He was soon clear in his mind that his mission needed some blood transfusion to revive and the blood had to be his own. He thus got himself mentally ready for the supreme sacrifice that was to lead him to the cross. Accordingly, he started moving towards Jerusalem with his companions on the quiet to be there at the time of the annual Passover.

Once there, he angrily upturned the tables of the money changers and removed the pigeon dealers from the Temple, as such commercial activities had the effect of degrading the sacred precincts. This proved to be a popular move and many of his old devotees mobbed him for his discourse. However, the issue of poll-tax to the Romans was rankling badly in the people's breast at the time. Jesus refused to speak against it and rather said, "Give Caesar what belongs to Caesar, give God what belongs to God". This did not go well with the gathering. He also threw a challenge to the Pharisees and the Sadducees that the tax-collectors and prostitutes would be admitted to the coming 'Kingdom of God' ahead of them. He thus seemed to be knowingly creating a case for his own prosecution.

That he clearly foresaw his death would be evident from what transpired during his historic Last Super with his twelve companions. Breaking his bread, he gave a piece to each of them saying that these were the pieces of his body. Similarly, while offering them a cup of wine, he said that the cups contained his blood. By taking these pieces and sips from the cups offered by him, they were to become one with him and he meant to live through them. Next day, he, having been betrayed by Judas, was seized by an armed mob sent by the high priest in the Garden of Gethsemane and dragged before the Jewish judicial body, Sanhedrin that promptly condemned him to death for blasphemy. He was taken to the Procurator, for execution. Pilate referred him to the Governor, Herod Antipas, who, however, felt his case to be a hot potato. He sent the case back post haste to Pilate for disposal under his own orders. Pilate made a last ditch effort to save him. One prisoner was traditionally released every year on occasion of the Pass-over. He wanted Jesus to be adjusted against this quota of clemency. The crowd, however, shouted instead for the release of Barabbas, a Zealot insurrectionist, rather than Jesus. Orders were thus finally passed for his crucifixion. All his companions had already deserted him. Rather, Peter, when identified as one of the follower of Jesus, by a woman in the gathering had denied the fact. Jesus was mercilessly flogged and made to wear a crown of thorns before being led to his crucifixion. A thorn from this crown is said to be preserved in the British Museum. It reached here via Constantinople, Paris and finally through Mary, the Queen of Scots. At the place where he was crucified and buried stands the Church of Holy Sepulchre and the trail that he walked on way to his execution is known as Via Dolorosa (the Way to Sorrow).

Jesus had left quite a few disciples behind who came out of their hiding shortly after his death to carry his message far and wide. Perhaps his blood on the cross had stung them in to action. The large following that Jesus had gathered during his own life time came handy for the purpose. Much above all else, his martyrdom caught the imagination of the people and he came to be seen as the much awaited Messiah. The earliest converts to Christianity were understandably the Jews. They endeavoured to have Jesus formally recognised as 'Christ' i.e. a messiah, but their rabbis would not have any of this. This, however, did not deter the apostles who went about preaching his gospel as the men possessed.

Besides the Jewish foundation to build upon, Christianity was lucky to have quite a few philosophically minded followers to inject rationality in to their creed. They provided the much needed ideological and mystical back-bone for the new religion to stand erect and prosper. This was fabricated out of the material provided by the sacrifice of Jesus. He was to be the focal point of the new spirituality. Henceforth, he was not just to be an extra-ordinary mortal, the son of Joseph and Mary, but to be the son of God, born to the virgin (Mary) through divine intervention. He thought of God as the Father of the entire mankind. This made eminent sense for, if we are not His children, whose children are we? His followers, however, made out that he alone was part of the Godhead and the rest of us were the ordinary beings, carrying the foul baggage of our sinful bodies. Our salvation lay in repentance and seeking the Grace of God, Christ and the Holy Spirit to guide us towards righteousness.

All this started with the building up a belief in the resurrection of the body of Jesus two days after his execution. It was considered inauspicious to let the body of Jesus hang on the cross on the holy days of the Passover. It was, therefore, removed and placed in a tomb. After two days when some women went to see it they did not find it there. The faithful say that they saw the resurrected Jesus being flown heavenwards by a bunch of fairies. This belief is now the cornerstone of Christianity and the occasion is celebrated all over the Christian world as 'Easter' and their ceremony of 'Baptism' is also based on this faith in renewal.

Baptism emerged as an initiation ceremony for the converts to Christianity and the children born to the Christians. It is carried out in running water outdoors or in 'baptisteries'. The sacred bath is accompanied by an oath to hold abiding faith in God, His Son and the Holy Spirit. What follows next are the blessings of a bishop, the pouring of consecrated oil (called 'Chrism'), prayers and the holy feast of the 'Eucharist'. After this, the convert gets formally admitted as a member of the Christian fraternity.

The Jewish hierarchy could never be expected to take kindly to the ideology of the man that they had had so ruthlessly executed. However, Jesus had quite a few illustrious companions to take care of his message after him. Paul and Peter who were later raised to sainthood by the Roman Church stand out among them and it is because of them that Rome eventually emerged as a sort of capital of the new creed. St. Paul was initially inimical towards Jesus but later got irresistibly drawn towards his personality. He spent the rest of his life not only as a carrier of his message but also as a weaver of divinity around him. Because of his relentless effort and his Roman connection, Christianity was able to spread its wings in Europe. It is sad that he also got eventually executed by the Romans. However, like his Lord, he had already done enough to guide his fraternity from the grave. Record of St. Peter is no less luminous among the fathers of the new faith. Many others who followed them had now a sound foundation to build upon.

After the struggle of a couple of centuries, the Christianity started coming in to its own. In AD 312, Emperor Constantine embraced the new faith. Political power in their backyard works as a magic potion for the religions. The conversion of the royalty to the new creed was thus a big leap forward for the Christianity. Then followed a string of holy men, preachers, philosophers and saints to concretize its canons and enhance its appeal. Athanasius of Alexandria (C. 293-373) worked out a rationale for incarnation of Jesus. According to him, mankind was capable of direct communion with God, but our flesh stood in the way. So, Christ had to descend among us in flesh and blood to secure our bond with the divinity. St. Augustine of Hippo in North Africa (AD 354-430) led a sensual life before he saw the light at the end of the tunnel. Some holy impulse drove him out of this groove. His journey from sensuality to spirituality is a source of inspiration to the Christian world. He has done a singular service to the cause of Christianity by producing a voluminous philosophy touching all areas of Christian concern. He believed that God had infinite capacity to wash off sin of any magnitude. He envisaged two societies—one of God and the other of human self-love. St. Benedict (C. 480-547) brought a touch of monasticism to the faith. The middle ages produced another galaxy of exponents of the Christian theology like St. Francis of Assisi—The Little Poor Man (AD 1181-1226), Thomas Aquinas (AD 1224-74) — known for his highly logical arguments for the existence of God and Julian of Norwich and a host of others.

Its apostolic connection through St. Peter and St. Paul turned Rome in to the sanctum sanctorum of Christendom and carried Roman Church to top prominence. Its Bishop came to be referred to as Pope. Before the Roman Empire fell to the barbarians, they themselves had been converted to Christianity. Thus the position of high prominence enjoyed by the church at the place was not adversely effected.

However, everything in the universe rotates around itself. This equally applies to the living beings also. So, rarely do the human beings and the institutions created by them are able to rise above self-interest. Power and privileges corrupt one and all— princes and priests alike. Thus, the high clout enjoyed by the Popes and the clergy around them vitiated the holy ambiance of the place periodically and left the faithful confused and wondering as to what was going around. A Pope is known to have sold a church built with enthusiastic donations by the devotees. Another Pope came down to selling admission tickets for paradise to the gullible believers. All this pointed towards a clear need for setting the Christian house in order by shifting the emphasis from sacraments to inner piety. Reformers like Martin Luther, Calvin and Fox sent out a call to the Christian world to look within and to go back to the original scriptures. It was forcefully made out that the ritual acts were no answer to the inherent sinfulness of man: he had to set Christ at his heart, if he really wanted to liberate himself.

This ecclesiastical earthquake in the Christian world goes by the name of Reformation. This led to the setting up of numerous Lutheran and Calvinist churches in the European continent. The Church of England, though still retaining many of the Catholic features, was also greatly influenced by both Lutheranism and Calvinism. Reformation was, thus, able to tear a large chunk of the faithful away from Rome. Roman Catholic Church was, however, too well entrenched to be shaken off its foundation. Despite all the upheaval, Rome continued to be a sort of 'kiblah' of the Christian world, like Jerusalem of the Jew and Mecca of the Muslim. Lately, some more unseemly features of the Christian clergy have also come out in the open in the form of prevalence of child abuse in their precincts. One hopes that the mighty institution would soon find a way to purge itself of this aberration also.

The Protestant movement soon started flowing along many channels and thus, the Congregationalists, Baptists, Quakers and Methodists etc. made appearance on the Christian firmament. Their common denominators are the emphasis on spirituality rather than the sacraments, individual interpretation of scriptures, easier relationship between church and the devotees, recognition of local congregations as the basic units of the faith and inwardness in devotion etc.

Roman Çatholics, however, seemed to believe that the priests and the established order of their church and their sacraments also had a role to play in getting the grace of God for the faithful. All shades of the Christian faith nonetheless have God and His son, Christ, at their core.

Another power-centre of Christianity, rivaling Rome, got established in the East at Constantinople. This finds mention in history as the Eastern Orthodox or the Greek Church. The areas of its influence were Greece, Cyprus and Balkans. Armenian Church and the Coptic churches of Egypt have also got affiliation with this body. Paganism dominated the Russian belief systems till the middle of the tenth century. It is said that around this time Russia felt impelled to have a state religion. A delegation was sent to select a creed suitable for the country. Its first stop was at Constantinople. The church there took pride in its antiquity, colourfulness, and liturgical magnificence that should suggest the existence of paradise on this very planet. The Russian delegates were so deeply impressed with the ambiance of the place that they felt that they did not have to look any further. The Eastern Orthodox Church was the order they could plunge into straight away. Thus, Russia joined the Greek Church formally in AD 988 during the reign of Vladimir of Kiev and in fact, it became its mainstay when the Turks overran Constantinople in AD 1453.

The Christian ecclesiastical institutions at Rome and Constantinople have mostly remained in unhealthy rivalry and have lost no opportunity to let each other down. Even during the historic crusades they did not cooperate with each other. At best of times they just tolerated each other. In fact, this inner rivalry on one hand and the cultural clash between Christianity and Islam on the other, has converted the Balkan region into the most incendiary spot of the earth where the Western, Slavic and Islamic civilisations have been in eyeball to eyeball confrontation. Sometimes two of these entities joined hands in marriage of convenience to get even with the third. In this context, one may call to mind the Crimean war of the nineteenth century or the more recent Kosovo war.

The Holy Bible, the sacred book of Christian belief, is the most widely circulated book on the earth. It is compiled from ancient scriptures and is a collection of sixty six separate and distinct writings. Almost every aspect of life and human thought has been dealt with on its pages. It is a compendium of poems, biographies, histories, prophecies, stories, speeches, letters, prayers, hymns, religious discourses and sermons.

Bible is in two parts, the Old and New Testaments. 'Testament' stands for covenant or agreement between God and His people. Old Testament relates to the period before Christ and is a compilation of some of the sacred Hebrew writings of the period from BC 750 to BC 150. For this reason, it is often referred to as the 'Bible of the Jews' also. It contains thirty nine books considered canonical or inspired. Another fourteen books earlier excluded by the Jews were added in the end as 'apocrypha' (a Greek word, standing for 'hidden away'). The book begins with the story of the cosmic creation and expulsion of man from paradise. It then goes on to cover the great deluge in the times of Noah, the exodus of the Jews under Prophet Moses from Egypt to Palestine and numerous other facets of human life and its relationship with God. The original language of the texts included in the Old Testament was, of course, Hebrew. As the Hebrew started getting extinct, these were translated into Arabic, Greek, Latin and other languages.

Throughout the Old Testament runs a promise that God would send a 'Messiah' to deliver His people of all their woes, provided they keep their part of the covenant with Him i.e. obey His commandments. Jesus is believed to have landed among them in performance of this promise. That is how he came to be referred to as 'Christ'. With his arrival the human history turned a new leaf and a fresh chapter was opened in the form of New Testament. Jesus thus stands as a bridge between the two epochs represented by the Old and new Testaments.

New Testament was not written by Jesus Christ, but his disciples long after his death. In fact, it started taking shape by the end of second century A.D. and finalised in the fourth century only. So, it is difficult to ascertain what comes in it directly from Jesus and what has been put in his mouth by his devoted disciples.

The New Testament is primarily about the life, acts, teachings, crucifixion and resurrection of Jesus Christ. It also contains the biographic account and epistles (letters) written by the earlier apostles——some of these letters written to various churches date from AD 70 to 100. This part of the Bible originally consisted of twenty-seven books. One hundred and nine books of 'apocryphal' nature were added subsequently. The canon of the New Testament was decided at Rome in AD 382 at a council held at Rome. The oldest manuscripts of some books included in the New Testament date back to around AD 350 and these are preserved in the Vatican Library.

The original language of the New Testament was Greek. St. Jerome who lived nearly four hundred years after Christ translated Bible in to Latin. This is the official version of the Bible of the Roman Catholic Church. The Greek text with Latin translation was first printed in AD 1516. Bible was translated in to English in AD 1382. The version of Bible prepared by a committee of forty seven scholars under the orders of King James I and published in AD 1611, is the authorised version of the English Protestants. The holy book has undergone numerous revisions after this. However, the authorised version of Bible has 1189 chapters, 31173 verses and 773746 words.

The distinctive feature of Christianity is its belief in incarnation. The faithful believe Jesus to be the son of God. God being the father of a human being naturally suggests that He Himself is also human and a male. The other two Semitic religions have chosen not to hazard a guess as to who or what God is. Christianity has definitely travelled far ahead of the others with regard to the number of adherents. Every third person in the world today is a Christian. The reason for it could not be its ideological pull alone. The political clout behind the faith and the sustained effort of its missionary cadres has a lot to do with its being able to spread its wings so fast. Some two thousand years back a lonely Jesus stood strung on the cross. Now, two billion crosses hang by the neck of humanity.

# 8

# Islam—A Case of the Sands Coming Alive

In the early years of the seventh century, a glorious era was waiting to dawn on the sandy solitude of Arabia. The people, of course, saw only the sand on the surface. They then neither had any idea about the huge oil wealth buried underneath nor the new prophet who had already landed among them to complete the unfinished agenda of his predecessors. The tribal population still held belief in the numerous Gods that they had created in the form of idols placed around the black stone in 'Kaaba' at Mecca. The black stone was possibly a meteorite that had ended up at the spot many centuries back and had since become an object of veneration among the locals. They believed it to have fallen straight from the Garden of Eden during the times of Adam.

Among these pagan deities, some 350 in number, were lined up the faceless Quresh idol known as 'Allah', the idol of Lat in human shape and also the idols of Uzza and Manat. These idols were to soon fall from grace. Allah, however, was to move to His magnificent throne on the seventh heaven, but not as an idol, but as the all-knowing and all-powerful Lord of the Islamic world. Henceforth, He was to be thought of as the Unique Being, the sole depository of all divinity. All the other living beings and elements were to be in master-slave relationship with Him.

From a mountain cave of 'Hira' where Prophet Mohammad had been in meditation was to come out a creed that was destined to home in by our time in a billion and half hearts.

The founder of the new faith, Abu al-Qasim Mohammad Ibn Adb al Muttalib Hashim, was from the Hashim clan of the Quresh tribe and was born at Mecca in AD 570 after the death of his father. He was brought up by his parental grandfather and after his death, by his uncle, Abu Talib. He lost his mother, Amina, when he was barely six years old. The Quresh claimed descent from Ishmael, the son of Abraham, a Jewish prophet who mooted the idea of God and monotheism among the Semites for the first time.

He lived the first forty years of his life as an ordinary mortal. However, he was a contemplative person like Jesus who appeared on earth many centuries before him. While in a transcendental state in a cave, he started receiving a series of revelations from Allah. Archangel Gabriel would appear in his vision as a being-of-light and download some divine messages in his consciousness. Mohammad himself could not write. But it appears that he had a phenomenal memory to retain what he had received. He would later dictate these revelations to his companions who inscribed these on dried palm leaves, bits of leather and whitened shoulder-blades of sheep and whatever else that came handy to them. Thus a record of what the Prophet envisioned eventually got compiled as the Holy Koran. His faithful believe the book to be composed of the lines fallen straight from the lips of Allah and they thus feel absolutely bound by every word of it. In fact, they also believe that the original copy of the Koran in some divine dialect lies preserved in heaven.

Incidentally, quite a few versions of the book were floating around after the death of the Prophet in AD 632. Caliph Abu Bekr (AD 573-634) called a conference of those who had heard the Prophet first hand and got an authentic version of the Koran drafted. All the variant versions of the book were destroyed and since then not a word has been changed in the Koran. The title of the treatise is drawn from the Arabic word 'Quran' meaning 'that should be read'. It consists of 114 'surahs' (chapters), each opening with the words, "In the name of Allah, the Merciful, the Compassionate." The book contains histories, legends and prophecies that mostly revolve around the Old Testament characters. It also incorporates moral precepts and laws.

Historically speaking, Mohammad, though an illiterate, was an intellectual giant and had an amazing capacity to influence people and win followers. He was concerned with the spiritual confusion prevailing among the tribal of his area and wanted to do something about it. Some ideas related to the uniqueness of God and how life should be lived started passing in a procession in his mind when he was in deep contemplation in the seclusion of his cave. A highly developed language and quite a few learned men were readily at hand to clothe his musings (his faithful, of course, would like to call these nothing but the divine revelations) in to a literary work of high order. The concept of oneness of God had already got rooted in the Jewish and Christian faiths. So something was already available for Mohammad to base his theology upon.

He picked up the name for the Divine Being from his tribal idol, Allah and declared Him to be the sole repository of divinity. This brought him in conflict with Christianity who believed that Jesus shared divinity with God as His son. However, Mohammad was quick not to question the virginity of Mary by accepting that Jesus was born to her through divine intervention and not through the normal human process. He laid great emphasis on the Day of Judgement when the dead would be made to rise from their graves to receive what they had earned during their lives. Every faithful would find himself surrounded by a bevy of seventy-two beauties in the blissful environs of heaven and the unbelievers would burn in hell. Besides, he laid down a regimen of ritual fasting, regular praying, charity, pilgrimage to Mecca. He also dwelt on the moral and jurisprudential aspects to regulate various areas and activities of life. Koran that he has left behind is thus a sort of 'Book of Life'.

The Prophet, however, was wise enough to understand that life was too complex a phenomenon to be fully covered by his treatise. So, he provided for 'ijma' (consensus), 'qiyas' (analogical thinking) and 'ijtehad' (systematic original thinking) to take care of the gaps and the new needs cropping up with the passage of time. What apparently seems to have escaped his attention is the need for change with the times. His ideology and codifications were perfectly suitable for the people among whom he lived. However, his faithful are now finding it difficult to administer civil societies in accordance with the codes decided a millennia and half back. In fact, only change is something permanent in this universe and everything else is temporary. The vital phenomenon of change has to be, therefore, taken due cognizance of, if vitality of a creed is to be maintained.

Many Islamic nations have thus found a way out of some of these stipulations. India itself was under the Islamic penal laws when the British got entrenched here. These were substantially modified by Warren Hastings, the Governor General, in the eighteenth century itself. The punishment of amputation of left hand was converted in to seven years imprisonment and that of two limbs to fourteen years incarceration. The offence of murder could no more be compounded by blood money nor its gravity related to whether it involved blood-letting or not. This meant that death caused by strangulation, poisoning, drowning and beating with a blunt weapon was to stand on the same footing as, say by beheading. Similarly, the punishment profile of many other crimes and the laws of evidence were suitably modified. By the mid-nineteenth century the Muslim codes ceased to be the law of the land all together.

Nevertheless, what the Prophet of Allah visualised was far superior to the pagan ideology of the place and the day. It gradually struck a chord in his people's heart and filled them with fervour that they had never experienced before. Islam, the new faith, just lighted up their lives. They felt as if they had been led from a desert of darkness to an oasis of enlightenment. The new found zeal brought victories and victories brought wealth to Arabia from its prosperous periphery. Thus a win-win situation emerged for the faithful out of nothing. If they won, wealth and women of the unbelievers were theirs. If they died, bliss and comforts of the paradise were just waiting to welcome them with seventy-two beautiful virgins, while their own virility was to get augmented hundred fold. What else a mortal on earth could wish for?

The belief worked wonders and carried the sword of Islam from Spain to India in less than a century. It is amazing to note that the steam worked into these soldiers of faith and fortune lasted for a full millennium. Eventually, however, it dissipated after running its course. In fact, later they suffered the ignominy of being enslaved by the colonial powers like the rest of the world. Now, with all the oil wealth in their coffers and numbers on their side, they are unable to deal with a tiny Israel. Israelites, the people persecuted for centuries, have, in turn, risen like a phoenix from the ashes of their past. The fire that once burned inside the Muslim seems to have passed on to the Jewish settlers. The wheel of fortune has thus turned a full circle.

To begin with, however, Mohammad's ideas meant a radical departure from the prevailing beliefs and practices. Therefore he straight away came in conflict with the pagan leadership that initially tried to belittle him and eventually decided to do away with him. This made him take shelter in a cave on Mt. Thaur and then escape to Yathrib (Later named as Medina in his honour) in AD 622. The great escape is commemorated as Hijra and the Hijri calendar corresponds to this historic flight. The political situation in Medina was ripe for him and he was able to collect a strong following there. He moved fast to establish himself both on the religious and political front. The first need was to give a cultic shape to his ideology. A mosque was erected at Medina for the purpose. The call for prayer was given from its roof and weekly prayers were held on Fridays prostrating towards Jerusalem to begin with and later towards Mecca. The practice of alms giving to the poor was also initiated.

A caravan from Mecca was looted to build up military strength. This resulted in the Meccans investing Medina with ten thousand men. A defensive ditch put around the town broke their advance and made them retire empty-handed after what is historically remembered as the Battle of the Ditch. This gave a decisive push to Mohammad's apostolic career. In AD 630, it was his turn to invade Mecca with a ten thousand strong army and secure a grand victory. The Prophet displayed great statesmanship and magnanimity by ordering general amnesty. He went around Kaaba in all reverence and kissed the black stone. He cleared the place of all idols and got the paintings of Abraham obliterated from the walls. He thus sanitised Kaaba, the 'undigested piece of Arab heathenism' suitably to henceforth serve as the abode of Islam on earth. There was to be no looking back from here. In the next few years, the whole of Arabia was brought at his feet and in another hundred years, Islam spread its sway over large tracts of Asia, Africa and Europe in the shape of a crescent. How these simple soldiers riding their camels and horses, with rudimentary weaponry and very little knowledge of battle tactics, could overrun so well-organised armies, is nothing short of a miracle. Surely, these desert warriors had some spark inside which their opponents could not stand up to.

It is time now to understand what Islam is about. The religion that literally means submission to God has, of course, evolved out of the commandments contained in the Koran and the Hadith i.e. the sayings and practices attributed to the Prophet and his companions. The following principal practices are generally considered as the five pillars (Al Arkan) of Islam:-

(a) The doctrine of certitude:

لا إله إلا الله محمد رسول الله

Lâ ilâha illallâh, Muhammad-ur-Rasûl-Allâh

(None other than Allah has the right to be worshipped and Mohammad is His messenger)

(b) Five daily prayers— before sunrise, at noon, immediately before sunset, between dusk and dark and before midnight.

(c) Giving of alms, especially during the month of 'Ramadan'.

(d) Ritual fasting during the 'Ramadan'.

(It is believed that Allah moves from the seventh to the first heaven during the month of 'Ramadan' to have a closer look at the world. So, the Muslims are enjoined upon to be at their best during this period.)

(e) 'Hajj' i.e. the pilgrimage to Mecca at least once in life time, if possible.

(This involves going round the 'Kaaba', kissing or touching or at least looking reverently at the Black Stone, imitating Hagar running frantically for water for her wailing infant Ishmael between the hills of Safa and Marwah, travelling to Mina and praying there till dawn, a long trek to the valley of Arafat, collection of stones at Mujdalifa for being thrown at the Satan, sacrifice of a goat or sheep or making a contribution towards this and return to Mecca for the second circumambulation of 'Kaaba' in satisfaction of having completed the holy mission of life.)

One could, however, say that all the more suggestive five pillars of Islam are rather: Allah, Mohammad, Equality, Fraternity and Simplicity. The creed inspires intense commitment. A Muslim has to mandatorily believe both in Allah as well as Mohammad and belief in Allah alone does not count for much. In other words, a person just cannot be a Muslim, if he does not believe in the Prophet, besides Allah. Prophet Mohammad thus stands inseparably bonded with Allah in Muslim consciousness. They rather believe:-

"BA KHUDA DIWANA BASHAD, BA MOHAMMAD HOSHIAR"

(You may take some liberties with God, but not with Mohammad)

There is thus no doubt in both Allah and Mohammad being the two primary pillars of Islam.

Let us now shift to equality and fraternity as the third and fourth pillars. Equality, as a theory, has universal appeal and almost all countries and faiths subscribe to it in principle. It happens to be the corner stone of the U.S., U.K., Indian and many other Constitutions of the world. The sting is, however, in the tail i.e. the implementation part of it. In Saudi Arabia, a role model for the Islamic order, a menial can merrily sit on the chair of his officer and may not vacate it in a hurry when he returns. The Saudi Arabian monarchs are just buried in sand without a memorial as commoners. Even markers on the graves of the Prophet and his family were removed for the reason that Mohammad also wished to be considered as no more than a slave of Allah.

But all this is only symbolic. It amounts to just following the letter of the law without bothering about its spirit. The basic fact is that most of the positions that count in the Saudi Arabian kingdom are occupied by the members of the royal family. There have been quite a few rebellions in the Islamic armies over the uneven distribution of loot. In fact, most of the Islamic nations have not been able to go very far in implementing this ideology. It is rather some democracies of the world that are trying to implement the law of equality in their societies by giving it a practical shape. Yet, there is no denying the fact that the concept of equality in the Islamic fraternity is a feel-good element of considerable consequence. Similarly, despite there being many fissures in the Islamic nations, the under-current of fraternity is clearly in evidence among them. The feelings of Muslim brotherhood often transcend the international borders. Same is the case at individual level.

Coming now to the fifth pillar, Koran itself encourages 'doing' rather than 'thinking'. For a common man, it is, in essence, a collection of 'DO's' and 'DON'T's' rather than a cross-web of intricate philosophies. It is unidirectional in its guidance and does not bother the faithful with options. They are just ordained to believe, pray, fast, give alms and pay obeisance at Mecca once in life, if possible. This, if done faithfully, would book a place for them in paradise. What could be simpler than this for a common man?

All the above notwithstanding, God has blessed man with brain which cannot just be shut down. Thinkers would keep thinking whatever barriers you put in their way. Some of them saw a few conspicuous contradictions in the Koran that needed to be clarified. The most apparent among these was that Allah guided only those who He willed and let those who He did not favour go astray. This superficially meant that He was unjust, arbitrary and biased. He had to be defended on this count. It was accordingly explained that man was blessed with a will of his own. If he considered too much of himself and was unwilling to be guided, Allah left him alone and those who wished to be guided, Allah was too happy to lead them to their salvation. The whole thing had a desert setting: one lost here humbly seeks the divine help and gets guided; while the other, crippled by his ego, not putting faith in Him gets perished in the sands.

Similarly, the eternity of Koran came to be questioned by the Mutazilites. In fact, in AD 827, the Abbasid caliph, Al Mamun, proclaimed it a heresy to assert the eternity of Koran.

Temple of Knossos — Greek Temple at Knossoss, Crete dating back to the time of King Minos (1700 BC). Attribution: With kind permission of Nick Leslie (bangers).

Wailing Wall — At least a wall to wail against— The Wailing Wall at Jerusalem, the holiest site of Judaism.

Church of Holy Sepulchre— The spot where Jesus was crucified and is believed to have been resurrected Attribution: Berthold Werner——Retrieved from the Wikipedia site.

Kaaba at Mecca-the holiest shrine of the Islamic faith
Attribution: Muhammad Mahdi Karim—www.micro2macro.net

The thinking during his regime was that the book was created when it was needed, i.e., it did not have any prior existence in heaven. However the next caliph over-turned this view. The Mutazilites also insisted that Allah did not sit on His throne in the heavens. Their view was that He was infinite, existing everywhere in the space and not confined to a particular spot. Mutazilites were, however, overthrown in the tenth century.

All religions need to be in a state of balance. They need reform, when the pendulum swings too much to one side and revival, when it moves to the other extreme. Islam produced a plethora of thinkers and theologians like Ashari, Abu Hanifa, Malik-ibn-Anas, Al Shafii, Ibn Hanbal, Ghazzali, Ibn Taimiya and Mohammad Ibd Adb al- Wahhab to keep their creed on course. A need was felt to compile the 'Sunna', the sayings and practices of the Prophet and his companions, to understand and interpret the Koran properly. Al Bhukhari of Persia thus compiled 7275 Hadiths that rank next to the Koran itself. Many other sets of such traditions are also afloat and enjoy considerable credence in the Muslim society.

Islam emerged as a massive fraternity all too soon and acquired quite a few ethnic strains in no time. There were, therefore, bound to be political upheavals among various interest groups and ideological clashes among the intellectuals here and there. The caliphate that emerged after the death of the Prophet itself became a bone of contention instantly. The Companions (close associates and supporters of the Prophet and Muhajirin) who wanted the mantle to fall on one of them succeeded and thus, Abu Bekr was installed as the first caliph (AD 632-34). This sent the Legitimists (Shi'ias) who wanted the blood relations of the Prophet to succeed him in to sulk. Abu Bekr was succeeded by Omar (AD 634-644) and Othman (AD 644-656). When finally, Ali, the cousin and son-in-law of Mohammad (husband of his daughter, Fatima) became the Caliph, the situation had become too hot for him to handle. On his failure to act decisively against his opponents, his own followers marched out of his military camp and he eventually got assassinated. On his death, his elder son, Hasan was eased out of power and the younger son, Hussain, fell fighting for his hereditary rights in the battle at Karbala.

The Shi'ia's have not forgotten these murderous intrigues for usurpation of the Islamic throne even to this day. They venerate Ali, Hasan, Hussain and the nine successors who followed them, as their Imams. The last of these Imams, Mohammad al-Muntazer went missing in AD 878. A vast majority of Shi'ites are living in the belief that he would show up as Mahdi one day to guide and deliver them. Many have since appeared on the scene pretending to be the much awaited Mahdi's, but only to disappoint the faithful. Down the line of their Imams, the Shi'ites sects, Zaidites and Ismailites branched off from the main line. The Zaidites have not drifted very far from the Sunnite position. The Ismailites were able to establish the Fatimid caliphate over Egypt, Syria and Tunis in AD 909. Another branch of Ismailites, the Karmatians, set up a kingdom on the western shore of the Persian Gulf extending from Yemen to the borders of Iraq. In a hair-raising raid these Karmatians were able to capture Mecca and carry away the holy black stone from there. It was returned after around twenty years on the request of Al Mansur, the Fatimid caliph.

Islam, after a while, began flowing along the mystic channels also. A number of 'Sufi's' and 'Darvesh's' appeared on the scene from time to time to lay bare the inner core of Islam. There was a sort of divine grace about them. They were the honest souls unprepared to yield either to clergy or nobility. They were the inward-looking spiritual personalities who have made a singular contribution in reducing the rigidities of Islam and promoting its acceptability. They set their mind directly on Allah and did not disregard the Prophet either, but otherwise bothered little about the outward symbols and sacraments of their faith. These ascetics periodically fell foul with the rulers and the orthodoxy. In AD 922, one such soul, Al Hallaj of Persia was scourged, nailed on cross and beheaded for blasphemy. In India itself, the dargah's of Nizam-ud-din Aulia at Delhi, Moin-ud-din Chisti at Ajmer and Salim-ud-din at Fatehpur Sikri have massive followings of their own.

As for the caliphates, they kept moving from place to place with every shift of the power nucleus of Islam. Medina, Damascus, Baghdad and a few other capital cities thus had the privilege of hosting the seat of the Islamic authority at various points of time. Finally, the Muslim caliphate first weakened and then disintegrated in to around sixty independent Islamic nations, owing allegiance, to none but Allah and his Prophet.

An overwhelming majority of humankind believes in God by one name or the other. So, there is really no problem with regard to Allah. But nobody can endear himself to the Muslim world, unless he endorses belief in the Prophet and his word also. Prophet Mohammad is thus the dividing line between the so called 'dar-ul-Islam' (abode of Islam) and 'dar-ul-harb' (abode of conflict). In the flush of their victories, the Muslim thought that they would bring the whole world to the feet of their Prophet. Their defeat in the Battle of Tour in France in AD 732 at the hands of Charles Martel put paid to this hope. Some radical elements of the faith, however, have still not abandoned this pursuit.

The Arab scholars composed Koran out of what the Prophet said. Its faith value apart, it speaks volumes about their high literary calibre. Later they triggered the first wave of the Renaissance in Europe and thus, made learning fashionable in this part of the world. However, at some point in its evolution, the Arab intellectualism lost its battle to their cleric interest groups. Their Prophet had done a world of good to them by producing a wonderful book of life in Koran. Instead of moving forward and making their own contribution to the progress of the world, these thinkers started whirling within the Koran, labouring to justify what is said in it. Koran does not need any justification by them— its value is self-evident. What a proud moment it would have been for them if they had instead themselves dug the Suez Canal and discovered the enormous wealth of oil buried under their soil!

Now, moving to our times, the European powers have reconciled to the loss of their colonies and clout without much of a grimace. Most of the Muslim nations have also adjusted to the new realities gracefully. However, it is sad that some Islamic states are unable to come to terms with the loss of eminence and power that they once enjoyed and are bent on 'jihad' to push the clock back.

The Muslims do have some genuine heart-burns at some spots. Palestine, for instance, is a case of a country being vacated of a nation to accommodate another. But, the point to be appreciated is that, like others, the long suffering Jews also deserved a home. This home had to be there around Jerusalem, to which they are historically and spiritually connected. It also needs to be understood that the Muslim lost their claim to Jerusalem when Prophet Mohammad stopped looking towards it for prayer. Both Palestinians and the Jews, undoubtedly, have a case to be there in this land. However, they have to coexist here in peace and not entertain the ideas of drowning each other in the Mediterranean. Left to themselves, they would find their way out of this difficult situation. It has to be necessarily based on the give-and-take principle. Perhaps the recognition for Israel to exist and an internationally guaranteed corridor to the Palestinians between Gaza strip and the West Bank is the key to the solution. One gets a feeling that the Muslim pride in the past is coming in the way of peace in the area and some of the surrounding Muslim states are complicating the matters by prompting the Palestinians to ask for the impossible.

Similarly, it is not Allah but history that installed the Muslim in the Kashmir valley. It is history alone that cast the lot of some of them with India. Pakistan may have some territorial ambitions there, but the issue is not in the nature of an unfinished agenda of the partition, as made out. The contours of the problem are simple. The Muslim dominated valley would have certainly been awarded to Pakistan had it not been one of the princely states of the country. The fate of these states was left in the hands of their rulers. Pakistan was itself a party to this decision. The Hindu ruler of the state cast his lot with India and the matter should have ended there. In any case, the problem has nothing to do with religion. In fact, wherever religion is used as a weapon, it often recoils. God does not want man to pass his own will as His will to his convenience.

Besides, terrorism can never lead to solution of any problem. It can keep the problem alive alright but cannot resolve it in favour of the terrorist in the end. Unfortunately, some misguided elements of the Islamic faith seem to be putting their faith in terrorism as a sort of weapon of the weak. The intensity of their faith is not in doubt, but so is the enormity of their crime. The worst part of it is not the violence that they have unleashed but the caution they have inflicted on the world, resulting in wasteful effort and expense. The good old world never needed the costly and time-consuming security checks that have become essential now. These would take ages to go, even if sanity were to dawn today. All the more tragic aspect of it is that some Muslim states have also fell for the temptation of fishing in the troubled waters in the hope of securing some of their national aims. There are some signs that the shortsightedness of this policy is getting realised belatedly now. The need of the moment is an internal 'jihad' against terrorism to restore Islam to its deserved glory.

Despite the fact that a few misguided elements, instigated by some interest groups, have done considerable harm to its image, Islam is still shining and attracting conversions. The God-given oil wealth under their soil has played its own part in enhancing the economic clout of many of their states as well as the Islamic appeal. The faithful still see Islam as the Highway to Heaven.

The story of the Semitics, however, does not come to an end here. Their love-hate relationship was to weave a lot of history after the death of Prophet Mohammad. Their internal conflict is going to be the subject matter of the next chapter.

# 9

# Crusades of the Cross and the Crescent

Jerusalem is of high spiritual interest to the Semitics. It has been the heartland of these religions at various points of time. Prophet Mohammad addressed his first prayers looking in this direction. He turned to Mecca only after he got disenchanted with the Jews who would not admit him to the exclusive gallery of their Prophets. He is also supposed to have visited the place on his way to meeting with Allah in person. (Koran- The Night Journey, XVII) Thus, despite shifting their 'kiblah' from here, the Muslim still retain some religious as well as political interest in Jerusalem. In fact, they have fought for centuries to maintain their claim over the holy land.

The city has been a place of pilgrimage for the Christians also as the place has a close association with Jesus, the founder of their faith. It bears his footprints and is haloed by his blood. The Jews, of course, have the strongest historical and emotional claim to it. After all it has been their spiritual capital for ages. However, being too few in numbers and being militarily weak, they were in no position to enforce their right over the place ever since they were dispersed from Palestine. The fighting over one of the holiest spots on earth thus fell to the share of the Muslims and the Christians. They have fought some of the bloodiest wars of the history to possess Jerusalem.

The Semitic faiths do have a common denominator in monotheism, but they have been in love-hate relationship right from the beginning. There are quite a few doctrinal differences among them. They do not see eye to eye in the matter of their Prophets either. The Christians and Muslims recognise the Hebrew Prophets, but assert their own to be the last and the best. The Jews, of course, do not accept any prophecy outside their scriptures which means that they do not recognise Jesus and Mohammad as prophets. All the three religions seem to believe that God went in to hibernation after revealing to their prophets whatever was worth revealing for the humankind. This belief, coupled with some territorial ambitions, has been a cause of mortal conflict among them.

Jerusalem and quite a few other places in Palestine, like Bethlehem, Galilee and Capernaum etc. have been settled deep in the Christian consciousness for their association with the life, death and believed resurrection of Jesus Christ. Over the centuries, these had been attracting a large number of pilgrims from the Christendom. The region was under the rule of the Abbasides Caliphs at Baghdad. However, the Islamic Caliphate by then had woefully weakened and real power had passed on to its governors. Thus, a Sultan from the Seljuk Turks was the real power in Palestine at the time. A lot of disconcerting news started pouring into Europe about the sufferings that the Christian pilgrims to the place were undergoing at the hands of these Muslim fanatics. Besides this, the Muslim states had blocked many of the trade routes to the East to the commercial jeopardy of the traders at Venice and Genoa. By the end of the eleventh century, the things came to a boiling point.

Pope Urban II summoned a conference of the European Christendom in AD 1095 and called upon the gathering that it was time to take up arms to defend their faith. This had immediate impact and the cries of 'Deus le volt' (It is God's will) went up in the air instantaneously. The delegates were roused to believe that God wanted them to retaliate hard against the humiliation being inflicted on their religion. Under their zeal to protect their faith many a man left home and parted with his properties. Many enlisted themselves as holy warriors with noble motives and many others came forward on the Pope's promise that the participants would have their sins forgiven and have their seat booked in heaven. Quite a few riffraff elements also joined the crusaders lured by the prospect of plunder.

Thus, a bloody chapter of the world history got opened in the form a series of the so called holy wars between the Christianity and Islam, symbolised respectively by the Cross and the Crescent. These were to keep Palestine and Asia Minor soaked in blood over the next few centuries. The initially launched hurried attempts, motivated both by genuine zeal as well as adventure and ambition, were too ill-organised to succeed. These got quickly crushed in Asia Minor itself by the Turkish cavalry. It then dawned on the Christian forces that the situation was not as simple as they had made out. Proper planning and organisation was necessary before venturing into the den of the powerful enemy.

Yahweh and their Prophets form the nucleus of Judaism, God and Christ that of Christianity, Allah and Mohammad of Islam and 'Om', identified with the primordial sound of the universe in motion, lies at the core of the Hindu belief. Otherwise, changing and splitting are the basic laws of nature. All religions get split in to sects in no time. Christianity also suffered a major split in the very first millennium. A patriarchate of the Greek Church came up at Constantinople to present a challenge to the papal establishment at Rome. In AD 1054, there was a complete severance of ties between them. In fact, the then Pope of Rome and the Patriarch of Constantinople excommunicated each other. Another incident of great significance is the crushing defeat that the Byzantine emperor ('Byzantium' was the old name of Constantinople), the traditional defender of the Christian faith, suffered in the Battle of Mauzikert. Despite their differences, the two Christian power centres were prepared to put up a united fight against the Turks in the beginning. This cooperation, however, remained half-hearted at the best of times.

Late in AD 1096, Bishop Le Puy took initiative to mobilize a powerful force to launch the first proper crusade for the Capture of Jerusalem and to make the city safe for Christian pilgrimage. This expeditionary force consisted of the contingents of Godfrey of Bouillon and his brother, Baldwin, Robert of Normandy, Raymond of Toulouse and the Normans Bohemund and Taucred from Italy. All these detachments converged at Constantinople to form a well-knit action group. They got fair cooperation from the Byzantine establishment and were ferried in ships to the Asia Minor. The battle for Jerusalem was ferociously fought. The Christian army was finally able to dislodge the Turks from the place. This was followed by a massive manslaughter for a full week. A French eyewitness testifies:

> "Under the portico of the mosque the blood was knee deep and reached the horses' bridles".

A Christian monarchy was set up at Jerusalem with Godfrey as the king. However, this kingdom had to live precariously on edge right from the beginning, surrounded as it was by hostile Muslim states on all sides. The Turks soon recovered, built up strength and over-ran a big chunk of the state.

This necessitated the launch of the second crusade to recapture the lost ground and stabilize the kingdom. A force was collected for the purpose under Louis VII of France. However, this army was not able to achieve much and returned home empty-handed and disillusioned. This caused wide-spread despondency in the Christian camp and Jerusalem was virtually left alone to live dangerously and fend for itself. In the circumstances, the Egyptian Sultan, Saladin, all but wiped off the Christian kingdom by AD 1187.

This made some states of Western Europe to sit up and act. Thus, troops were mustered for the third crusade (1189-92) under the legendary Richard Coeur de Lion and Phillip Augustus of France. This expeditionary force fought well and hard. But, despite the incredible courage and military genius of Richard, all that it achieved in the end was a treaty with Saladin for the safe passage of pilgrims.

The expeditionary force collected for the fourth crusade (AD 1204) thought it wise to first settle scores with Constantinople. It lost its steam there itself and could not proceed further to deliver Jerusalem. However, the Greek emperor of Constantinople was driven away and a Latin kingdom established in its place. This monarchy lasted for a little over fifty years. The fifth crusade launched in AD 1217-21 similarly wasted its energies in the Nile Valley down south without being able to bring any succour to the Christian enclave on the verge of total collapse. The diplomacy of Frederick II, the emperor of the Holy Roman Empire, secured a short respite for Jerusalem, but the failure of yet another crusade under Louis of France in 1249 sealed the fate of whatever was left of the Christian kingdom. Edward I, however, was able to win another temporary retrieve for the encircled enclave for ten years. After this the crusading kingdom had to depend upon its own devices to exist.

Some more bad news followed. In AD 1289, Tripoli fell to the Sultan of Egypt. Two years later the Christian stronghold of Acre also fell after heroic resistance by the Grand Master of the Templars and the Marshall of the Hospitallers. The Christian population had to sail to the safety of Cyprus. That mercifully brought to an end the longest war of the world history, with the privilege of the last laugh falling to the share of the Muslim. It was only with the dawn of the colonial era some centuries later that the tables started turning against them. In AD1489, Caterina, the last nominal queen, surrendered her crown to the Republic of Venice. With that died the last flickers of the deadly religious rivalry in the region.

The crusades, besides being a saga of heroic struggle to defend faith, are also a tale of treachery, exploitation, underhand deals and wrong priorities. Many times the Christian crusaders turned on the Jews and even on their own fraternity. Often they were opposed by the Christian populations and thrown out of their areas in disgust. During the crusades a large number of young boys, mostly from France and Germany, left their homes in their enthusiasm to participate in the holy war. Many died and got lost on the way. A large bulk of them reached Marseilles where their zeal was taken advantage of by the slave traders. They were tricked by them and taken to Egypt for being sold in to slavery. The incident is known in the history as the Children's Crusade. With such incidents coming to public notice the remaining glamour also went out of the crusades.

Though these holy wars are mostly remembered for their ferocity where no quarter could be given or sought, yet some heart-warming incidents of chivalry also took place during the period that speak of the general goodness of human heart. It is on record that once when Richard, the Lion, was down with heat-stroke during the fighting with Sultan Saladin, the generous Sultan sent him ice and snow collected from the hilltops to facilitate his recovery. Needless to mention, that the technology to manufacture ice artificially was not existent then and high hills were the only source of it. Besides a few more such incidents where human touch was conspicuously in evidence, the other positive feature of the otherwise futile wars was the sense of oneness that these generated in the Christendom in the Western Europe.

# 10

# Religions of South Asia

## (a) HINDUISM—The Himalayan Faith

The Hindu religion, besides with many things else, has a strong connection with the Himalayas also. It has lived in its courtyard and under its shadow for centuries. The towering presence of the Himalayan ranges has given it lofty ideas. Many of its sons have been disappearing in its caves in search of solitude to think hard to uncover the mysteries of life and delve deep into the metaphysics of the universe. It is home to numerous Hindu shrines also.

Hindus have been in a thinking mode for ages. Hinduism is thus full of ideas about God and His universe, soul and its salvation, mind and matter and in fact, all that is relevant to living of life well and gainfully. Massive brain work has been done in this part of the world to remove some of the layers of mystery surrounding the Divine reality. God, no doubt, remains still undiscovered. Yet, a lot of food for thought has been generated to encourage further effort at demystifying life, nature and also the One who creates and controls everything. Nothing like this has perhaps happened anywhere else.

The British masters, however, did not think very highly of the religious and cultural traditions of India. Rather, they regarded Indians as some sort of primitive people mired in backwardness and in need of modern education. When in the fourth decade of the nineteenth century, the East India Company was struggling to justify before the British Parliament why a small sum of money earmarked earlier for educating the natives in India could not be spent, it came forward with the plea that they could not decide (during their earlier charter period of twenty years!) as to in what medium of language this 'White Man's Burden' should be discharged. When the reluctant heads could think of no more excuses to avoid spending this budgetary allocation, Lord Macaulay, the Law Member of the Governor's General Council came up with the recommendation that the medium of instruction should be English. He loftily proclaimed that one shelf of a good European library was worth more than the entire literature of India and Arabia. The learned Law Member happened to overlook that India had given the world its first book, the Rig Veda and Arabia had triggered the first wave of Renaissance in Europe that made learning fashionable in his part of the world. Incidentally, this common language, though foreign, united the nation. Once some semblance of unity was there, it became impossible for the minuscule British minority to overlord a nation of the size and stature of India.

The Indian subcontinent, for a long while, had been the knowledge capital of the world. However, for becoming too reclusive, individualistic and casual about their security concerns or just because of the natural law of averages, the Hindus not only just lost their prominence but also had to bear with slavery of around one thousand years. It is aptly said about India, "She let the legions thunder past and plunged in thought again". All man-made gods live by the sword and die by the hammer. When you lose wars, not only your men get massacred or enslaved, women ravished, wealth looted but also your idols get trampled. This is what happened to the Hindus also. However, there seems to be some mysterious life-force in their folds. This has enabled them to survive the slavery of a thousand years, with almost everything intact, their Vedas and values, their fairs and festivals, their rituals and 'ragas', their cuisine and culture, their dances and dress, and above all their pride in the past.

However, there are quite a few misconceptions floating about this faith. Some even doubt whether Hinduism qualifies to be called a religion or it is simply a way of life. For being a Hindu, one has to be just born a Hindu. There are no other stipulations. A person born to a Hindu thus continues to be a Hindu, even if he does not go to any temple even once in his life, does not fast on any of the religious occasions, does not give alms ever, does not read any of his scriptures, does not obey any of the predetermined codes of conduct, does not follow any of the other rites and practices of his religion or even does not believe in God.

A common Hindu is certainly casual and relaxed about his faith. In fact, his religion just shows the way. It does not lead anybody by the ear. A Hindu enjoys enormous amount of intellectual freedom to grow spiritually as per his own choice. He stays a Hindu till he is proud of being one. Otherwise, he is even free to convert.

A Hindu may not be very particular in marking his presence in his temples. But the soothing notes of the evening 'arti' (Hindu prayer), issuing out from their sacred precincts, never fail to evoke a resonance in his soul. The same is the case with the 'azan's echoing from the mosques five times in a day for a Muslim, the ringing of the church gongs for a Christian and the sight of people in silent prayer in the synagogues for a Jew. In fact, the religious rigidities are wearing off with the passage of time. The attendance in the churches and synagogues is thinning with every passing day. Many of the Muslims also do not go to the mosques or pray five times a day regularly. People have either gone materialistic or look for spiritual inspiration more and more from within.

All the religions have their rituals right from birth to death and even beyond. Similarly they have their elaborately laid down religious ceremonies, fairs and festivals. Their adherents observe these traditions and participate in these practices mostly when they feel inwardly impelled. Hardly anybody is excommunicated for non-observance of the religious codes. In fact, no religion would like to lose on numbers by doing anything like this. Rather, Islam provides for death penalty for anybody deciding to leave its ranks.

Hinduism has its set beliefs and a system of worship. Despite there being no compulsion, a common Hindu habitually follows most of his religious rites and practices. He is incredibly enthusiastic about some of his ceremonies. Just think of two hundred million of the Hindu devotees, with their faces lit by the same light, congregating on the banks of the holy Ganges on the occasion of the 'Kumbh' festival this year. Some sixteen million of them stood at the spot on the day of the concluding ceremony ('shahi snan') on the fourteenth of April, two thousand and ten. Has anybody ever heard of a spectacle of this magnitude being enacted anywhere else on earth? Surely, such a massive show of faith would be unthinkable, if Hinduism were not a religion, pulsating with devotion within.[1]

The other wrong notion floating around is that Hindus are confused about their God. Various sections of the Hindu society have created different Gods of their own preference for their worship. If such observations are meant to suggest that the Hindus do not believe in oneness of God, these are based on incorrect understanding of the Hindu system of belief and deserve to be dismissed out of hand. It is true that the Hindus see God peeping through plants, stones, stars and in fact everything around. They also believe that He cannot be in a master-slave relationship with the creation that He has fathered. In fact, nothing gets created unless God so wills. They thus find a dash of divinity scattered all over the universe, because everything in it bears His touch.

They worship many heavenly bodies, natural elements and other beings that they feel the humankind should be beholden to and even those that need to be propitiated to keep themselves out of the harm's way. They are, however, worshipped only as the agencies of God. The prayers are ultimately directed to the same Supreme Being who the Muslims know as Allah, the Christians as God, the Jews as Yahweh and Hindus by varied names. Hindus also believe that God alone is worthy of worship, but they see the universe as God incarnate. Prophet Mohammad was against the worship of the tribal idols at Mecca, because these were worshipped as God and these were deemed to be in competition with Allah. Amir Khusrao, the legendary laureate of Sultan Ala-ud-din Khalji, understood this position well. He says something like this in Chapter-III of his 'Nuh Sipihr':

(a) Hindus are very much the pantheists who believe in the eternal phenomena of God and His capacity to create out of nothing.

(b) The atheists are those who do not believe in God. The

Brahmins are not the atheists, by any reckoning, as they believe in his existence.

(c) No doubt, they worship sun, stones, cattle (cow, for instance) and plants ('Tulsi' or Basil) quite ardently. Yet, they do so because they see the divine spirit in them. Their prayer is, thus, always directed towards Him alone.

The Rig Vedic Sutra-129 from the 10th Mandalam itself makes it evident that the Hindus made a clear distinction between gods and God. It says that gods appeared only after the universe had already been created by some nameless Eternal. Perhaps only He knows as to when, how and why the universe was brought in to being. Rather, we do not have any means of knowing whether even He knows about the 'when', 'how' and 'why' part of the Creation. A verse from the same scripture, known as 'Gayatri Mantra' refers to the nameless Eternal as 'Om'. This name is based on the primordial sound that our galaxies produce while in motion at a terrific speed of twenty thousand mile per second. We, being far away from the source of the sound, do not hear it in the normal course. Rishi Vishvamitra while in deep meditation heard this unending echo as 'Om'. Greek philosophers of the Hellenic era also talk about the music in the movement of celestial bodies as the 'music of spheres'. The highly revered 'Gayatri Mantra' that is loaded with lot of relevance to the issue under discussion is reproduced below:

ओम भूर्भुवः स्वः
तत्सवितुर्वरेण्यं
भर्गो देवस्य धीमहि
धियो यो नः प्रचोदयात्।

*Om bhur bhuvah swah*
*Tat savitur varenyam*
*Bhargo devasya dheemahi*
*Dhiyo yo nah prachodayat*

(Formless God is referred to here as 'Om', the Lord of 'Bhur' (earth), 'Bhuvah' (the planets) and 'Svah' (the galaxies). 'Savitur' (Sun and stars) reflect His 'Bhargo' (light). He is 'devasya' (deity) that is 'dheemahi' (worthy of being meditated about). His grace has been sought to 'parchodayat' (guide) our 'dhiyo' (intellects) on right lines.)

Thus, 'Om' is the initial name that the Hindus gave to God. Later, of course, they picked up a plethora of other names to suggest in various ways that He is omnipotent, omniscient and omnipresent. Man likes to see God in his own image, so that he may be able to focus on Him more easily. Thus, in course of time, the idea of the Divine Trinity, Brahma for creation, Vishnu for preservation and Shiva for destruction and renewal, entered the Hindu mind. They were given the privilege of consorts also and thus, lot of legends could be woven around them and their families.

Brahma has since faded somewhat in Hindu consciousness, as his work of creation is believed to be over. Shiva has his roots extending very deep into the Indus Valley civilisation. Afterwards he finds a mention in the early part of Vedas as, Rudra. Vishnu was also known as a subsidiary god in this Vedic period. Later he rose to the highest prominence when the idea of the Trinity came to be conceived. Vishnu chose to incarnate Himself nine times, five of his 'Avtars' (incarnations) being in human form. Rama and Krishna among them have caught the Hindu imagination most and they are worshipped as God proper. Gautama Buddha is believed to be his last incarnation. By the side of the Divine Trinity stands a huge pantheon of gods who just represent the numerous ministries of God. If this divine hierarchical arrangement, devised by the Hindu thinkers, is grasped many things would fall in place and many of the cobwebs of confusion around Hinduism would get cleared.

After these cosmogonic conceptions, we can proceed to the philosophical aspects, where Hinduism is at its best. The Faith has given some highly loaded words like 'Lila' (Games that God plays with His universe), 'Maya' (Cosmic illusion) and host of others for brainstorming by the mankind. This is what the American President, Barack Obama said in the Indian Parliament during his visit to the country on 8th November, 2010:-

> "Indians unlocked the intricacies of the human body and the vastness of the universe."

The earliest Hindu literature exists in the form of a compendium of 1017 hymns known as the Rig Veda. It was composed at least 3500 years back and reduced to writing somewhere around the eighth century BC or later. Rig Veda was followed by three more compilations of the same genre, Yajur Veda, Atharva Veda and Sama Veda. It must be admitted that bulk of the Vedas is devoted to the praise of the natural gods like Indra, Agni, Vayu and Sun etc. This portion of the works is monotonous, repetitive and ordinary. The bulk of Its value lies in its antiquity. Nevertheless, their philosophic content at times rises to such dizzy heights as would make the modern man feel proud of his ancestry. The way they have described the phenomenon of God has proved to be the last word on the subject. Nobody has so far been able to improve upon that.

The Vedas also give us a glimpse into the Indus Valley civilisation. But for this and the uncovering of the ruins of their cities through archeological excavations in the early part of the last century, the story of these wonderful people would have been completely lost to the world. Since it has not been possible to decipher their script, the scanty archeological information that we have about this civilisation can only be supplemented by the Vedic literature.

The Vedic psalms generated interest in writing a few addendums in the form of commentaries and elaborative literature. The prose works known as 'Brahamanas' that followed lay down the duties of the priesthood. Got added after this were the 'Sutras', setting out laws and ceremonies; the Upanishads, dwelling on the link between God and soul; the 'Aranyakas', setting out the requirements for leading an ascetic life and finally, the Puranas listing the sacred traditions.

The Upanishads that were written mostly by Kashtriyas and later acquired ready recognition from the Brahmins contain some of the deepest strains of the Hindu philosophy. The Upanishads talk about the oneness of the Brahmn (God) and the Atamn (soul). They conceive the Supreme Being as an ocean and the souls as waves that do not have any independent existence. The separate selfhood is, thus an illusion according to the monistic philosophy of the Upanishads. Should you ask a Vedic scholar if God is there, he would tell you that only God exists and everything else that seems to exist is an illusion. Along with their profound philosophical thought, the Upanishads also talk about some mystical speculations and mysterious rites that really do not count for much. A few extracts from these works have already been reproduced in the earlier chapters. This should suffice keeping in view the general area of thrust of this book.

The Hindu philosophy suggests three ways of getting to God—Jnana Yoga (the pursuit of knowledge), Bhakti Yoga (through devotion) and Karma Yoga (just by doing well one's duty by life). He who enunciated this philosophy must be a great genius. These options not only appeal to logic, but sound to be practical for all classes of people. If the words— 'Jnana', 'Karma' and 'Bhakti' are given their natural meaning, people should have no difficulty in understanding the simple philosophy that these convey. What exactly is meant by acquisition of knowledge is an effort at gradual demystification of life and nature to get closer to the Creator. People can just choose their own way to deliverance according to their individual inclinations and convenience. Speaking in practical terms, 'Jnana Yoga' is meant for intellectuals, 'Karma Yoga' for doers and 'Bhakti Yoga' for believers. As 'believing' is far simpler than 'knowing' or even 'doing', 'Bhakti Yoga' is the popular choice with the masses.

Those blessed with intelligence in good measure and also the will to apply it, could go for attainment of knowledge. The requisites for this choice are the clearest minds and strongest wills. They are to be the people who would cut their own paths that would be subsequently available for others to follow. The doctrine having been conceived during the Upanishad period, it got intertwined with monism. It was then thought that those who were in ignorance of the truth that 'Brahmn' and 'Atamn' are one, were the ones in a state of 'Avidya'. A 'Jnana Yogi' was expected to work to clear the things up for such people. However, the monist view is just one dimension of the doctrine. There are in fact many more angles to it that need to be explored.

In the first phase of his life (Brahamcharya Ashram), a person was supposed to absorb the knowledge already available in the scriptures. After finishing with his 'Ghristha Ashram, he was expected to enter 'Vanaprastha Ashram' and make his way for the solitude of forests to come up with a thesis of his own. In the fourth and last phase of his life, he was to return as a 'sanyasi' to give the benefit of his knowledge to the world.

'Karma Yoga' seems to be based on the premise that God expects every being to do his duty by life. If he discharges this duty honestly and diligently, he does not have to bother about anything else. This in itself is enough to pave his way to salvation. This way of life is particularly relevant to the 'Ghristha' phase of one's life. Here again, the priesthood has made life difficult for man by listing a plethora of duties that he is bound to perform. He is told that he is under various debts, like the 'deva wrin', 'Pitri wrin' and 'Guru wrin' etc. that he is required to discharge, if he wishes a blissful next life for himself and his ancestors. All this involves considerable effort and expense in the form of regular worship, numerous ceremonies and dans/dakshinas i.e. donations etc. The main beneficiaries of these gifts are obviously to be the priests rather than the poor. Man is also enjoined never to stretch his neck out of the confines of his caste. Similarly, women must serve their men meekly and never try to out-reach them.

The author of the theory perhaps intended something very different. Lord Krishna's discourse to the conscience-stricken Arjuna in Bhagavad Gita gives a much better idea about what in fact is meant by 'karma yoga'. A karma yogi must fight against inappropriateness with a detached mind. Thus, while doing so he should neither bother about who he is up against nor should he be looking for reward through the corner of his eyes. He has the right to act only, but not to any reward. The reward part of it has to be left to the Lord. If he is on the right side of 'dharma', the consequences are bound to be beneficial. Our natural talents are in the nature of a trust committed to us. It is our sacred duty to live up to these. The following verse from the celebrated scripture is relevant in this regard:

> कर्मण्येवाधिकारस्ते मा फलेषु कदाचन।
> मा कर्मफलहेतुर्भूर्मा ते सङ्गोऽस्त्वकर्मणि।।
>
> —*Bhagavad Gita*, Chapter II, Verse-47.

(Your right just extends to performing your dutiful deeds and not at all to the reward for such actions. You neither consider yourself as the originator of actions that have borne fruit nor be disinclined to perform your duty i.e. keep doing your duty without an eye on immediate reward.)

'Bhakti Yoga' is seeking salvation through sheer devotion. It is living in a world of faith and the surrender of self to the Divine. Bhagavad Gita, besides deftly answering many other spiritual queries, also dwells upon the devotional way of getting to one's goal. In fact, Krishna finally brought Arjuna around in the action mode by displaying His 'Virat Roop' as the universe incarnate, into which everything is born, blooms, withers and renews in an eternal cycle. That reaffirmed his faith both in karma and bhakti. The finest exponent of the cult of devotion is god Hanuman. The way of devotion is most popular with the masses. They broadly fall in two categories—the ones who believe in silent meditation in the privacy of their homes and the others who like to congregate in temples for prayer, yajya and 'keertan' (full-throated chanting of hymns) or organize social functions elsewhere on holy occasions. The more ardent among them sometimes get in to a state of trance while singing high volume paeans in praise of God.

Numerous streams of thought flow in the Hindu society that sometimes make you forget the differences between Hindus and humans. Hindu thought often rises to such dizzy heights as would suggest, as if Hinduism is speaking not only for whole of the humanity but about the creation of God in its entirety.

Orthodox Hinduism stands divided into many systems. Among these, Sankhya, Yoga, Vedanta, Nyaya, Vaisheshika and Purva Mimansa are particularly noticeable. However, all these systems and philosophies are beyond the mental reach of a common Hindu. His spiritual activities are limited to having small temples at home where he worships God through the deities of his choice. Then, he often goes to temples where all sorts of deities are placed for worship. Occasionally, he also finds time and money to mark his presence at various places of pilgrimage and to be part of the holy congregations. He bows his head before many idols, objects and elements. For instance, he worships Hanuman as an ideal devotee of God and sun, during the festival of 'Chhat', as a gift of God to the living on earth. There should, however, be no confusion that all his prayers are ultimately directed to the one and only one Divine Being.

### (b) BUDHHISM—The Way out of Sadness to Salvation

Religions develop a lot of unwanted undergrowth with passage of time and there is a constant need for removal of these weeds to ensure their healthy growth. Some socially smart people crop up in no time to feed on faith and to distort the religious message in line with their interest. Reform and renewal are, therefore, necessary to keep religions alive and in shape. All religions eventually accept the need to change with the times, though some make it a painfully labourious process. It must go to the credit of Hinduism that it has been much less jealous about its dogma. In fact, it has been endlessly hospitable rather than hostile to good ideas and has always welcomed light from whatever source it came.

Buddhism and Jainism were born with quite some rebellious content in their ideologies. In fact, these were in the nature of a strong reaction to the elitism in the Hindu belief system where the Brahmin occupied bulk of the privileged space and the other castes felt themselves squeesed into an area, too small for their proper spiritual growth. Only the Kashtriyas were in some position to take on them and they did it well and proper, giving birth to two great heresies. The Vedas, the Brahmin way of worshipping and the caste structure put in place in the Hindu society so assiduously, were all challenged. Yet, it happened to be a tolerant land where the heretics were not meant to burn at the stake. Rather, these heresies were viewed with equanimity and finally defeated by owning them as part of the Hindu faith. The good ideas they generated were promptly absorbed into the Hindu philosophy itself. To top it all, Prince Siddhartha who founded Buddhism was pronounced as the ninth 'avtar' (incarnation) of Lord Vishnu. Some are of the opinion that these developments were, in fact, quite well anticipated in the Vedic literature itself and so these did not evoke any sort of extraordinary shock or surprise in the Hindu society, as these were not against the grain of Hindu nature in essence.

Siddhartha Gautama was born in the Sakya clan in BC 560. His father, a chieftain of some consequence, had his principality in the foothills of Himalayas (now in Nepal), around one hundred miles to the north of Varanasi in India. Had he decided to spend his life in the usual princely comfort, he would have ended up somewhere in the vast landfill of history like the numerous others. He was, however, not a man of this world. Keeping in view the streak of high sensitivity in his character, all efforts were made to keep him away from the unseemly sights of life. However, this was something impossible to do. Soon the broody young prince became starkly aware about debilities, disease and death in the mortal world. This robbed him of his peace of mind. His marriage to a charming princess and the birth of a lovely son to them failed to soothe his uneasy mind. He knew that all this would not last and ultimately end in decay and death. He developed an overpowering desire to decipher life and find a way out of the misery and morbidity.

Finally, he made up his mind and left for the solitude of forests, throwing a last look at his sleeping wife and son. During the next six years, he sat at the feet of many seers of his time to have a proper idea about the existent philosophies. He, however, could not make much out of these. He exposed himself to all sorts of austerities in the course of his meditation. This extreme asceticism reduced his body almost to skin and bones, but he could still see no light at the end of the tunnel. In this near dead state, he concluded that hara-kiri was not exactly the answer to the questions that sat on his mind. He thus decided to choose a 'middle path' to the great consternation of his five ascetic associates whom he had picked up in the course of his sojourn in the forests. They felt let down and deserted him at Uruvela.

Mahaparinirvana — Ancient excavated Buddha image at Mahaparinirvana at Kushinagar (India)
Attribution: Retrieved from the Wikipedia site

Gautama remained in the denial mode so far as the worldly life was concerned, but he decided to keep his body in health so that he could continue with his quest. At long last, while in deep meditation under a tree in Bodh Gaya, he found what he had been looking for all these years as a monk. The cause of all human misery was the desires— the desire to live; the desire to have; the desire to count and so on. One could get in to a state of permanent bliss, if he could find a way to rid himself of the worldly desires. For this, a man had to depend on his own devices. The scriptures, Brahmins, ritual worship and religious practices could not guide him to his emancipation. The path to salvation did not lead to the world or through the world. One had to fly off the tangent from here. Each individual must work out his own way to 'nirvana' through 'self-discipline, self-purification, study, meditation and concentration'.

After his enlightenment, Gautama came to be referred to as Buddha. His sermon at the Deer Park at Varanasi brought his five companions back to his fold. They got convinced about his theory of 'middle path' and were the first to convert to what later came to be called as Buddhism. The number of adherents soon rose from five to sixty. Most of them were the people from his own clan. They were followed by a good number of converts from all castes. Gautama Buddha kept preaching his faith for about forty five years till his death at the age of eighty. The Sangha (Buddhist organisation) was now in place and in the centuries to come, it was to carry Gautama Buddha's message to most of Asia.

All adherents to the new faith had to take a vow of seeking refuge in Buddha, Dharma and Sangha. They were also required to follow its ten basic precepts i.e. non-violence, not taking what was not given, chaste life, no lying, no deceiving, no intoxicants, moderate eating, no dancing/ singing/ dramas, no garlands/scents/unguents/ ornaments and no acceptance of gold or silver. The lay members of the order were required to accept the first five of these. The others were meant for the monks.

Buddhism was not convinced about redemption through Vedic rituals, prayers and practices, nature worship and seeking guidance of the priesthood. It viewed the gods as finite entities, subject to the laws of nature and themselves in need of redemption. The new faith was, in fact, not interested much in the metaphysical aspects of Hindu religion. It rather concerned itself more with the psychological dimension of human life. Man lived uneasy in mind over the vagaries of life. The idea of Buddhism was to put him at ease at moderate physical cost. Buddhism displayed no particular curiosity to know about the Being who existed prior to the Creation. It thus had an agnostic view about God.

Otherwise, Buddhism does believe in two major precepts of Hinduism, the law of 'karma' and transmigration of souls in its own modified way. The Buddhist variations to these doctrines are that beings are reborn alright, but those who reach the stage of 'arahatship' in life through sustained piety, break out of the vicious cycle of rebirths and just get extinguished like a lamp on death to attain the blissful state of 'nirvana'. Buddhism also believes that no 'soul substance' accompanies a person on rebirth. This is rather confusing. If a person does not carry his self along when he is reborn, then whose soul does he contain inside? Is it then really a rebirth or just a replacement of one person by another? Buddhist theoreticians, however, explain the phenomenon like this. It is a case of a new wick getting lighted by an already lighted wick or learning passing from Guru to his disciple. In both the cases nothing goes away from the original holders—neither the light nor the learning. In other words, the reborn being just bears the stamp of the 'karma' of his earlier life like a seal on the wax.

Common man is, however, interested more in philosophers themselves rather than their philosophies. Buddhism made impact on the mass mind, because from behind its precepts, peeped the image of a young prince sneaking away from the luxuries of palace to a state of homelessness in search of truth. What particularly touched a chord in people's heart was his walking away from his charming wife and a lovely son at the prime of his youth. Masses always have an urge to deify such extraordinariness and supernaturalism. Buddha also got eventually deified and that helped to push his message far and wide.

After Gautama's 'nirvana', his disciples took over from where he had left. The first Buddhist Council was held under Kassapa to discuss, develop and consolidate the philosophies and canons of the creed. The second was held a century later at Vaishali. An idea of making the faith less rigorous was mooted during the confabulations. The dissensions eventually split the faith in to sixteen sects. The religion, however, remained alive and kicking with more laymen than monks subscribing to its message. After several centuries, oral traditions were reduced to writing in the form of texts like Vinay Pitaka, Sutra Pitaka and Adi-dharma Pitaka (jointly known as Tripitaka). Besides these, voluminous other literature was produced to give scriptural support to the creed and to provide guidance to the monasteries, monks and the lay followers of the faith.

The big leap forward for the faith, however, came when the profoundly remorseful Emperor of India, Ashok, embraced the faith in the aftermath of his bloody victory over Kalinga. The mighty Emperor, however, was not interested in becoming a monk to work towards his 'nirvana'. He believed more in piety than prayer and wished to store up enough merit points for a happy rebirth. He called the third Buddhist Council to consider some reforms and to globalize the faith. In BC 256, he issued a series of edicts based on Buddhist principles and piety and had these inscribed on rocks, pillars and caves etc. for information and enlightenment of people.

His Sacred Majesty had a global vision for the religion. He sent his son (or brother), Mahindra, to Ceylon with a band of missionaries to perpetuate and popularize Buddhism in the country. The land took to the new faith like a fish takes to water. The country had been free from any serious conflict and remained so during the next over two millennia. The peaceful ethos helped it to emerge as the biggest depository of the faith. It still holds many holy relics connected with Buddha, including his canine tooth, collar bone, begging bowl, besides some priceless volumes of archival literature. The country predominantly subscribes to the Hinayana (i.e. the older or orthodox) order of Buddhism that emphasizes the message of the founder, rather than his divinity. Hinayana initially believed, quite in line with the Buddha's own thinking, that he had attained 'nirvana' and ceased to exist in this world. What was now important was the message that he had left behind.

Man's nature is, however, oriented towards magic, miracles and supernatural things. He is not happy to believe that all who take birth in the world are just mortals. He likes to think that those who have done unusual things are either gods or demons. To satisfy this human need many myths were invented about Buddha. The followers of this offshoot of the faith now believe Buddha to be a supernatural soul who reached this position through pious, perfect and sinless conduct over a number of births. He had descended on earth from Tushita heaven and would appear again at an appropriate time as Maitreya. The neighbouring countries of the south-east Asia like Burma, Thailand and Cambodia where Buddhism penetrated peacefully in course of time predominantly believe in this Hinayana brand of faith.

People are always willing and eager to see God in anyone or anything. All that is required is a little spark to fire their imagination. A person of the lofty stature of Buddha could not escape being deified in course of time. This led to the birth of 'Mahayana' order of the faith that believes in worshipping Buddha as a deity. Emphasis thus shifted from his message to the man himself. This gave a touch of glamour to the religion, made it more agreeable and brought it closer to the parent faith in its country of origin to finally melt back into it.

Buddhism enjoyed a position of high prestige throughout the Indian subcontinent during the reign of Ashok. During the next few centuries, an unending stream of highly motivated intellectual missionaries kept overflowing India to throughout the length and breadth of Asia. They mingled smoothly with the local populations. Working their way with them patiently and peacefully, they eventually won them to their ideology. The faith thus found permanent settlements in China, Japan, Korea, Tibet, Mongolia, Bhutan and a host of other Asian countries. Philip Batchelor, a Buddhist scholar of renown from the West, writes in this regard: "Wherever the Buddhist teachings went, to Tibet or Japan, it adapted and mutated according to the circumstances in the host countries." We shall be dwelling upon the development of Buddhism in these lands when we have a look at the faith profiles of the East Asia in the next chapter. However, by the end of the seventh century, Buddhism had nearly been uprooted from the land of its birth. The Chinese traveler, Fa Hien, who visited India in AD 405-11 found it flourishing. Around two centuries later another Chinese, Hsuan Tsang who was here from AD 629 to 645 saw it floundering. It was a curious case of somebody winning the world and losing himself.

As far as India is concerned, with the ascendency of the Gupta's in central India, nucleus of Buddhism shifted northwestwards. Kanishka, the Kushan king, who ruled from Peshawar, emerged as the biggest patron of the faith. This provided an opportunity for cross-fertilisation of the faith with Greco-Bactrian cultures. A lot many gorgeous images of Buddha in Greco-Buddhist style thus got sculpted on the rocks of Bamiyan in Afghanistan. These were recently blasted by some boorish elements that are bent upon bringing Islam in conflict with the world. Buddhism does not believe in God, creation and revelation, the premises that are at the root of Hinduism. Yet, it is so completely soaked in spirituality, ethics and the urge to understand life in all its dimensions that Hinduism feels quite comfortable with its ideology and, in fact considers it as an integral part of itself. Stephen Batchelor, the Buddhist scholar, rightly observes:-

> "Buddhists do not believe in God but they are able to lead a life devoted to spiritual values and practices, ethics and morals without any recourse to the word god or anything remotely similar to the word god. In Buddhism, the core values are wisdom, compassion, tolerance, commitment to an ethical way of life and reflection on the meaning and purpose of life."[2]

### (c) JAINISM—The Search for Solace through Self-Pain

Jainism preceded Buddhism by around a generation. Founder of the faith, Nataputta Vardhamana, better known by the honorific name of Mahavira, was a contemporary of Gautama. He was born at a place near Vaishali to a Kashtriya king in BC 599. His adherents, however, believe that he was the twenty-fourth 'Jina' (the conqueror of self) in the long line of 'Tirathankaras' of the faith— the first being Rishabha and the last before him being Parshva. Their belief gets some support from the Indus Valley artifacts which point towards a possible connection with this religion. The earlier twenty-three jinas must have also lived a perfectly pious and highly disciplined life and must have gathered considerable following around them. Yet, the credit for founding the new faith historically goes to Mahavira.

Vardhamana was not the eldest son of his parents. So, he was a freer man to nurse the ideas of renouncing the world. Still, he did not wish to create a commotion by getting in to the state of homelessness while his parents were alive. He waited patiently and in the meanwhile got married. A daughter was also born to him. As soon as his parents were no more, he sought the approval of his brother to turn a monk. He asked Vardhamana to wait for one year to be sure that he was really ready for the final plunge out of the palace. Sure enough, the broody prince, now about thirty, broke all his attachments, discarded all ornaments and fineries and walked out of the worldly life, wrapped in just one ordinary garment. After a while he got rid of even this piece of clothing. He first made his way to an ashram run by the disciples of Parshva in a forested area. He then got lost in meditation, moving from place to place and accepting no hospitalities, so as not to develop fresh attachments. He exposed his body to severest discomforts in the course of the next twelve years. Finally, at the age of forty-two he attained the trance state of a jina. He devoted the next thirty years to preaching. On his death in BC 427, Mahavira is believed to have merged into Isatpragbhara, a congregation of liberated souls and thus, got released from the cycle of rebirths.

Jainism broadly believes that salvation is attainable only through self-effort. Praying to gods cannot serve any purpose. Vedas and priests could also be of no help in this endeavour. In fact, the creed raises a pertinent question, "Why wishest thou for a friend beyond thyself?"

Jainism does not believe in Brahmn-atamn theory of the Upanishads, though it does believe in atamn, as an independent element. Its idea of Isatpragbhara is quite different from that of Brahmn which reflects the Supreme Being. As per the Upanishad theory Atamn (individual souls) does not have any independent existence. Individuals are like the drops spraying up from the ocean. They may have an illusion of separateness for a while, but they soon fall back and lose their identity completely. On the other hand, Isatpragbhaga, is a collection of liberated souls, all retaining their consciousness. It is like a heap of grain in which each grain has a personality of its own, whereas the heap does not have any identity. It would be pertinent to note here that Buddhism does not believe in atamn either.

The followers of Jainism carry an intense desire for salvation within and believe in extreme asceticism. They believe that soul gets lot of dirt wrapped on to it when the body goes for relentless search for sensual pleasures. That makes it heavy and it gets trapped in the vicious cycle of rebirths. The purity of mind and deeds can remove all dirt from round the soul and make it light enough to fly away to join the Isatpragbhaga. They also lay utmost, rather obsessive, emphasis on nonviolence. The staunch among them would not even scratch their bodies, so as not to harm the bug that might be causing the itch.

The Jain monks have to take five vows: strict adherence to non-violence; no lying out of anger, greed, fear or mirth; not taking anything that is not given; no sexual pleasures and no attachments i.e. getting delighted or disturbed by anything. The last one is most inclusive: as if the monk while in the world, is not in it in his mind. There are twelve softer vows for the lay adherents. Because of the austerities that it expects its appeal is limited, but otherwise quite intense. Jains are just a few million in number, but its survival has never been at stake. Their monks have been carrying on contentedly with their austere existence and queer way of life for ages. Their lay followers have, however, been flowing along smoothly with the Hindu mainstream.

Jains are particularly known for their stellar contribution in the fields of literature, sculpture and architecture in India. Jainism is presently divided in to three main sects. Shvetambaras among them wear white clothes and mostly inhabit the northern region of the country. Digambaras, found mostly in the South, are more orthodox and wear no clothes. They do not admit women in to their order. Sthanakvasis do not believe in idols and worship in the open mostly in the form of meditation.

The creed has many common features with Buddhism. Both are quite in conflict with Brahamanism, deny the revelatory nature and special sacredness of the Vedas, have little belief in Vedanta philosophy, have agnostic view about God though they are highly spiritual in their approach to life, are in world denying mode and are founded by Kashtriya princes, uneasy with earthly existence and in search of inner peace. Many of their precepts and principle are also common. However, the dissimilarities between them are equally striking. Jainism believes in extreme asceticism, Buddhism has chosen the 'middle path'. Buddhism is much less obsessive about nonviolence compared to Jainism. As brought out earlier, Jainism does believe in atamn (soul), but not in Brahmn (the phenomenon of God), whereas Buddhism believes in neither. Jainism is strictly a local phenomenon while Buddhism has a vast number of adherents all over Asia and only a few at home.

### (d) SIKHISM—An effort at Syncretism and Simplification

Sikhism revolves around one God, ten Gurus and the holy Granth Sahib. God, in the absence of a more expressive name, has been referred to as 'Sat Nam', based on the view, that more than anything else, He is Truth. This finds further elaboration in the preamble of 'Japji Sahib', a composition of thirty eight verses (pouri's or steps), containing in essence, the spiritual experiences of its founder :-

ੴ ਸਤਿ ਨਾਮੁ ਕਰਤਾ ਪੁਰਖੁ
ਨਿਰਭਉ ਨਿਰਵੈਰੁ ਅਕਾਲ ਮੂਰਤਿ
ਅਜੂਨੀ ਸੈਭੰ ਗੁਰ ਪ੍ਰਸਾਦਿ ॥

(There is but one God. He is Truth. He is the Uncreated Being who has created all. He is above all fear and enmities. Guidance of Guru can get you to Him.)

This is perhaps the best description of the Divine, thought of anywhere in the world.

The importance of a Guru, as a guide, has been given high emphasis in the religion. One could not hope to break out of the vicious cycle of rebirths through mere observance of fasts, giving of alms, austerities, penance, pilgrimages, holy baths, renunciation and rituals etc. Only the inner piety, noble deeds and grace of Guru can guide a man to his goal. All that he needs to get to God is recitation of His name from the depth of his soul.

The faith was founded by Guru Nanak, born in a Khatri family at Talwandi in AD 1469. He was born in his 'Nanake' (Mother's parents' place) and that is how he got his name—Nanak Chand. The roots of the religion rather lie deeper in the earlier centuries. Nanak had precursors in Jaidev, Namdev, Ramananda and his illustrious disciple, Kabir. The thrust of their message was that Hinduism needed to be simplified and brought closer to the understanding level of the masses. Common man was interested in home truths, rather than intricate philosophies. In 12$^{th}$ century, Hindi poet Jaidev advocated a shift away from the ceremonies and rituals to just 'the pious repetition of God's name'. This was to later reflect in the key word of the Sikh faith— 'Namsimran'.

Nanak, as a youth, must have been a disappointment to his parents who were always worried about his professional carrier. He was sincere and hardworking alright, but worldly affairs hardly interested him. His heart seemed to be set on something higher. He flopped as a herdsman and a store-keeper. These were the two professions initially chosen for him. He was hardly a success on the domestic front either, though he did marry in obedience to his parents' wish and was blessed with two sons also. Finally, he was persuaded to join a government job at Sultanpur. A spiritually inclined Muslim, Mardana, became his soul-mate at the place. He was destined to remain hyphenated with him in the rest of his life. In fact, he continues to remain so in Sikh consciousness even today.

Once during his meditation, Nanak had an unworldly experience that changed the course of his life. In this vision, he found himself in audience before the Almighty who offered him a cup of 'amrit' (nectar). He was enjoined to devote the rest of his life in motivating people towards spirituality through recitation of 'Sat Nam'. Thereafter, he kept moving in the manner of a mendicant to cities like Haridwar, Benaras, Jagannath and many other holy places ensconced in the Himalayas. Wherever he went, he spent his time in preaching and singing in praise of God. Mardana gave him instrumental support by playing on his rebeck. Later, his spiritual curiosity is said to have taken him to Mecca, Medina and Baghdad also. It is said that while the travel weary Nanak was resting at Mecca, a Muslim faithful rebuked him for his temerity of sleeping with his feet towards the holy Kaaba, the abode of Allah. Nanak humbly asked him to turn his feet in the direction where God was not there. The legend has it that in whatever direction his feet were moved 'Kaaba' was seen to be right in front. Possibly, what is meant is that the Muslim faithful felt enlightened that God after all was there everywhere.

Nanak then made his way to his country. By this time he had picked up a sizeable following, mostly in Punjab. Mardana parted company with him on his death at Kartarpur. Nanak also did not survive long after that. He breathed his last in AD 1538. There is another legend related to his death. While on his death bed, he found some Hindus and Muslim arguing over his last rites. He asked the two groups to place their flowers to his right and left sides. He told them that whosesoever flowers were found to be fresh the next morning shall have the privilege of performing his rites. Next day when the sheet covering him was removed there was no body underneath it, while the flowers were in bloom on both the sides.

The core features of the Sikh religion are the Unity of God, Equality, Faith in the Gurus, Love of God, Morality and 'Namsimran' (reciting the name of God) on every available moment. An attempt has thus been made to syncretise many existing faiths without going into the intricacies of their philosophic content and without offering any arguments with regard to the selection of the creedal matter from these faiths.

Emperor Akbar made a similar effort while launching his own religion, Deen-e-Ilahi, by borrowing beneficial features from many religions of the world. A faith gets a boost from its followers. Quite a few followers of sort had gathered round him during his life time. The new faith, however, died with his death. Perhaps Akbar could not set a very shiny example of personal piety and his harem life did not go well with his spiritual adventure. Also, there is quite some difference between the followers with genuine conviction and the mere flatterers. The otherwise great Akbar must have felt uneasy in his grave that his word could not become the word of God. Significantly, Nanak and his illustrious successors, all commoners, succeeded where the mighty emperor had failed.

Sikhism is a faith of hope and cheer. Universe is 'Maya' alright, but this illusion is the creation of none other than God. One has to be therefore in peace with this situation. Man does not have to walk out on what is on offer to him in the world. Life is a great gift of God to him and it is meant to be enjoyed to the hilt. He, being the choicest creation of God, all other living beings are supposed to be at his service. Meat eating could thus not be a taboo for him. However, he had to avoid any attachments and lures that divert his attention from the higher goals of life.

The faith believes in the basic Hindu doctrines of the transmigration of souls and the law of 'Karma'. Nanak advocated that one should not live apart from God. Keeping Him in mind all the time and repeated recitation of His name was the way to absorption in Him. The Sikh mode of worship is thus tailored to send the prayer directly to the Divine, rather than this being relayed through numerous gods. At least in the beginning, it looked to be the reformed face of Hinduism, washed clean of all mazelike philosophies and mysticisms. The faith is also opposed to the caste system of the Hindu society. Guru Amar Das says in this context, "The world is all made out of the same clay".

Sikhism was initially seen as an amalgam of the Hindu and Muslim faiths. For some years, this perception kept it out of the harm's way in the Muslim dominated India and provided it an opportunity to grow in peace. The Muslim felt that their ideology of monotheism was gradually pushing a section of the Hindus towards their own faith. However, this illusion was soon dissipated. The new faith was too intricately hyphenated with Hinduism to get sucked into Islam. The Hindus and Sikhs never had any difficulty in worshipping together, paying obeisance at each other's places of pilgrimage or even entering in to matrimonial relationships. The strain of monotheism has also been very much present in Hinduism itself in good measure. The real difference between Hinduism and Islam, in fact, does not relate to monotheism, but the Islamic belief that Allah does not share divinity with anybody and Hindu thinking that it lies sprinkled all over His universe. Their close affinity, however, does not mean that Sikhism is an adjunct of Hinduism. In fact, such suggestions can result in agitation in the mind of the minority community. After all, nobody relishes the idea of his faith being referred to as a sub-religion.

The Muslim eventually started discerning traces of blaspheme in the Sikh religion. The first four Gurus of the faith were pacifists who believed in quiet prayer. The fifth Guru, Arjun Dev, compiled Sri Granth Sahib that is a compendium of devotional hymns written by the Gurus and the saintly souls of the earlier era like Jaidev, Namdev, Kabir and others. Some influential elements of the Muslim clergy found the volume blasphemous and took the matter before Emperor Akbar. He, however, found nothing objectionable in the book. Guru Arjun Dev is also credited with the completion of the holiest Sikh shrine, the Golden Temple at Amritsar.

Akbar initially wanted his grandson, Khusrao to accede to the throne after him, as his son, Salim (Jehangir) was addicted to hard drinking. However, he changed his mind while breathing his last and suddenly declared Salim as his successor. On this, Khusrao rose in rebellion that got crushed. Khusrao had obtained the blessings of Guru Arjun Dev before launching his rebellion. This brought the wrath of the new emperor on the Guru. He had him tortured to death. Before dying, Guru Arjun Dev enjoined upon his son, Har Govind, to raise an army to defend the faith. This brought the Sikhs in conflict with the Muslims which culminated in the martyrdom of the ninth Guru, Teg Bahadur. By the time of the last Guru, Govind Singh, a situation of undeclared war between the Sikhs and the Muslims had developed in Punjab. The heroic Guru was able to breathe a miraculous spirit of militancy in his followers. He ordained that his followers would henceforth use 'Singh' (standing for lion) after their initial name and after his death, Guru Granth Sahib would be regarded as the last Guru. Though he himself did not live to see his efforts getting crowned with success, he had already sowed seeds of the Sikh victory. He died of the stab wounds inflicted on him by a Muslim in AD 1708. After Aurangzev, the Muslim rulers of the country were reduced to the pale shadow of their past. Finally, Maharaja Ranjit Singh was able to set up a powerful empire in Punjab that turned the tables on the Muslim invaders and put them on the defensive on the north-west periphery of his empire, from where they had been making frequent forays into India over the centuries.

The last Guru also enjoined upon his devotees to adhere to the five 'K's'. These are: (a) 'Kesh' (letting the natural hair grow to comply with the God's will), (b) Kangha or comb (signifying controlled spirituality), (c) Khanda or sword (to declare the determination to defend truth), (d) Kara, a steel bracelet (to imply unity with God) and Kachha or the under garment (to connote moral strength). This was possibly intended to provide a distinct identity to the followers of the new faith. Besides, all these happen to be the utility items to cater to the needs of the situation that they were then in. The Tenth Guru saw his end drawing near. Taking stock of the situation in his religious order as obtaining at the time, he enjoined upon his followers:-

> "I have raised the Sikh Panth in compliance with the will of the Eternal Father. I now desire you, my followers, to regard the Holy Granth Sahib as your Guru after me and have the faith in it, as if it were your living Guru. The faithful shall henceforth seek guidance from its holy text."

The message that Sikhism radiates is simple. With God in your heart and His name on your lips, you could do no wrong. It takes care of both God and morality. No water can wash your inner impurities. A prayer not rising from the depth of your heart cannot reach the Divine Being. It is as simple as that. Sikhism thus reduces a mountain of philosophies and rituals to a mere mole hill.

## Notes

1. Figures based on the report of Sh. Ramesh Pokheryal, a former Chief Minister of the state of Uttrakhanda in India.
2. The Speaking Tree section of 'The Times of India' dated 6th February, 2011.

# 11

# The Faith Profiles of the Far-East

## (a) CHINA—Life and Nature to the Fore

The most striking feature of the Chinese religions is that they have not allowed any sort of revelatory strains to enter into their system. In the first millennium BC, they produced a galaxy of illustrious thinkers and commentators like Confucius, Lao Tzu, Chuang Tzu, Mo Tzu, Mencius, Chung Yung, Hsun Tzu and a host of others who still rule the Chinese mind from their graves. However, none of them had any pretentions to being a prophet. They did not even claim to be the reformers, but only the researchers of the rituals and belief systems of the country's past. This is what Confucius has to say about his work, "My attempt is just to follow and explain our ancient traditions and I do not try to create something of my own".

As regards God, the Chinese have a generally agnostic attitude. They do not deny the possibility of God being there somewhere. However, they also seem to bear in mind that He is an unknowable phenomenon. It is thus futile to make an effort to know him. This Chinese view is quite clearly reflected in the following two passages of Lao Tzu, the founder of the Taoism in the land:-

> "Quite truly, there is one supreme power that holds the universe together."

> "It is more or less clear that there is a Supreme Being; but knowing about the origin of all things is far beyond the human brain. There is One from whom I derive my life breath. I, however, have never seen His form. He is real, has thoughts and feelings, but is shapeless otherwise".

The truth is somewhere close to this view. Earlier the Aryans also thought the same way. Many have presented this thesis since then again and again with not very significant variations. I feel very humble on being late on this by two and a half millennia.

The working of nature and nuances of life might also be difficult to understand but these are not beyond the reach of human brain. So, the Chinese philosophers have concentrated hard in these knowable areas with good results that are there for all to see. One could discern a marked resemblance between these Chinese intellectuals and the Greek philosophers of the time like Plato, Socrates and Aristotle etc. The common cross-thread that runs through them is the philosophic vision and wisdom.

The ideologies of Confucius (BC 551-479) and his elder contemporary, Lao Tzu (born BC 604) brought in to being two major religious faiths in the region, Confucianism and Taoism. These were to permeate the Chinese psyche for all time to come. There is no element of revelation in either of these. These have just risen out of the wisdom of man. Confucianism advocates respect for family, tradition and society. The believers look to 'Tien' or High Heaven as the source of all cosmic order. The concept of High Heaven comes closest to what is understood as the Divine in other parts of the world. Sacrifices were regularly offered to the Spirit of Heaven at state, community and private levels.

The reigning emperor was considered to be the next in command to the High Heaven in the spiritual order. Even the deceased emperors of the ruling dynasties took precedence over the spirits of the Sun and Moon. A plethora of spirits like that of the hills, rivers, soil and so on, followed next. These spirits were duly graded and had a flexible order of precedence based on their performance. The emperor had the authority to upgrade or downgrade the status of these spirits. If, for instance, the spirit of the soil did not play up, despite proper propitiation, and this resulted in inadequate crop and consequent famine, it could face down-gradation. These spirits were neither idolised nor provided temples. Their worship, mostly in the form of sacrifice, was performed under the open skies. Interestingly, however, Confucius himself was deified a few centuries after his death and temples were raised all over the country to offer sacrifices to his spirit. The reigning emperors often graced these ceremonies with their personal presence. Still, Confucius is worshipped for his wisdom and virtue and not for any Godly links.

Some books written by Confucius or compiled by his disciples on the basis of his discourses have a canonical character, but these do not, even remotely, seek the authority of the Divine to reinforce their message. These are primarily concerned with morality, ethics, education and cosmic harmony. These books have very little metaphysical content in them. In fact, this is what his disciples say about him, "The subjects on which the Master (Confucius) did not speak were the supernatural phenomena, feats of (superhuman) strength, disorderliness and spiritual beings". All this equally applies to the other indigenous canonical literature of China. George Foot Moore is absolutely right and on course when he writes:-

> "In China, certain books for many centuries have been accepted as regulative in religions, morals and government. They are not regarded as revealed or inspired: their authority is due solely to the prescription of antiquity or the wisdom and virtue of their reputed authors".[1]

Confucius–The great Chinese thinker

The disciples of Confucius describe him as, "mild mannered but dignified; majestic, and yet not awe-inspiring; respectful, yet relaxed". The Confucian literature consists of the highly regarded Five Classics and Four Books. The Classics, that are sometimes referred to by the Western scholars as the Confucian Old Testament, are Shih Ching (The Book of Poetry), Shu Ching (The Book of History), Yi-Ching (The Book of Changes), Li Chi (The Book of Rites), Chun Chiu (The Spring and Autumn) and Yueh Chi (The Record of Music). The last of these has since gone extinct and has been forgotten about. These have been compiled from very old materials and are in the nature of odes in praise of the rulers, their histories, speeches, ancient rites, beliefs and archival records. These also deal with the etiquettes to be observed during public and private ceremonies.

The Four Books carry even greater prominence than the Classics and are regarded as the New Testament part of the Confucian Bible. The first of these, Lun Yu (The Analects of Confucius) is a compilation of the discourses of the sage to his disciples. "Look not at what is at odds with propriety; listen not to what is at odds with propriety; speak not what is at odds with propriety", advises the sage to his disciples in Book-XII/Chapter I/Para-2. (Incidentally, this also gives an indication where the famous three wise monkeys of Mahatama Gandhi come from). "To know what is right and not to do it, is indicative of lack of courage", is another typical observation from the great master (Book II/Chapter-XXIV/Para-2). The second one, Ta Hsueh (The Great Learning) is based on the politico-moral philosophy of Confucius. It was meant for the education of the princes and young nobles. The third book, Chung Yung (The Doctrine of the Mean) relates to harmonising the human conduct with the 'Will of Heaven'. The last one, The Meng-tsu (The Works of Mencius) deals with the views of the early Confucian commentator, Mencius, on the rules for righteous government, qualities of a good ruler and duties of the subjects etc.

A few typical excerpts from these Books would give a more accurate idea about what a wealth of human wisdom that lies buried in this ancient literature:

爲政第二 子曰、爲政以德、譬如北辰、居其所、而衆星共之。

(The Master (Confucius) said, "He who governs on the strength of his virtue holds a position similar to the polar star to our north which always stays stationary, whereas the other stars look towards it—.

行必果、硜硜然小人哉、抑亦可以爲次矣。曰、今之從政者何如。子曰、噫、斗筲之人、何足算也。

—Confucian Analects: Book II, Chapter-I.

(He who is always conscious about his conduct and when sent on a mission would not bring disgrace to his commission, is fit to be called an officer.)

齊其家、欲
齊其家者、
先脩其身、
欲脩其身
者、先正其

—Confucian Analects: Book XIII/Chapters-XIII & XX

者、先正其
心、欲正其，
心者、先誠
其意、欲誠
其意者、先
致其知、致
知、在格物。

(The ancients who desired to bring home resplendent virtue to whole of their kingdom, first made a beginning in their states. Wishing to restore their states to good order, they took up the families first. Wishing to regulate families, they first thought of cleansing their own hearts. With the goal of cleansing the hearts, they made an effort for being sincere in their thoughts. Wishing to be sincere in their thoughts, they went for extending the frontiers of their knowledge. This extension of knowledge came through inquiry in to the things.)

— The Great Learning (The text of Confucius)/Para-4

其憂、樂以天下、憂以
天下、然而不王者、未

(When a ruler rejoices in the happiness of his subjects, they join him in his happiness; when the ruler grieves in their sorrow, he finds his people by his side in his hour of grief——.)

—The Works of Mencius, Book I, Chapter IV/Para-3

子貢問政。子曰足
食、足兵、民信之矣。

(The Master said, "The requisites of government are that the state should have sufficient food and military equipment and it must enjoy the trust of its people.")

—Confucian Analects, Chapter 7, Para-1

子曰、飯疏食
飲水、曲肱而枕
之、樂亦在其中
矣、不義而富且
貴、於我如浮雲。

(The Master said, "I shall still feel joyful if I were to manage by eating course rice, drinking just water and sleeping with my bended arm as pillow. I shall take the riches and honours acquired by inappropriate means as illusionary like a passing cloud.)

—Confucian Analects, Chapter-XV.

[illegible]子曰、恭而無禮則勞、愼而無禮則葸、勇而無禮則亂、直而無禮則絞。

(The Master said, "If principles of propriety are not observed, respectfulness gets reduced to just laborious bustle; carefulness to timidity; boldness to insubordination and straightforwardness to rudeness."

—Confucian Analects, Chapter II, Para-1.

Confucius was born in the age of political disintegration, social unrest, intellectual anarchy and moral disorder. He took upon himself the task of mending matters through a sort of moral revolution. He persuaded the rulers to live up to their high responsibilities towards their subjects and exhorted the people to extend all cooperation to their rulers through righteous conduct and unflinching loyalty. He stressed on uprightness (Chih), benevolence (Jen), conscientiousness (Chung), righteousness (Yi) and filial piety (Hsiao) as the cardinal human virtues that could enable the governments to earn love of and peace with their people. Their subjects could also, in turn, live happy and contented lives under royal benevolence.

As already stressed, both Confucianism and Taoism are born out of brain and wisdom. They do not seek any revelatory support to reinforce their preaching. Neither of them claims that what they say was put in their ears by any supernatural being. Their thinking thus stands on its own legs. The Chinese have been practical people. What has always occupied their mindscape is the fecundity of earth and the blessings of the heavenly forces. Confucius mostly talked about man and morals. But he also saw the natural forces under the Tien suggesting a particular way of life. He wanted life to be lived

Kumbh Mela site at Haridwar (India) where millions of Hindu Devotees congregate every twelfth year.
Attribution: Edson Walker from Brazil—Retrieved from the Wikipedia site.

The Golden Temple at Amritsar (India), the holiest shrine of Sikhism Attribution: Paulrudd—Retrieved from the Wikipedia site.

Temple at Bali — Hindu temple of Dalem Agung Pedangtegal, Bali, Indonesia
Attribution: Site http://en.wikipedia.org.

The Japanese temple at Kangawa.

and the states to be governed in harmony with nature or the 'Will of Heaven'.

Lao Tzu who ushered Taoism in the land, however, was excessively obsessed with nature. He posits a world order based exclusively on the understanding of nature. He wanted man to live the innocent life of a new born baby. Unlike Confucius who thought education was the answer to the problems of life, Lao Tzu did not relish knowledge. He thought that it led to artificiality. Skills that were profit-oriented also complicated life. He advocated, "Banish wisdom, discard knowledge, and the people will be benefited a hundred folds—— Banish skill and discard profit, and thieves and robbers will disappear."

The philosophy of Lao Tzu is simple. It advises man to just flow with nature. He seems to believe that Adam and Eve did commit a great sin by eating the forbidden fruit of knowledge, whereby they lost their innocence and were rightly condemned to live a life full of concerns and toil. Thus, the Taoist slogan is, "Back to the Nature". Acquisition of knowledge promotes the scheming instincts of a man. Manipulations inflict unnecessary care and caution on him, leading to uneasiness. Taoism advises man to sit in forgetfulness to avoid stress. It says that emptiness of spirit is in the nature of a fast of the mind. Confucius is also all for harmonising life with nature. However, he insists that we should first try to understand what nature seems to suggest and then act accordingly. Lao Tzu, however, is of the view that there is no need for man to rack his brain. He should just follow what appeals to him instinctively. What nature requires him to do is already present in his blood and breath. The fourth verse of Tao Te Ching that seems to contain Lao Tze's views in essence is reproduced below:-

"The Tao is empty, yet inexhaustible, bottomless, the source of all that exists.

The sharp edges would smoothen, angular things straighten, severity of Sun soften as it does under a cloud cover and all dust would settle serenely on ground (if you are able to put your thoughts in line with nature).

The spirit of nature is hidden, but always present. I know not to whom it was born. But it, as a father figure, is in ancestral relationship with all."

The two great contemporaries did not see eye to eye with each other and felt that they were poles apart. However, they have, more or less, left the same philosophies behind. At least the ultimate moral message of the two is broadly similar. The only dividing line between the two is the Confucius's emphasis on education and enlightenment and Lao Tzu's aversion for knowledge, skills and sophistication. That way, Taoism would appear to be some sort of anti-intellectualism. It, however, could not be so, comes as it from a brilliant intellectual himself. The other difference between the two is that Confucius always remained down to earth and did not lift his eyes to the eternal reality of the universe, whereas Lao Tzu has paid some attention to this invisible area of knowledge also.

However, Taoism has a definite element of quietism in it. It believes in avoiding conflict by restraining overweening ambitions. The Taoist view is that the best government is the one that governs the least. Too many institutions, laws, restrictions and prohibitions eventually prove counterproductive. Uniformity should not be forced, as the individuals are all naturally different. Confucius, on the other hands believed that individualism could not be allowed a free run all the time. Some laws were necessary for collective living. Some of the age old views of Confucius and Lao Tzu find an echo in the constitutions of all democratic countries today. These statutes constantly struggle to strike a balance between Confucianism (social interest) and Taoism (individual liberty).

The most highly regarded Taoist book is 'Tao-te-king'. It was either authored by him personally or at least it records his sayings faithfully. Moral content is dominant in Taoism. It contains commandments like: Do not promote your own cause at the cost of others; do not discard public good for private interest; do not suck the brain of others; do not hold back the virtue of others and expose their defects; do not reveal private affairs etc.

Taoism urges equanimity in the face of adversity. It is of the view that even death is the natural result of life and nothing more than a change from one existence form to another. Here, it coincides with the Hindu belief articulated in the Bhagawat Gita. Interestingly, Chuang Tzu, a famous Taoist, was found singing merrily on the death of his beloved wife. He justified this unusual reaction by saying, "While she thus sleeps in the Great House (the universe), my going about weeping and wailing would betray ignorance of the scheme of nature on my part."

Three foreign faiths, Buddhism, Islam and Christianity, found their way to China. Out of them, only Buddhism could get properly naturalised here. It has since made profound impact on the Chinese psyche. Himalayas have been a formidable barrier between India and China. To a degree, the situation is still so. Despite this, the two countries had been in constant contact at least since the third century BC. Buddhism was also somehow able to seep through these mountain ranges from India to china. The faith did not come on a tourist visa, but for a permanent settlement here. A steady stream of selfless missionaries with loads of patience, personal virtue and high intelligence started pouring into the country from the sides i.e. over the sea route as well as through central Asian lands. It is nothing short of a miracle that the people who they converted were not the pagans with a mental vacuum. The society where they found acceptance already boasted of a highly advanced civilisation. They also did not have victorious armies advancing ahead of them.

As a legend has it, the Han emperor, Ming Ti (AD 58-75) saw the golden image of Buddha entering into his sleeping chamber, brilliantly alight as Sun. Out of his burning curiosity, he dispatched twelve special envoys to India to bring detailed information about the Blessed One. This delegation returned with a load of holy books, images of Buddha and two missionaries of the faith. The emperor got a monastery constructed for the Buddhist guests and had their books translated in Chinese. That is how they believe the faith germinated in their land. The more credible version, however, is that some Buddhist missionaries arrived in the country sometimes around AD 75 and Ming Ti allowed them to install Buddha's statue and propagate their faith. It is, however, doubtful if the emperor converted to Buddhism himself. His curiosity for the new creed nonetheless is quite evident. He was perhaps also fascinated with the fact of the Buddha bartering princely comforts with monastic piety.

It was the Hinayana cult of Buddhism that appeared in the land at that point of time. It did not catch the imagination of the people much, as the Chinese, with their jest for life and love for family bonds, could not appreciate the world denying doctrines of the new faith. Their materialism just could not reconcile with the Buddhist mysticism. The joyous people could not understand what miseries of the worldly existence and transitoriness of being the Buddhists were talking about, the Taoists among them though found the new ideology somewhat close to their own thinking. Confucians were, however, hardly enthused with what Buddhism had on offer.

By AD 220, the Han dynasty dissipated and China got divided in to three kingdoms and consequently weakened. The next few centuries saw the nomads breaking through the Great Chinese Wall in huge numbers and causing colossal political and intellectual upheaval in the land. When the cheer got thus robbed from their present life, the fascination for next life assumed importance. Confucianism, in this regard, just offered that you would be remembered and respected after your death by your descendents out of filial piety. The nomadic tribes entering China brought the Mahayana strain of Buddhism with them. This carried optimistic conceptions about the afterlife. Thus, by the fourth century AD, Buddhism started blossoming rapidly.

The good results were first noticed in North China where the local and barbarian bloods had mixed. The progress in the south was slow as the nationalistic pride provided considerable staying power to the Confucians and even the Taoists there. However, Buddhism had such a great porosity in it that it would readily absorb into itself all positive features from any source. Also, its inbuilt adaptability made it discover a good many commonalties both with Taoism and Confucianism. It gelled so well with the local creeds that it itself started appearing to be indigenous. Later it came to be said that the Chinese were 'Confucian in office, Taoist in retirement and Buddhist as death drew near'.

Buddhism did get a rousing reception in China. However, this is not to say that it did not face any trials and travail there at all. There were times when the Confucian or Taoist emperors went after them real hard. The Tang emperor, Wu Tsung, for instance, destroyed thousands of Buddhist buildings, melted down tens of thousands of Buddha images and deported around half a million monks, nuns and servitors. All this notwithstanding, there were nearly two hundred and fifty million Buddhists in China on the eve of the Communist take-over.

A significantly different variety of Buddhism took root in Tibet and Mongolia. Around AD 630, the Tibetan prince, Srong Tsan Gan developed interest in the faith, possibly under the influence of his two wives, one from China and the other from Nepal. He sent some emissaries to North India to explore the feasibility of inviting a few exponents of the Buddhist ideology to his kingdom. His mission did not make much headway as the Buddhist ideas were seen to be at odds with the prevailing ethos of demonology in the land. The wind-swept high plateau faced inclement weather most of the time. The difficult environment of the region had generated lot of demonic apprehensions and fears in the native psyche. The Tibetans considered it necessary to propitiate various elemental devils to live in peace and comfort.

A tantric brand of Buddhism was prevalent in Bengal around this time. The creed underwent some reform and refit in course of time. When Padma Sambhava took it to Tibet in the eighth century it met quite some acceptance there, because it seemed to suggest means and mantras of keeping Tibetans out of the harm's way. By invoking the protective power of the Buddhist divinities, they could always keep the demons of mountains, desert plateaus, cemeteries, winds, cold, hearths and homes away. These beliefs brought the priestly power to the fore and the priests came to exercise civil authority also in their areas. Thus the institution of Lamaism where the sacred and secular streams meet in the person of a high Buddhist priest got firmly established.

In the thirteenth century, the legendary Mongol chieftain, Kublai Khan was looking for a religion to reinforce his disciplinary control over his vast army. He had a look at many religions including Islam and Christianity and finally found Tibetan variety of Buddhism most suitable to his needs. He himself converted formally to this faith, giving it a great boost.

In the second half of the fourteenth century, Tibetan monk, Tsong-kha-pa, organised what the Westerns now call the Yellow Church. The name comes from the colour of their hats and girdles. This brought celibacy and added piety to their system. As the Lamas could not marry now, their successors came to be selected on the principle of believed incarnation rather than heredity. The Dalai Lama (the High Lama of Lhasa) visited Mongolia on the invitation of the powerful Mongol chieftain of the place. He was given a rousing welcome. He revived Buddhism in the land by working out some hierarchical arrangements, introducing new rites, festivals, practices and traditions which still survive. The prelates of Urga there, in fact, claim to be incarnates of Taranatha, an Indian historian who visited Mongolia and is held in highest esteem there.

The so called Yellow Church soon spread to the fringes of Siberia, China and India (Sikkim and Bengal Areas) and has since been settled in peace in the Tibetan plateau for centuries. However, with the Communism coming to power in China, politics has driven religion to the backyard and the Communist propensity for tighter control over their administered territories has forced the present Dalai Lama to seek shelter in India.

### (b) JAPAN—The confluence of two Holy Streams.

When two mighty rivers meet there is quite some watery turbulence, but after a while they flow together smoothly in friendly embrace. It is slightly different in case of religions. Even after initial acceptability of a foreign faith, the societal ego keeps on creating periodic problems. This is what happened everywhere when Buddhism overflowed the borders of India into many alien lands. The places where it poured had difficulty in deciding whether to allow the new religious ideas to cross-fertilize their existing beliefs or they needed to shield their prevalent system against the influx of foreign influences.

In Japan, it was a case of heart and head being unable to reconcile with each other. The patriotic hearts thought that they should stick on to their past; the progressive heads propelled them to welcome the light wherever it came from. As we shall see, ultimately the indigenous Shinto and Buddhism fused to form a mixed faith called 'Ryobu'. Occasionally, the Japanese national pride came to the fore in the matter of faith and efforts were made to purge the alien strains from out of their system. However, over the centuries, Buddhism had intermixed with the native belief system so thoroughly that it just could not be sieved out of the Japanese psyche.

Though the Japanese are intensely proud of their past and really love their land they are people of mixed ethnicity who came to the country from the neighbouring areas. They are an amalgam of Koreans, Mongolians, Malayans and people from various Pacific islands. They had to fight fierce battles with the Ainu tribal, the original inhabitants to get a foothold in their adopted land. This happened in the distant past and right from then the Japanese acquired a martial mentality and came to hold their warriors and weapons in high esteem.

They believe that their islands were brought in to being by Isanagi (the sky father) and Isanami (the mother earth). Quite some mythology lies woven around this origin. Then, there is a pantheon of 'kami' gods and goddesses occupying their consciousness. On the top is, of course, the Sun goddess, 'Amaterasu'. The Japanese believe that their emperors have descended from this deity and they themselves also have divine origin, being the descendents of the lesser 'kami' gods. The Amaterasu temple at Ise is their holiest shrine. Shinto religion is thus soaked in a concept of holy land, thronging with deities representing various elements of nature like Sun, Moon, sea, storms, stars, lightening, thunder, rain, rivers, rocks, mist, trees, earthquakes and volcanoes etc. Besides, there are grain, food, fertility, health, phallic and even some animal deities. Their list is, in fact, unending.

In course of time, around the fourth century AD, Confucian influences from china started making their way into the Islands. They brought a new way of life, arts and skills to the Japanese. Being quick learners and progressive people, they smoothly assimilated whatever they thought was good for them. They already venerated their emperors and respected their chieftains. Confucian ideas reinforced their belief in morality and filial piety. Various schools of Buddhism had cropped up in China by then. Some of these eventually penetrated into the Japanese islands also. The most important among these being the 'Chan' school which in Japan came to be known as 'Zen'.

Buddhism that came to them through the Korean peninsula brought even bigger changes in their outlook and beliefs. Buddhism, with its wonderful capacity to merge with any land, seeped deep into Shinto shrines, affecting their system of worship and architectural designs. After initial reservations, the Japanese took to Buddhism, as if it was their own religion. This merger of Shinto and Buddhism, as already noted, produced a mixed faith 'Ryobu'. This harmony held for centuries, but eventually got disturbed by a patriotic surge towards pure Shinto. However, hard Buddhism tried to indigenize itself and gel with the local sentiments, it could not get rid of the tag of being an imported faith. Nevertheless, over the centuries, the indigenous and the alien faiths had dissolved in each other so thoroughly that it was just not possible to separate the two. Thus Buddhism is still very much alive in the Land of the Rising Sun and is also kicking. In fact, it stands proved here that a person could be a Buddhist, Shinto and Confucian all at the same time. Shinto relates to national heritage and Confucianism to social ethics, while Buddhism takes care of the after-life concerns.

The Japanese believe that their indigenous religious system may be primitive, but it is of divine origin. They have both the primitive and progressive traits in their genes. Their intense pride in everything Japanese prevents them from moving along with others, but it does not stop them from moving ahead of others, by beating the best in their own game.

### (c) The Other Countries

The other Far Eastern countries had their own tribal cultures before Hinduism and Buddhism penetrated there. Later, however, Islam and Christianity also made inroads into these lands in a big way. Today Indonesia and Malaysia are predominantly Muslim, though Hinduism also has a sizeable presence there. Buddhism permeates the religious ethos in Thailand, Myanmar and Kampuchea. The other countries of the region have mixed profiles. However, their past Indo-Chinese connection is manifestly evident everywhere.

## Note

1. 'History of Religions', Vol. I, p. 4, Charles Scribbler's son, New York, 1948.

# 12

# The Question Mark Over Conversions

People always have a propensity to believe that their own religion is superior to that of others. This illusion is born out of a sense of vain ego or some mental limitation. They seem to feel that the founders of their faith had better knowledge of God and His ways and they themselves at least have the basic wisdom to understand this. They have thus been able to select the correct way of life for themselves, while the others are groping in ignorance. The fact of the matter, however, is that a man belongs to a particular religion mostly because of the accident of birth and sticks on to it because he gets habituated to it. His religion is almost always a matter of tradition coming down from his ancestry or some inducement offered to him for conversion. Only a miniscule minority of people belong to a particular faith out of personal choice.

Religions, with passage of time, become less spiritual and more worldly. They often need politico-military back up to thrive. Hinduism spread in the south-east Asia because its princes held political sway in the region at that point of time. Later, as the Muslim came to acquire political clout in the area, the tide turned in favour of Islam. Likewise, Buddhism dissipated in India as soon as it lost political patronage. The miraculous thing about this faith, however, is that it was able to spread its wings in so many surrounding countries without any victorious armies marching ahead of it. It was a rare case of genuine change of heart on part of the converts to it. It seemed to have a miraculous capacity to seep into the soul of people on the quiet. Yet, had the political patronage not played truant to it periodically, the world would have been predominantly Buddhist today. Similarly, if the Muslim had won the Battle of Tours in AD 732, the whole of Europe and most of the world would have been living under the shadow of the Crescent these days. All this goes to prove that politics and religions just complement each other in the worldly power-play and hardly any divinity is involved in this process. Divinity, in fact, resides deep in the consciousness of the common people.

The worth of a religion depends on the intellectual level of its adherents and their capacity to review their past objectively. Those who are able to pick up the pearls scattered in the heritage behind them and have the wisdom to quickly discard what blocks their minds on way to enlightenment, move forward. The others just keep going round and round in the grooves of their making, believing that nothing exists beyond the arc of their belief. The message of all the religions is broadly the same. It is, however, mostly not the message, but the communities behind the religions that draw the converts into them. Sometimes the personalities of the founders also play a big part in the religious migrations.

Judaism permits conversions in and out of it. For conversions into it, the faith is very selective. Hinduism is equally fussy about admitting the outsiders in its fold. It is generally believed that for being a Hindu one has to be born as a Hindu. However, this is not strictly true. Even the Indian apex court has recently ruled that a person following Hindu precepts and practices and acceptable to the community, is a Hindu. The Muslims try to keep their flock together on pain of death for the proselytizer out of it. Both Islam and Christianity nurse the ideas of eventually converting the entire world to their faith. The other religions do not entertain any such aspirations and are quite happy with the following that they already have. The following statistics about the religious migrations should help us to understand what is happening on this front in the world today:-

| *Religion* | *Number of adherents (AD 2000)* | *Growth from 1990 to 2000* | *Rate (%)* | | *Coun-tries* |
|---|---|---|---|---|---|
| | | | *Natural* | *Conv-ersions* | |
| Christianity | 1999 | 23 | 2.50 | 1.36 | 238 |
| Islam | 1188 | 22 | 0.87 | 2.13 | 204 |
| Hinduism | 811 | 13 | (-) 0.66 | 1.69 | 114 |
| Buddhism | 360 | 3.5 | 0.15 | 1.00 - | |
| Judaism | 15 | 0.19 | (-) 0.071.25 | | |

The global population in the beginning of the present millennium was 6005
Figures in millions.
**Source:** David A Barrett, World Christian Encyclopedia, 2001/p. 4.

Judaism is one religion that welcomes conversions into it only after carefully ensuring that the person desirous of joining them in their faith is coming with a genuine change of heart. They make it abundantly clear to him that he will have to wipe his mind clean of his past beliefs. For instance, a Christian wanting to join them shall have to forget about Jesus completely. He would also have to look for an Orthodox Rabbi to guide him. The Rabbi will try to explore his heart and dissuade him, if he finds him even slightly double-minded. He would then expect him to study the Hebrew Scriptures and move into some Jewish neighbourhood to have a feel of their life. If all goes well, he will be prȯduced before 'Bais Din' (a Jewish court) who will again test his sincerity and resolve. One has to be thus a real diehard to persist on joining the Jewish community.

The conversion ceremonies include circumcision (This is done again in case of the persons already circumcised by making a small cut to let out a drop of blood.) and dipping in the holy water of a 'mikvah', which is symbolic of the person having got a new soul. The covert is thus like a new born in the Jewish community. One positive feature about the Jewish conversions is that a candidate could come from any religious, regional, linguistic or ethnic background. He may be a Christian, Muslim, Hindu, non-Semitic or even a pagan. Once they are sure that he genuinely wishes to be a Jew, they admit him.

This attitude of exclusiveness and the hassles involved in conversion into their faith have ensured that the Jews remain a miniscule minority on earth, hardly about 0.25% of the humanity. They have in fact been losing on their numbers all through. All initial converts to Christianity were Jews. In the last decade of the previous century, they lost seventy thousand adherents, mostly to Christianity. It was out of this concern that Israel sought an assurance from the Pope when he visited Jerusalem recently that the Christian missionary activity to convert Jews would henceforth stop.

Hinduism also does not believe in contrived conversions. When the Aryans landed in the Indian subcontinent four millennia back, the Panees (Indus Valley people), Dravidians and various tribal communities seem to have eventually adjusted themselves with one another to co-exist in peace. In course of time, they came to be called Hindus. Later, a steady stream of caravans of diverse ethnicity, the Kushans, Hoons, Sakas and others, came pouring down the Hindukush in search of permanent home. All these ingresses were also smoothly absorbed by the hospitable motherland. All became Hindus seemingly without any effort on anybody's part.

There is no evidence that Hindus ever made any conscious effort to convert any communities. Whatever inward migration occurred that came in the natural course. They, however, became concerned when they started losing numbers to the Buddhists at an alarmingly rapid rate. It was then that the policy and practice of reconversions came in to vogue. Serious efforts were made to draw the Buddhists back into the Hindu fold during the reign of the Gupta dynasty. This was also done largely in a peaceful manner. As the Communism was defeated by the West by joining it, the Brahmanism defeated native Buddhism in much the same way. The parent faith appears to have sucked back Buddhism in the land by making it seem, as though the two were in fact the one. Just imagine, Gautama Buddha, the founder of Buddhism and a heretic by Semitic standards, was formally declared as the ninth incarnation of Vishnu!

The Indus Valley people had a huge mercantile presence towards the west right up to Mesopotamia (the present day Iraq). It appears that these magnificent people got involved in turf war with the hardy Aryan migrants and got subdued or some natural calamity took a toll of them. Their highly advanced civilisation got buried under thick layers of silt and historical change. With their disappearance from the scene, the Indian maritime activity in the West vastly diminished. Millennia later, the Bay of Bengal was to see lot of seafaring surge from southern India. The Indian migrants to the south-east Asia set up quite a few principalities there. The region kept bristling with Hindu presence for quite a few centuries. Some Hindu legacy still subsists in places like Bali, Kampuchea and Thailand etc. It seems that large sections of the local populace moved into the Hindu fold because they saw advantage in being with the ruling elite. With the Muslim coming to power in the area many of them converted to Islam.

Another round of conversions was unleashed with the East India Company coming to power in India. Close on the heels of the military successes of the Company followed the British missionaries. They largely went for the soft belly of Hinduism. With the political patronage and financial clout at their back they were really unstoppable. The selfless humanitarian work they did in the difficult tribal areas further enhanced the quotient of their irresistibility. The result was the mass conversions in the north-east of the country—the three states of the region, Nagaland, Mizoram and Meghalaya with 90%, 90.5% and 70.3 % Christian population respectively got almost completely Christianised. Besides these, the Christians have significant presence in Goa (26%) which has been under prolonged Portuguese rule and Kerala (19%), the first port of the Christian call in the subcontinent.

Lot of Christian missionary activity continues in India even after its Independence. Perhaps the country is considered quite a fertile land for religious poaching. In fact, India is presently teeming with secular fanatics who want all religions to have a free run. Since Hinduism is not interested in inward conversions, it has to be, in the situation, at the losing end of the game. In 1999, His Holiness, the late Pope John Paul II openly declared that the Christian objective was to Christianize the entire world. Supposing, this really happens and we wake up one fine morning to find that whole of the world has turned Christian, would this mean an end to conflict in the world or solve any of the human problems? Considering the fact that both the World Wars were in the nature of a deadly conflict within the Christendom, it appears that entertaining any such hope would be nothing but an illusion. In fact, it is not clear why this mad game of securing conversions by hook or crook has to be played at all. Interestingly, however, the so called secularists, occupying positions of power in India, still advise the Hindus not to sully their tolerant image by opposing the conversions!

Lot of resistance has nonetheless lately developed against the conversions through allurements of various sorts, including soft power, such as humanitarian work. According to one claim, nearly one hundred and fifty thousand tribal converts have been reconverted to Hinduism. All this occasionally results in violence against the missionaries. The ghastly burning alive of Graham Staines and his kids in Mayurbhanj in 1998 is, of course, an awful tragedy and a colossal crime, but it is also a sad example of how the missionary activity has come to be viewed. Considerable violence against Christian missionaries again erupted after the unfortunate killing of a Hindu monk, Swami Laxmananda, on 23rd of August, 2008.

All this violence certainly has to be condemned and the perpetrators adequately punished. Simultaneously, however, something also needs to be done to regulate religious migrations, to ensure that no conversions take place through force, fraud (the claims of faith healing etc.), money power and other dubious means. Faith must not be allowed to be bought with anything whatsoever, except the genuine change of heart. Even doing something good with bad intention is bad. What needs to be considered is that after all 660 thousand Hindus have been poached out of their faith from 1990 to 2000 and the poor tribal form a large bulk of them. This would be clear from the fact that the scheduled tribes constitute just 9.1% of the country's population, while the Indian Christians have 32.8% tribal among them (The Sachar Committee Report). If one believes that all this has happened with no inducements being involved in any form, it is absolutely fine. Otherwise, it is terribly wrong and something needs to be done about it. M.K. Gandhi had highly enlightened views on this issue. This is what the Mahatama writes about conversions:-

"I am against the modern method of proselytising. Years of experience of proselytising both in South Africa and India has convinced me that it has not raised the general moral tone of the converts who have imbibed the superficialities of European civilisation, and have missed the teachings of Jesus. I must be understood to refer to the general tendency and not to brilliant exception.....

Why should I change my religion because a doctor who professes a certain faith has cured me of a disease or why should the doctor expect or suggest such a change whilst I am under his influence? ...... Method of conversion must be like Caesar's wife, above suspicion. Faith is not imparted like secular subjects. It is given through the language of heart...."

Jesus himself was a Jew and the first people to convert to Christianity were also mostly Jews. His martyrdom acted as a magnet to draw both Jews and Gentiles (non-Jews) to his ideology. The Gentiles, in fact, had to first become Jews to get admitted to Christianity. This obviously involved circumcision also. St. Paul soon put an end to this mode of conversion. Baptism (bathing in holy water) was adopted as the principle ceremony for initiation into Christianity.

The companions and disciples of Jesus became the nucleus of the Christian clergy. Many of them were eventually raised to sainthood. They first tried to persuade the Jews to accept Jesus as one in the long line of their Prophets. They stubbornly refused to recognize Jesus as Christ (messiah). The new faith, however, turned the tables on them in course of time. A good number of Jews came in the Christian fold. When Christianity was able to get royal patronage at Rome, there was to be no looking back for it. Conversion of Emperor Constantine to it and the Christian victory in the Battle of Tours were other big leaps forward for the faith.

The colonial ventures of the West in the second half of the last millennium took Christianity to all corners of the world. During this era the Christian missionaries, with Bible in hand, made it a point to move close on the heels of their armies. While the armies captured territories, they endeavoured to capture the minds of the vanquished. This worked wonderfully well to secure mass conversions. When the missionaries were resisted and expelled, that became an added excuse for further military exploits. The primary causes behind the two Opium Wars in China in the nineteenth century related to an attempt at forced market ingress and missionary access to the land.

Even after the collapse of the colonial empires, the religion continues to spread its wings at a rapid pace. During the period 1990-2000, Christianity has been able to push two and a half million people into its portals. Maximum conversions to Christianity during 1990-2000, 2.4 million came from Asia. Strangely, the Faith is in a state of flux in its own strongholds. It is losing numbers in North America, Latin America and Oceana.

Prophet Mohammad had a tolerant attitude towards other religions at least to begin with. It would be amply evident from the following verses of Koran:-

يٰٓاَيُّهَا الْكٰفِرُوْنَ ۝١

لَكُمْ دِيْنُكُمْ وَلِيَ دِيْنِ ۝٦

(Say: O' Mohammad (to unbelievers i.e. disbelievers in oneness of Allah) to you, your religion and to me, my religion.)

—The unbelievers, CIX- 1&6

۞ لَيْسَ عَلَيْكَ هُدَاهُمْ وَلَٰكِنَّ اللَّهَ يَهْدِي
مَن يَشَاءُ ۗ وَمَا تُنفِقُوا مِنْ خَيْرٍ
فَلِأَنفُسِكُمْ ۚ وَمَا تُنفِقُونَ إِلَّا ابْتِغَاءَ
وَجْهِ اللَّهِ ۚ وَمَا تُنفِقُوا مِنْ خَيْرٍ يُوَفَّ
إِلَيْكُمْ وَأَنتُمْ لَا تُظْلَمُونَ ﴿٢٧٢﴾

It is further laid down in Surah II: 256 that there cannot be any compulsion in the matter of faith.)

> (It is not for you (Mohammad) to guide them (non-Muslims), but Allah guides whomsoever He wills—.)
>
> —Surah II, Verse-272

The Prophet has made reverential mentions about many of the Jewish Prophets in his Koran. In turn, he expected them to promote his message and recognise him as the last in the line of their Prophets. The Jews, as is their wont, declined to go with him. It appears that this attitude enraged him and he then gave them a 'convert, quit or get killed' ultimatum. The Arabian Peninsula was, thus, all but vacated of them. Some of the Jews converted, quite a few got massacred and the others migrated from the place.

Islam does enjoin the Muslim to convert as many people to their faith as possible, but it does not suggest that this should be done by force or through allurements in any form. This notwithstanding, there is hardly any doubt that military successes and coercion have played a big part in securing conversions to Islam. The Muslim, in the first flush of their victories, acted much in the same way as all colonialists do. They went for conversions in a big way. All sorts of pressures were brought to bear on the local populations to secure migrations to their faith. The Hindus were often treated as 'zimmi's' who were required to buy back their lives by paying a tax called 'zazia'. The hated levy had to be offered humbly in person. As a result of this, nearly a third of the Hindu population was converted to Islam during the Muslim rule in the Indian subcontinent. An overwhelming bulk of the Muslim population in Pakistan and Bangladesh consists of Hindu converts. As against this, the conversions to Islam got reduced to a trickle when the Muslim started losing their political clout in the country. These days we just about hear some odd Hindu couples embracing Islam to evade the legal consequences of bigamy. In fact, this fraud on the faith has recently come to be frowned upon both by the Indian judiciary as well as the Muslim clergy.

With the passage of time, the Muslim got naturalised to the land. After all they had come here to stay. Besides, the portion of the local converts among them started swelling. These converts, in any case, were the sons of this very soil. Cemented by their soil, but fragmented by their faiths, the two communities kept living through the centuries in a love-and hate relationship. Nonetheless, a realisation gradually dawned on them that they could not wish each other away. So they started getting somewhat comfortable with each other. 'Bharat Mata' of the Hindus thus became the 'Madr-e-watan' of the Muslim also. Despite all the colonial efforts to keep them divided, they eventually joined hands to rid the motherland of the alien rule.

Proselytising out of Islam is a capital offence in the Muslim eyes. The Muslim intelligentsia perhaps needs to have another look at the Koranic literature on this issue and see if the Prophet would have really liked to hold on to a person even after he had lost faith in the precepts and practices of the religion. Trying to stop proselytising out of the faith on pain of death seems to be a counter-productive policy for the following reasons:-

(a) It gives an image of unreasonableness to the religion.

(b) Strikes fear in the heart of potential converts.

(c) It is against the modern thinking on freedom of faith.

(d) Conveys an impression that the Faith is not confident of keeping its flock together by non-violent means.

(e) If other Faiths adopt a similar policy, doors would get shut on all religious migrations.

Conversion has become a highly controversial issue because most of the religious migrations have taken place in the world through force, fraud and allurements, rather than any genuine change of heart. Political ascendency has often been used to push the ruling faith down the unwilling throats. Otherwise, every religion has a right to preach peacefully. If its message goes home to any heart and the person feels convinced that the new faith presents a more enlightened view of life and responds to his spiritual urges more satisfactorily, he should be free to convert. It is a matter of conscience and the decision must come from there. Preaching and even acting good Samaritans, with the sole aim of poaching cannot be justified. In any case, the holier-than-thou attitude of the religions is purely a communal propensity. There is nothing spiritual about it and no good can ever come out of it.

# 13

# Man's Natural Need for Focus

As believed by the Jews and the early Aryans, God is a Formless Eternal. This human formulation, though worked out millennia earlier, is surely nearest to the truth. Yet, this also could not be but true that He is capable of assuming any form. After all, He has created all the boundless matter and energy and countless life forms that we are physically aware of. Such a formless Being could be presumed to be capable of incarnating Himself in any way that He might will. Whether He has actually done it in a particular instance or ever at all, is another matter. Whatever be the truth, man needs to relate Him to something known to him. He has to address his prayers to somebody who can be focused on. Even nothingness has to be something, if the human mind is to latch on to it. There has to be an address to which the petitions can be addressed.

Our parents, grandparents and may be great grand parents also, who we have seen, are faces and figures to us. Their visuals in our mind help us to think of them clearly without any difficulty. Our earlier unseen ancestors are just names to us. In fact, we are quite familiar with this 'Out of sight, out of mind' phenomenon. We have to thus think of God as something, so as to be able to concentrate on him conveniently. This is where the temples, idols and pictures lend us a helping hand. This is what Pope, Gregory the Great, wrote in this context, "A painting can do for the illiterate what writing does for those who can read". One of the ancient Fathers of the Christian Church, John of Damascus, explained the relevance of the icons equally aptly in his words, "What a book is to the literate, that an image is to the illiterate". He went on to suggest that all the rites, creeds and institutions of the church also similarly convey divine grace to the believers. Concurring with the reverend Father, the Seventh General Council of the Greek and Roman churches that was held in AD 787, declared that pictures, images, cross and Gospels should be held in reverent regard for "the honour which is paid to the image passes on to that which the image represents and he who shows reverence to the image shows reverence to the subject represented in it".

Thus He was set in varied forms for human convenience from time to time. In fact, there seems to be hardly anything wrong with it. At least no sin could be attributed to sending the prayer to the Unknown through the agents and elements that we know about. Prophet Mohammad's thinking was in conflict with the idols placed around Kaaba that were worshipped as God and not against the humankind trying to focus on Him through mediums that appeal to man. In fact, he himself picked up the name of the Formless Eternal from a featureless Quresh idol lined up there. All the hue and cry over idolatry resulted from the bitter conflict that the Prophet had with the earlier tribal beliefs. It eventually turned in to the Allah versus the Idols struggle. The idols placed around Kaaba had to go, if the new order in the mind of Mohammad was to make a head way. It thus needs to be appreciated that the Prophet was against the idols set in competition with Allah and not with those providing a medium to the human mind to focus on God. In fact, what the Prophet propounded for the benefit of the tribal around Mecca, was already known to the Jews and Hindus nearly twenty five thousand years earlier.

We shall not talk about the times when the clear concept of God had not entered the human mind and begin with the monotheist phase of the Hebrew history. The Jewish God, Yahweh, is believed to have descended on Mount Sinai hidden in a swirling storm of fire and smoke to leave His message with Moses in the form of some commandments. This ball of fire was, however, so benign that it did not burn or even singe anything on the mountain. His first commandment was, "You must not make any molten gods for yourself". Two things are evident from this Biblical narration: Yahweh did not allow even Moses to have a look at Him and thus he wished to remain invisible to man. Secondly, He also did not relish sharing worship with any other being. The idea again was to usher in a new monotheist creed, with single revelatory God, Yahweh, as its nucleus, by discarding the old beliefs based on the worship of a multitude of idols representing various gods, goddesses and spirits.

The Jews, therefore, do not set up any idols in their synagogues. They satisfy their artistic urges by preparing their primary religious symbols— six pointed Star of David, Menorah (seven-branched candelabrum) and Torah mantles— in all sorts of richly ornamented designs. When they pray to Yahweh and focus on these symbols, their mind must be quietly slipping on to that benign ball of fire that descended on Mount Sinai before Prophet Moses. Another focus available to them for prayer is the site of their historic temple at Jerusalem. The haloed spot reflects the glory of God to them.

Hindus began with silent meditations out in the open. They soon picked up a focus for their prayer in the form of a primordial sound that the cosmos produces in the course of its eternal motion at unimaginably high speed. This celestial revolution takes place around the biggest mass of matter cast out after the Big Bang or the biggest star of the universe, which is yet to be identified. One of their seers is believed to have heard it echoing endlessly from the far off cosmic regions something like 'O o o o——m'. All else emanates in the Hindu consciousness from this phenomenon, whether it is 'The Trinity', various 'Avatars and their consorts/progeny and the countless gods and goddesses. The multi-focal way of looking at the God's universe does not detract them from their belief in oneness of God and it also does not, in any way, affect the amazing depth of their philosophy. All that it indicates is that they believe that everything in the cosmos— the living beings, Sun, stars, stones, plants, wind, water, fire and so on— bears His touch and divinity lies scattered everywhere. You just focus on anything that appeals to you and you will find God peeping out of it. A saintly soul, Sarmad, used to be moving around naked at public places during the Aurangzeb era. The emperor had no stomach for such things. He ordered him to be beheaded. The godly man walked to the execution chamber with the excitement of a child being taken to Disneyland. Once there, he saw the executioner's sword reflecting the image of God and exclaimed that he would not miss to recognize Him in whatever form He cared to come. If divinity could be seen in the executioner's sword, it could surely be seen in everything else.

Formless 'Om' was difficult to concentrate on by the common man. Faces, figures and familiar objects were thus brought in for the convenience of his worship. These beings and objects are just suggestive of His presence and serve as focal devices for man to concentrate his mind on their Creator. What falls to their share is just the veneration and the worship part of it is meant solely for the divinity that they reflect. It is true that sometimes temples are exclusively dedicated to various deities and the rites that are performed there amount to worship. But it is equally true that they are not worshipped as God. If anybody thinks that Hindus worship Surya Dev (Sun God), Hanuman (Monkey god), various planets, plants and cow etc. as God, he is mistaken. They are just venerated as God's gift to man and as the reflectors of His glory. This becomes abundantly manifest when worshipers of all hues periodically congregate in millions during the Kumbh festivals on the banks of sacred rivers, with their faces lit with just one light and their eyes bespeaking of just one belief. It is a sea of humanity surging to touch the feet of God, the Creator of all in the universe.

Buddhism and Jainism also needed images to flourish. Memories have a tendency to fade and vanish with time. Images help to keep these alive. Millions of Buddha icons were thus cast in various metals and sculpted in stones to sustain him in the mind of his faithful. Same was the case with Mahavira and the earlier Tirathankars. The vandals sometimes felt that they could destroy the human heritage by melting the statues, blasting the sculptures and throwing the idols out of the temples for being ruthlessly trampled. But all this physical damage could not obliterate their images stamped on human psyche. After all, man needs to think of God as something, even if he cannot see Him. It is not in the power of anybody to deprive him of the focus of his prayer. Human mind just cannot reconcile to the view that He is nothing.

The Jew thought of Yahweh as their private God. They believed that if they worshipped Him and kept their word given to Him, He would ensure their prosperity and keep them out of the harm's way. Jesus universalised Yahweh in to everybody's God and paid for this with his life. His hanging on the cross made the hideous wood holy and provided the Christian world a focus for their prayer, the Holy Cross. Jesus often lovingly referred to God as 'Father'. By that he meant the 'Universal Father' that He actually is. On his death, however, his companions and disciples fondly declared him to be the 'Son of God', born to Virgin Mary through some divine intervention. Joseph, his worldly father, got pushed out of the frame. The faithful, thus, found another focus, a celestial baby held in the arms of the Virgin who could be brought before mind while engaging with the Divine.

The Christian claim of Jesus being the son of God did cause a ripple in the Semitic belief in the formlessness of God. This theory of incarnation, however, added to the appeal of Christianity in popular consciousness. The images of Jesus, Mary and various Saints in the churches went a long way in promoting the lustre of Christianity. Man has some inborn artistic urges. If God could be written about out of imagination, He could surely also be similarly sketched and cast through other mediums. A mention has already been made of a Russian delegation sent out to select a suitable religion for their state and these delegates having been deeply impressed by the grandeur of the Greek Church architecture at Constantinople and the magnificence of its ceremonies. It is, therefore, not the ideas alone, but also the spectacles, sounds, smells, feels and flavours that leave their impact on human mind. Colourful visuals, scented smoke rising heavenward, the gentle touch of the droplets of fragrant water being sprinkled, the sound of soothing music and the taste of the holy offering (Prasad) have an effect of their own on the devotees. Minds always have a tendency to latch on to the environment around them.

Athanasius of Alexandria (AD 293-373) theorizes in this context that mankind, in theory, is capable of direct communion with God, but our flesh often comes in the way of this. It was thus necessary for Jesus to appear in flesh and blood for human convenience. It is extremely difficult for an average man to concentrate on something formless. Forms have thus to be invented for man to be able to focus his attention on the Divine.

Even when a Muslim prays to Allah, what rises before his mind is the image of a radiant young man, with long and thick beard, sitting on his magnificent throne high in the heavens. He may be praying out in the open, thousands of miles away from Mecca. But what flashes before his mind is the 'Kaaba' that bears the kiss of the Prophet. Mohammad did not wish to leave his images behind so that the faithful did not get distracted in their prayer to Allah. He projected himself as a mere slave of the Almighty like all other mortals. Yet, he was no ordinary human. He reflects the glory of God in Muslim consciousness. Everything connected with him is holy to the Muslims and helps them to focus their attention towards Allah who alone, of course, is worthy of worship.

Similarly, the Sikhs have their ten Gurus and holy Granth Sahib to settle their mind on the 'Sat Purakh'. Besides, they have the Golden Temple and other magnificent shrines to help them feel in audience with God as they pray. The melodious chanting of hymns in His praise (gurubani) lifts their mind to a loftier plain where they can feel themselves to be in communion with the Divine.

Man has to, thus, think of God as something. This imperative need for focus has given rise to numerous shrines of breathtaking architectural beauty in the world. God is, of course, right there in the heart of man. Yet, it is difficult for a common man to locate Him within. It is much easier for him to believe that He has His abode in temples, churches, mosques, synagogues, Gurudwaras and other shrines. Certain symbols available there help him to feel His presence there. Icons and symbols, thus, have an importance of their own in the world of faith. Religions surely need images to reinforce their message. You remove all the shrines, religious sculptures and paintings etc. from the world, the religions would feel orphaned.

# 14

# Woman – The Worshipped Victim

Borrowing a lament from Wordsworth and replacing 'woman' for 'man' in the end, one could say, "much it grieved my heart to think what man has made of woman". In fact, both man and religions have been unfair to woman all through— one more reason to believe that the religions are the creation of man and not God who could never be cruel to His most sophisticated creation. O.A. Wall has expressed a similar sentiment in his celebrated book 'Eroticism in the Religions of the World'. This is what he writes in this regard:

> "It is largely due to the debased position assigned to women that I have lost faith in any 'inspired' nature of man-made Bibles, whether they be the sacred writings of Greeks or Brahmans, of Jews or Christians."

The suffering and subjugation that woman has undergone all through and the pain that she has been made to swallow for centuries, should drive any sensitive being to tears. So far as woman is concerned, every society has blood on its hands. Man has space in his mind for a plethora of goddesses, even independent of their gods. Thus, on one side, he has been worshipping woman ritually. On the other, he has misused to the hilt his stronger muscles to hold his female in cruel bondage.

Woman is the most sophisticated creation of nature. God has provided her a face and figure that is matched only by the poetry, paintings and sculptures that they have inspired over the ages. One such face (Helen of Troy) once 'launched a thousand ships and burnt the topless towers of Ilium'. This, however, is not the case with other female species. Their males certainly look more gorgeous. Pope Gregory the Great (AD 540-604) once saw some English slaves being sold in to slavery in a Roman market. As per the prevailing practice, they were exhibited for sale naked. Gregory who was then only a Benedictine monk was so impressed with their beauty and grace that he spontaneously remarked:-

> "Non Angli, sed Angeli sunt." (They are not English, but angels.)

He felt like going to England to convert the country to Christianity. Somehow, he could not make it. The task was left to his successors. Milton writes in an identical vein:-

> "O woman! Fairest of Creation! Last and best
> Of all God's works! Creature in whom excelled
> Whatever can to sight or thought be formed
> Holy, Divine, Good, Amiable and Sweet."

Struck with a similar sentiment, Thomas Peacock also pens the following lines in lavish praise of woman:-

> "To chase the clouds of life's tempestuous hours,
> To strew its short but weary way with flow'rs
> New hopes to raise, new feelings to impart,
> And pour celestial balsam on the heart;
> For this to man was lovely woman giv'n,
> The last best work, the noblest gift of Heav'n.

Woman, in fact, is a biological wonder. Nature has provided her body three separate orifices, one for sex and procreation and the other two for the normal excretory functions, whereas man has to manage with two and the birds with just one. She is physically more stable and in the normal course, she would live longer than man. In the beginning of this century, out of about five thousand centenarians in France, around four thousand were women. As per the Gerontology Research Group (U.S.A.) 31 oldest persons on earth on 13.6.2013 were women. Besides, she can procreate independent of man and keep the world going, though she cannot produce male offspring without male chromosomes. Man is totally incapable of anything like this. Her ovum is thus a must, while his sperm is not so for procreation. However, this biological superiority of woman has hardly ever been recognised.

In fact, man thinks otherwise. According to Spencer, woman is nothing more than an undeveloped man, arrested in her evolution to fullness because of menstruation, pregnancy and procreation. Darwin says the same thing a little differently. According to him, man is a sort of fully evolved woman. Tiedman thought that every embryo was meant to be male, but quite a few of these degenerated to the female state for some reason. Starkweather was among the first to challenge these atrocious views about the biology of woman.

Societies, politics and religions often move in tandem. We may now proceed to examine what woman really means to them. In the early phase, some doubts were raised in the Semitic religions whether woman really had a soul. Saint Augustine (AD 354-430) posed a question whether woman had a soul or was just a lump of flesh separated from Adam. Strangely, this was taken seriously and discussed in the Provincial Council of Macon in the sixth century. There were quite a few who came to the conclusion that woman had no soul. The issue continued to be discussed in the coming centuries. As late as AD 1895, a minister of the Christian church preached that woman was a soulless being. A few of the Muslim sects also held the same view. This meant that woman could be treated as a commodity and if tormented, she would feel no pain and if killed, no case of culpability would be made out. What bigger cruelty than this could be perpetrated on a living being?

This was not just a theoretical preposition. It was followed up in practice in some regions. Whenever a woman was felt to be an encumbrance moneywise or otherwise, she could be disposed of by being thrown in the sea, with adequate weight tied to her to ensure her drowning. This attracted no penal law as the affairs of the harem were not considered to be in public domain. The highest degree of fiendishness was in evidence when Turks or Kurds laid bets on the pregnant Armenian women in their slavery over whether they were carrying male or female embryos. These luckless victims had their abdomens cut open to decide the bets. Female infanticide was quite in vogue in China and in India, particularly among the Rajput community. Even in Europe, a practice prevailed where the newborn babies were shown to father to decide whether they were to be raised or not. Some female babies thus often got culled. Another horrendous fact is also on record that, during a great famine in China, many grown up girls were sold to the butchers for around $ 3 each as meat-on-hoof!

In many parts of the world, it was thought that the husband had an inalienable right to beat his wife. Even today, in sub-Saharan Africa, from Sudan to South Africa and from Mali to Mozambique, spousal abuse is still an ugly fact of life. There is a practice there among some ethnic groups that if a woman has not been thrashed enough during her life time, the husband should beat her corpse to prove his manhood! In Iran, the Islamic judges are said to have issued orders that a young girl awarded capital punishment must be raped first, since 'if executed while still a virgin, she would go to heaven'. Fatwa-e-Alamgiri, a sort of multipurpose code, enacted by Emperor Aurangzeb, prescribed that, once a wife had been promised to be paid her Mehr (bridal money), she must respond positively whenever she was summoned to bed by the husband. If she refused, she could be beaten up. Just recently, the U.A.E. Supreme Court has held that husband has a right to beat his wife, but the beating must not leave any marks on her body. In England also the husband's right in this regard was restricted to the extent that he should not use a rod thicker than his thumb. In Russia, birch rods used to be part of a bride's trousseau which she dutifully presented to the husband to beat her with whenever he felt the need for that. Even in the most enlightened democracy of the world, the U.S.A, domestic violence is the single biggest cause of injury to women, ahead of rapes, muggings and road accidents all put together.

All this atrocity against woman stems from the fact that she has all through been treated as the property of man. An extract from Shakespeare's 'Taming of the Shrew' would be in order here:-

"I will be master of what is mine own;
She is my goods, my chattels; she is my house
My household stuff, my field my barn;
My horse, my ox, my ass, my anything;
And here she stands, touch her whoever dares."

In some countries, France for instance, the women were deemed to be the property of the state. The king could keep any number of them for his pleasure. The others could be disposed of as per his wish. As late as the eighteenth century, the then King Louis XV could summon any lady of his court to his bed. As per the law in force before the French Revolution, the king had the right to sleep with any maiden on the first night of her marriage. Most of the brides, in whom the ruler was not personally interested, were passed on to others on consideration. It was not for nothing that the general perception of the people then was that 'the court was the tomb of the nation'. The court, of course, referred to the king's durbar where the king, clergy and feudal lords ran the show. Even Plato, the Greek philosopher, considered women to be property. He did not approve of the idea of monogamy, as he considered it monopolistic. With his socialistic bent, he thought that women should be the property of the community as a whole and all should be able to enjoy them freely.

Most of the canonist laws are heavily weighted against women. The Mosaic law of the Jews, for instance, allows a husband to divorce his wife at will. Wives have not been permitted any such privilege in turn. The following passages extracted from the Law of Moses would help understand the Jewish position with regard to woman:-

> "— when thy Lord Yahweh has delivered it (a captured city) in thy hands— ————women, children and the cattle, and all that is in the city, even all the spoil thereof shalt thou take unto thyself."
>
> — Deuteronomy xx, 13&14.

(Mercifully, however, the Mosaic law also declares that man must not make a merchandise of women in whom he loses interest.)

> "When thou goest forth to war against thine enemies— ——and seest among the captives a beautiful woman and hast a desire unto her————thou shalt go unto her and be her husband———."
>
> — Deuteronomy xxi, 10.

> " If a man finds a damsel that is a virgin which is not betrothed , and lay hold on her and lie with her, and they be found; then the man that lay with her shall give unto the damsel's father fifty shekels of silver, and she shall be his wife."
>
> — Deuteronomy xxii, 22.

Hinduism also does not have all that bright record so far as behaviour towards woman is concerned. It is true that during the early Aryan period, the women enjoyed considerable freedom and respect. They participated in many socio-religious ceremonies by the side of their men-folk. However, there should be no illusion that even then there was no parity between the two sexes. Women were definitely deemed to be in subordinate position in relation to men. Brhadaranayaka Upanishad suggests that if a husband intended to have a son of particular attributes, he should make the necessary preparation for that in terms of dietary stipulations and chanting of 'mantras' etc. The prior consent of wife in this regard was unnecessary. Once he was ready, the wife was also expected to be ready. He was then enjoined to invite the wife to bed and thereafter proceed as below:

> सा चेदस्मै न दद्यात्, काममेनामचक्रीणीयात्; सा चेदस्मै नैव दद्यात, काममेनां यष्टया घा पाणिना वोपह-त्यातिक्रामेत्, ईन्द्रियेण ते यशसा यश आदद इति ; अयशा एव भवति।। ७।।
>
> —— Brahadaranyaka Upanishad, Verse-7

(If she was not willing, he should buy her over (obviously with some inducements like the offer of ornaments); if she was still unyielding, he should strike her with hand or stick. If she finally did not cooperate, he should curse her saying that I take away your honour (of being my wife). She would then stand actually discredited.)

With the passage of time the things deteriorated further for her. The country suffered the invasion of Alexander in fourth century BC and many others afterwards. This brought the vulnerability of women in sharp focus. They came to be seen as potential source of family dishonour. This led to many pernicious practices in the India like child-marriages, female infanticide and 'sati' etc. This also generated a feeling in the Hindu society that women were not meant by nature to be independent. They should stay under the care of father in childhood, husband in young age and son in old age. Particularly, her stature in relation to husband sank very low. She was obliged to treat him as god, even if he happened to be old or ugly, debauch or devilish, crippled or a criminal. The matrimonial rituals where the father-in-law is required to touch the feet of his son-in-law reflect this malady. Woman has been in demand here both as 'Pativrata'(devotee of husband) and prostitute but sadly, not as a person. However, a saving grace with the Hindu society is that there has never been any debate here at least with regard to her being with or without soul. Hindus have never regarded her solely as an object of sex either. If a Hindu wishes to be treated as god by woman as wife, he, in turn, is not shy of deifying her as mother.

As for Christianity, St. Paul talks in terms of the 'natural use' of woman being just for coition. The general outlook of the Christian Church has been that original sin originated from woman, in that she was the one who persuaded Adam to eat the forbidden fruit. Jesus proclaimed in this context, "I have come to abolish the deeds of women". (Apocrypha, Egyptian Gospel) Let us follow it a little further in Father Tertullian's words:-

> "—— the woman should wear a simple dress, be mournful and full of repentance to suffer her inheritance from Eve, the shame of being the one who committed the original sin and the guilt of being the cause of mankind's condemnation."

Here are a few extracts from Bible to understand where the sacred book places the women:-

> "He (thy husband) shall rule over thee."
>
> — Genesis iii, 6.

> "Wives, submit yourselves unto your husband as unto the Lord. Therefore, as the church is subject unto Christ, so let wives be to their husbands in everything (which naturally, includes her submission to his sexual appetites and even perversities.)"
>
> — Ephes. V, 22 &24.

> "Let the woman learn in silence, with all subjection, for I suffer not a woman to teach or usurp authority"
>
> — Tim. ii, 11& 13.

The Old Testament prescribes that delivering a girl makes the mother twice more unclean than giving birth to a boy and accordingly, she must abstain from certain things for 66 days instead of 33 days. It is believed that the covenant with Yahweh at Sinai was with the men only and the women do not enjoy this great privilege. The Church Fathers further argue that word 'female' comes from the Latin word 'femina' which when dissected in to 'fe' (faith) and 'mina' (minus or less) means a being of lesser faith. Pope John Paul II declared that the debate on female priests was over, as there was nothing to discuss. After all, Jesus chose only men as apostles. To sum it up, woman could at best be allowed to breathe only as a passive believer.

The disparities between man and woman are all the more glaring in Islam. Daughters are authorised only half the share in the parental property, as compared to the sons. (Still, this is much better than the position in many other religions, including Hinduism, where women were not entitled to immovable property at all). A woman's testimony is considered having just half the weight of that of the male counterparts. In case of rape, a woman is required to produce four witnesses. In the absence of satisfactory evidence, she gets exposed to the charge of fornication for which she can be stoned to death.

Koran leaves it in no doubt that men are superior to woman. Let us have a look at Surah-4, Verse-34:-

> "————Allah has made men superior to women as they spend from their means (to maintain them). Thus, the virtuous women are obedient (to their husbands),

> and Allah desires them to safeguard their Chastity in their absence (because it is deemed to be their husbands property). Those who do not conduct themselves properly can first be admonished. Next, the husband can refuse to share their beds and beat them. If they come round, husband need not do anything further (to cause them any further pain).Surely, Allah is Ever Most High, Most Great."

The Koran also stipulates that the slaves rounded up in wars are in as helpless a position as the stone idols around Kaaba that were removed unceremoniously by the Prophet. They are therefore the lawful property of their master. He has all the authority to take for himself a female slave, either married or single.

All religions have occasionally felt that the inferior position assigned to woman is not justified. However, their clergies think that all this has come straight from God and so they are powerless in the matter. The silver-lining is that things have moved some distance towards emancipation of woman, despite various scriptural constraints. Christian and Hindu world has already worked out some measures to bring her relief. Lately, there has been some progress in this area in many Islamic states also.

One very specific reason for woman's misery has been the man's excessive obsession with her virginity. Chastity is, indeed, something that could be cherished. The sexual act does not involve the baring of the bodies alone, but the entire being. The sweet sounds and silences shared during those moments of intense joy would ring hollow, if replicated with a new partner. However, why woman alone should bear all the burdens of virginity? It has somehow got stuck in social psyche that an impermissible sexual act pollutes the woman, while the man stays pure or at least comes out of it, as if nothing had happened. Superficially perhaps, sex is a messier affair for woman as the secretions get dumped into her. It also involves rupture of the hymen on the first occasion and may even lead to unwanted pregnancies. Thus, for her, snakes hiss where the grass is green. However, the primary sexual organ is the brain. Pollution, if any, occurs there. It does not need any emphasising that brain is common to both the sexes.

Yet, often losing sight of their own licentiousness, men have been excessively concerned with the purity of their women. In the medieval age, wives were fitted with metal frames called 'chastity belts' with padlocks to ensure chastity on their part while the husbands were away. It is on record that a German emperor had a blacksmith fit such a steel frame on his queen while he was leaving for a campaign against the Saracens during the Crusades. In some harems when the husbands permitted their wives to meet friends and eunuchs were not at hand to escort them, they had one end of a stick, four or five inches long, pushed in their vagina while the other end reached up to their knees. The stick was tightly held in place by an iron or leather contraption securely locked. Similarly, it was customary for the Roman girls to be fitted with a girdle (virginalis) round their loins and waists, so that their abdomen could not expand abnormally, as in the case of pregnancy. This girdle was removed by the husband on the nuptial night, indicating that then onward she had the permission to mate and conceive.

So, this has been the lot of woman since the dawn of civilisation in the world. Mercifully, some winds of change, favourable to the human female, have started blowing now. At least on paper, she is the equal of man in many countries. Habits, however, die hard and societal psyches evolve at painfully slow pace. The battle to raise her from the state of 'property' to 'person' is, thus, going to be a long drawn one. Conditions shall have to be created for her to walk alone without fear. She would then be able to come out in the open freely for education, employment and entertainment. Other things would then follow automatically. Religions can atone themselves by lending a helping hand in this noble mission.

# 15

# Sex and Spirituality

Sex has two very distinct angles to it — procreation and pleasure. Both are inseparably entwined in something like a mystical bond. In fact, nature has provided for pleasure in the act so that the vital job of procreation does not get neglected and the world keeps going. Nonetheless, these two aspects are viewed differently by the religions. The first is considered not only to be acceptable but also sacred by some. The second is often seen as a sin or something in the nature of a weakness of flesh. Nonetheless, if anything comes anywhere near the spiritual bliss; it is the sexual sensation. But for rising above lust, sex has to incline towards love.

Hindu scriptures idealize those who engage in sex only for procreation. Roman Catholics have proclaimed sex as a taboo for their priesthood in the western churches—— it is another matter that some unseemly things keep happening in the haloed precincts on the sly every now and then. Celibacy has, indeed, proved to be a tall order, as it involves swimming against the current. Many times a question has been raised whether the option of marriage should be thrown open to their clergy. They, however, have been in a dilemma over the issue and not been able to decide it yet.

Celibacy has, nonetheless, been held in high esteem in most of the religious as well as social orders from the very early age. It is considered to be 'the better, nobler and higher condition in this life'. Some early Christians even believed that the married forfeited the chance of going to heaven. In any case, since celibacy is far beyond the will-power of the ordinary, those known to practise it inspire awe and adoration, even above the war heroes. Yet, should everybody were to go for celibacy (which mercifully would never happen), this world would get vacated of human footfalls in about a hundred years or so. With that, all religions would also obviously die an unnatural death.

There is, therefore, something organically wrong with the concept of considering sex a sin. In fact, Osho (Bhagwan Rajnish) in his 'Sex to Super Consciousness, Full Circle' goes to the length of asserting that if this be so, there would be no greater sinner in the universe than God. The sexual pleasure seems to be meant for promoting procreation and is possibly also intended for achieving some still higher goals in life. In any case, the denial of this pleasure to self, in the ordinary course, is against the will of nature. O.A.Wall writes in this context:-

> "All excellence of character, all loveliness and all seductiveness of body serve but to attract two individuals through love, in order that a spermatozoon may come in contact with an ovum, to produce a new being."

Thus, the basic truth is that 'what is natural, cannot be obscene', though the human societies wish this to be done in privacy and have laid some other norms for it also. An old Roman saying, "Et musca habet penem" (even a fly has a penis) also points to the fact that sex is a God-given impulse. Gay relationships, that find mention as Greek Love in old texts, also do not seem to have anything unnatural about them and have been widely practised over the ages. Even the legendary Julius Caesar is known to have been used to this kind of love.

The religions, however, have a counter to these views. They do grudgingly admit that sex has some relationship with spirituality. However, they feel that the idea of celibacy is not flawed either and the sexual energy can be channelised in to something much loftier than orgasm i.e. the spiritual bliss. Mahatma Gandhi, who turned a celibate in his later life, writes:-

"The scientists of the old have put great value upon the vital fluid (semen), and they have insisted upon its strong transmutation into the highest form of energy for the benefit of society."

Swami Vivekananda is also of the view in his 'Raja Yoga' that the energy stored in the sexual organs can be shifted to brain as 'ojas' through celibacy. This transformed energy can then work wonders.

The value of semen as energy is not universally accepted, especially in the present times when it has been fully examined for its chemical composition. In any case, celibacy has to come in as natural a course as the sex act itself. If the religious celibates have to struggle in the matter, not understanding the deeper nuances of celibacy, the better course for them would be to find a natural outlet for their sexual urges—suppression always leads to outbursts at some point of time. They have thus to be completely convinced about the superiority of their spiritual option. Not just this, they have to be actually able to feel the bliss involved in conversion of their sexual energy in to spiritual solace. Otherwise, if they feel suppressed inside, they should come out of it all and choose instead to go the way of all flesh. There is no third course available in the matter. This observation would find a perfect echo in what is stated in the verse below:

कर्मेन्द्रियाणि संयम्य य आस्ते मनसा स्मरन्।
इन्द्रियार्थान्विमूढात्मा मिथ्याचार: स उच्यते।।

—Bhagavad Gita, Cpapter-III,Verse-6.

(A person's having been physically able to abstain from sensual desires does not count for much, if these keep churning constantly in his mind. In this situation, he is just deceiving himself and he cannot be considered genuinely clean in his conduct.)

There are many other doctrines floating in this regard. Plato and Philo (a contemporary of Jesus) have tried to explain that all human beings were first androgynous. They got separated in to unisexual halves through some divine intervention — this view finds an echo in the Biblical version of Eve having been created out of the rib of Adam. The two halves, therefore, have an overpowering urge to unite. This, according to them, explains the amorous instincts and inclinations of the sexes to get merged into each other, at least momentarily, through coition. One does not have any idea whether God is male or female. Perhaps He is both i.e. an androgynous. In fact, as an all-powerful Being, He should be capable of being anybody or anything at will.

The next theory is that sex is the starting point of all life. All living beings are born out of 'kama' (desire)— one of the four 'purusharthas' (strivings for lofty goals of life), the other ones in the ascending order, being the 'artha' (prosperity), 'dharma' (virtuous life) and 'moksha' (salvation). In fact, as per the Indic line of philosophy, the cosmos has also originated out of 'kama'. This is how this idea has been elaborated. What existed in the primordial times was an inert mass of matter or 'sadvastu' surrounded by kham' or space. At some point of time and somehow, it got invested with an element of 'kama' that caused a colossal churning inside it. The impregnated mass soon started bubbling with enormous amount of energy within. This ultimately burst forth in 'bindu visphota' or what is now referred to as the Big Bang. 'Bindu' here, points to semen and 'Visphota', to its discharge in an orgasm. This doctrine, thus, visualizes the birth of this universe through the Big Bang as a sort of cosmic orgasm that, in course of time, resulted in sprouting of life in the universe.

Osho is of the view that sex deprivation can lead to many unpleasant consequences. After all, sex is the starting point of love and life. If the sexual urge gets suppressed, the subsequent stages of love and procreation would also get squashed. According to him, the blooming of flowers, a girl growing in to a comely damsel and a boy developing in to a strapping youth etc. are all manifestations and expressions of sexual energy. Sex is thus God's creative force at work. The dancing of a peacock and singing of a cuckoo are, in fact, mostly in the nature of mating calls. The sexual energy ultimately transforms and transmutes into love. He thus concludes that 'sex' is love's Gangotri (source of the holy Ganges) and love is something sublime. Once you get in to relation of love with someone, you begin seeing certain things in that person which others cannot see. He or she radiates such charm and loveliness, as only you can notice and there is such a sweet humming coming from him as only you can hear. All said, sex is at least something far different and higher than mere joint masturbation by the partners. Something in the same genre was once said by Robert Browning, "God be thanked, the meanest of creatures boasts two soul- sides— one to face the world with, one to show a woman when he loves her!" Daisaku Ikeda, president of the Japanese Buddhist sect, Soka Gakki, also observes:-

> "It is natural to feel attracted to, be interested in, and fall in love with members of the opposite sex during one's youth as it for flowers to bloom in spring or snow to fall in winter."[1]

We may now move to have an idea in what light sexuality is actually seen by various religions. Judaism has a generally healthy attitude towards sex, except for the fact that it considers male to male homosexuality as a capital offence and male masturbation also as something sinister. In fact, Talmud prescribes, "In the case of man, the hand that reaches below the navel should be chopped off". For some curious reason, the Jewish religion considers 'spilling of the seed' outside the vagina as sinful. Since lesbian sex and female masturbation do not involve any such thing, the Jewish law on the subject is silent. In any case, since it frowns upon all sorts of licentiousness and sexual immorality, these two practices are also traditionally considered undesirable. Same is the position with regard to premarital sex, though Torah does not prohibit it specifically.

Both Bible (the Old Testament- Genesis 19: 24-25) and Koran (Surah 21: Verses 70 to 75) record that the Jewish cities of Sodom (word 'sodomy' has originated from this notorious place) and Gomorrah were handed down a terrible punishment by God for practising sodomy. These urban clusters were flattened by raining brimstone and fire and now lie annihilated near the southern end of the Dead Sea. Judaism also prohibits illicit sexual relationships. One of the commandments) given to the community is:-

> "You shall not commit adultery." (Exodus- 20: 13)

Otherwise, Judaism does not see any virtue or purpose in celibacy. In fact, it considers marriage and procreation as something sacred. Even its high priests are expected to marry. Legitimate Sex in Jewish order, even for the purposes of pleasure alone, is not conceived as shameful, sinful or obscene. It is admitted that sexual desire rises out of 'yetzer ra' (evil impulse), but so do hunger and thirst. So long as the appropriateness in the matter is not lost sight of, satiation of sex is well in order. In fact, the primary purpose of sex is seen as reinforcing the loving marital bond. Jews rightly feel that the act involves mind and heart also to it and not the body alone. Talmud declares, "A man may do whatever he pleases with his wife" (Nedarim- 20b) and it also encourages foreplay (Nedarim- 20a). Wife also has been given right to sex from her husband (onah), just like the right to food and clothing. Divorce and abortion are also permitted.

One unusual thing about the Jewish religion is that Torah does not permit sex during the 'Niddah' period which not only covers the five days of the menstrual cycle, but also seven days thereafter. It is a fairly long period for sexual abstention. Thus, the marriages have to be scheduled carefully, so that the nuptial night does not fall during the prohibited period.

It may, however, be clarified that all these stipulations apply to Orthodox Judaism. The other branches of Judaism have somewhat different thinking on this issue and follow their own rules and interpretations.

Hinduism attaches high sanctity to procreation and all that is involved in the process. This seems to have been the situation since the Indus Valley Civilisation where indications of phallic worship are quite in evidence. The celestial creators, Shiva and his consort Parvati, represented by 'Linga' and 'yoni', have been worshipped by the Hindus since times immemorial. This sort of worship has also been in practice in many other parts of the world, including Europe. The question is, if it arouses any sort of prurient ideas or it stands at a higher plain, loaded with deeper meaning for humanity. The answer is that the faithful see it as something sublime, the starting point of life and its renewal. Those who are unprepared to understand its real meaning would, however, have none of the sanctity attached to the Linga and Yoni culture as symbolic of the universal renewal. The Portuguese and Muslim, in fact, had many engravings with phallic and Yoni connotations at the Elephanta caves of Mumbai mutilated.

The Hindus have studied sex in all its dimensions, including the cosmic one. When this was done, Hinduism was far ahead of the world in this area. Some of the conclusions reached at by them are still relevant and some, of course, have gone obsolete. The Semitic religions relate sex primarily to the private parts of human body and its psychological and moral aspects. They, however, miss on its sublimity amplitude, related to the God's will to keep universe going and renewing itself constantly. The political ascendency of the Semitics in the Indian subcontinent for nearly thousand years created an impression, as if Hindus were the tribal, caught far behind in time.

Some aberrations in their system like the 'devadasi' tradition of the South and the beliefs like the eunuchs, primarily in the profession of prostitution, being auspicious, were seen as propagation of free sex. Hinduism, however, neither approves free sex nor condones premarital sex. These are rather considered a sacrilege. It is another matter that Hinduism does not enforce its scriptures. The ancient book of the high genre of 'Kamasutra' is generally accepted by the Western world for its 'kick' value rather than its knowledge quotient. Vatsayana, the author, of Kamasutra' states, "'Kama' is the enjoyment of appropriate objects by the five senses of hearing, feeling, seeing, tasting and smelling, assisted by mind together with the soul." The deeper meaning behind this thought was not appreciated, not because that it went over their heads, but for the reasons that:-

(a) The Christianity and Islam both follow an agenda of globalising their religions and Hinduism has been one of their primary targets for poaching.

(b) They are unable to peep into the times when this knowledge was poured forth and understand where they themselves stood at the time.

(c) They relate private parts only to pleasure, procreation and excretory functions and nothing higher than that.

The most striking feature of the Christian attitude towards sex has been its strict insistence on celibacy on part of its clergy in the Roman Catholic world of the West, especially after the two Lateran Councils of AD 1123 and 1139. (The clergy of the Protestants, Roman Catholics of eastern rite churches and priests below bishops in Orthodox Church are allowed to marry). This is based on the ideal of renouncing familial ties for the 'Kingdom of God'. Body has often been described as "a pit of dung", "a container of all things rotten" and "a snow covered pile of manure" by Church Fathers like John of Aviola. The Christian clergy has thus been making valiant efforts to sustain its belief in celibacy. There are instances on record when monks dived in ice-cold waters, whipped themselves to unconsciousness, rolled over thorny bushes or colonies of ants, wrapped heavy iron pieces to their penises and tortured their bodies in many other ways, just to keep at bay the periodic evil sensation in their groins. Saint Symeon Styites from Syria (AD 390-459) is said to have spent thirty six years on a pillar for prayer, exposed to all sort of inclement weather conditions. A Church Father, Origenes, castrated himself to stay sexually pious.

The fear of female contact in the Church tradition has also something to do with its views 'on sex, celibacy and chastity ideals'. However, it has never been easy to fight nature. Despite all its effort, Church has not entirely succeeded in suppressing the overpowering human urge for sex. All sorts of unseemly things have been happening on the sly and sometimes even openly. Popes, cardinals and bishops are all known to have occasionally succumbed to the female flesh. Pope Paul III had three sons from the women, other than his wife. His sister was, in fact, a concubine of an earlier Pope, Alexander VI. Pope Sixtus IV ran a brothel and earned around twenty thousand ducats out of it. Papal Rome in AD 1490 had just about a hundred thousand citizens and around 6800 prostitutes. In the sixteenth century some male monasteries were teeming with women and children. In the eighteenth, a famous brothel owner in France, Marguerite Gourdan, designed a sex toy (wooden penis), popularly known as 'Nun heirlooms'. When she died in AD 1783, she had hundreds of pending this gadget from the nun monasteries. The cases of homosexuality and masturbation have also not been all that uncommon in the holy precincts. These revelations testify to the fact that even the Catholic clergy is also very much human. However, being human is no sin. These few aberrations notwithstanding, what the Christian clergy have been able to achieve in the difficult area of celibacy is not only amazing, but also awe-inspiring. After all, they have been able to swim quite some distance against the powerful natural current.

Nevertheless, the scriptural position of Christianity with regard to sex is as follows: The legitimacy of sex within marriage is acknowledged, though in the medieval period, sex for around eight months in a year on various counts was forbidden. Sex involves satisfaction, passion, pleasure, closeness and climax. Biblical commandments, however, imply that becoming one flesh with one partner provides the best setting for satisfying sexual intimacy. Adultery is strictly prohibited. Jesus proclaimed in his Sermon on the Mount that even a lustful thought about a woman amounted to adultery with her. Fornication and premarital sex are also considered evil and so are homosexuality, bestiality and incest. Book of Leviticus talks about many prohibitions, but oral sex has not been specifically condemned or barred.

The Christian society at the moment seems to be at war with itself, fighting against its scriptural Puritanism on one side and the licentiousness of the modern culture on the other extreme. It may now appear promiscuous to some, but it is, undoubtedly, the most progressive also. It is, in a way, the first to break out of the prison of their religion. Rather, it has been largely able to confine the religion to the precincts of the Church, where it belongs.

Like Judaism, Islam also does not feel that celibacy has any spiritual content. On the other hand, it holds that denial of sex is against the grain of nature and affront to Allah. It also believes that sex is beneficial for the following reasons:-

(a) It is essential for preservation of the human race.

(b) Non-ejection of semen (water of life) can lead to many complications and diseases like obsession, habitude, lunacy, insanity. It also believes that it can help recovery in such disorders.

(c) Sex is necessary for fulfillment and pleasure.

Islam therefore, provides lavishly for legitimate sex in this life, at least for the well-placed males, and the faithful, in the next one. Its views on legitimacy are also quite different from those of others. Those who can afford to pay 'Mahr' and are in a position to treat wives equally, can have four legally wedded women at one time. Marriage to more women is also not 'haram', but only irregular. That is how, emperors like Akbar, Jahangir and Shahjahan were able to stuff hundreds of women in their harems without any problem. Female slaves in any case were available to their masters without any count. A look at Verse- 3 (Surah-IV) of Koran would be in order here:

وَإِنْ خِفْتُمْ أَلَّا تُقْسِطُوا فِي الْيَتَامَىٰ فَانْكِحُوا مَا طَابَ
لَكُمْ مِنَ النِّسَاءِ مَثْنَىٰ وَثُلَاثَ وَرُبَاعَ فَإِنْ خِفْتُمْ
أَلَّا تَعْدِلُوا فَوَاحِدَةً أَوْ مَا مَلَكَتْ أَيْمَانُكُمْ ذَٰلِكَ أَدْنَىٰ
أَلَّا تَعُولُوا

( —— then marry (other) women of your choice, two or three or four ; but if you have an apprehension that you shall not be able to be equitable (to them), then only one or that your right hands possess i.e. the slaves. ——)

Similarly the devout Muslims can look forward to landing in heaven after death and seventy two exquisitely beautiful virgins being provided to them, in addition to numerous other privileges.

At the same time, however, the faith provides for very harsh penalties for sexual transgressions like rape, fornication and adultery etc. It also enjoins on the adherents to guard their private parts i.e. chastity, except from their spouses and slaves. Here are a few extracts from the holy Koran to explain this position:

وَالَّذِينَ هُمْ لِفُرُوجِهِمْ حَافِظُونَ ﴿٥﴾

إِلَّا عَلَىٰ أَزْوَاجِهِمْ أَوْ مَا مَلَكَتْ أَيْمَانُهُمْ
فَإِنَّهُمْ غَيْرُ مَلُومِينَ ﴿٦﴾

فَمَنِ ابْتَغَىٰ وَرَاءَ ذَٰلِكَ فَأُولَٰئِكَ هُمُ الْعَادُونَ ﴿٧﴾

((Successful, indeed, are those believers) who guard their private parts (from illegitimate sex acts), except from their wives and that their right hands possess i.e. slaves, for then they are free from blame. But, whoever indulges (in sex) beyond that is a transgressor)

— Surah XXIII/ Verses 5 to 7.

Women are required to cover themselves well from top to toe. Even their shaking of hands with the strangers is prohibited, especially when it is likely to generate any sort of titillation. Sodomy is forbidden (though the position on the ground has been very different from the scriptural stipulations), but oral sex has not been proclaimed as 'haram'. The religion also does not have a view on masturbation.

The Chinese never had a God to please or sin against. So, there is no scope to attach sin or shame to sex in this part of the world. They, however, do have religions — Confucianism, Taoism and Buddhism— that have a definite view on sexuality. We could study this in the light of appropriateness, rather than any sort of religious taboos.

The Chinese sexual concepts in ancient China revolved around 'Yang' and 'Yin', the mystical elements connected with health and general wellbeing. Males were believed to have a limited quantity of 'Yang' and females were supposed to have 'Yin' in abundance. Interestingly, one important objective of sexual intercourse for the male was to acquire as much of the female "Yin' as possible. This could be supposedly done by prolonging the act so that the woman had quite a few orgasms before the man had his own. Since male masturbation involved loss of 'Yang', it was forbidden. Nocturnal wet dreams were also considered unhealthy for the same reason. Women, however, could resort to masturbation without any harm because they had unlimited amount of 'Yin' in them. They were, however, advised not to use any foreign objects for the purpose.

Prostitution was acceptable in the society as this enabled the patrons to collect some extra 'Yin' from the women who had collected abundant 'Yang' from multiple partners. However later, when the medical knowledge advanced to the next level, prostitution came to be seen as harmful, because it could lead to various infectious diseases. Male homosexuality was earlier rare while the female one was widespread. However, later in the Han Period, both were practised regularly in the land as elsewhere.

The sex was also supposed to have political implications. According to Goldin, "Sexual relations had to be orderly and regulated because sexual aberrations— like all aberrations— threatened the fragile unity of the new empire, and so were tantamount to rebellion. This was the early imperial sex ideology; it is one of the outstanding features of the Hans intellectual world."

Taoism believed in flowing with the nature. Whenever, there were Taoist monarchies in China, for instance during the Han and Sui Dynasties, people felt free to enjoy the pleasures of sex and the art of love making. A number of books on sex like 'The handbook of the Plain Girl', 'The Art of Bedchamber', 'The Secret Methods of the Plain Girl', 'Recipes of the Plain Girl' and 'Secrets of the Jade Chamber' etc came into circulation. An emperor is believed to have himself practised some breathing techniques in his bed chamber in line with this literature to prolong the sex act and to attain immortality through sex. The Confucian culture, however, believed that sex was primarily meant for raising families. It advocated restrictions and regulations. Sex, purely for pleasure, was looked at as something undesirable. Concubines were permitted, though elaborate rules to regulate their conduct were duly put in place.

The present day China enjoys considerable freedom in the sphere of sex. In a recent survey over a fairly wide spectrum, only 15.26 % of the participants were found to hold the view that premarital sex was immoral. This percentage was as low as less than 7% in the 20-29 years age-group. No wonder, China meets 70% of the demand of sex toys in the world these days.

Buddhism generally takes the line that sex between two people who genuinely love each other is fair. The formality of marriage is inconsequential in this regard. The faith does lay down some principles in the area of sex, but no rules. Even homosexuality is not specifically barred. Aberrations are just 'akushala' (unskillful acts). Buddha once said, "Be a lamp onto yourself". Adherents are thus left alone to seek guidance in the matter from their own good sense. Some precautions have, no doubt, been talked about, but these are largely vague.

This, however, is the position with regard to the lay only. Otherwise, 'Vinay Pitaka' prohibits sex by monks and nuns. Touching females between collar bones and knees is also considered inappropriate. In Japan, celibacy has not generally been mandatory for monks. In AD 1872, the Meiji Government particularly allowed Buddhist monks and priests to marry. Nuns, however, were not granted this liberty. Monastic celibacy is now decided from sect to sect and in fact, from monk to monk basis.

Religions are deeply concerned with life that 'manifests itself in motion, growth, sensation and self-preservation'. After all, we have come to the world with mind, senses, desires and attachments. All religions, therefore, have a view on sex because it happens to be a biologic urge and is really inseparable from life. Many of them permit sex for the lay, both for pleasure and procreation. It is generally realised that celibacy is meant for the saints only and it is well beyond the capacity of the common. Some faiths place a much deeper meaning on sex. They see it as a Godly instrument of natural renewal.

## Note

1. Interview recorded under the title, "Love Makes you Flower" in the Speaking Tree section of the *Times of India* dated 13th February, 2011.

# 16

# Quest for Immortality

Both seers and scientists have been after the cosmic secrets for ages. They have tried to unravel the mysteries of life and universe in their own preferred ways. What they have said about the origin of life and all else that we see and imagine, has been constantly under review, the dogged insistence of religions about their own infallibility notwithstanding. In fact, the way science has been going for the last about a century or so, holds the hope that many more mysteries related to mind and universe, that earlier seemed to be beyond human comprehension, may well come within our grasp. Simultaneously, many of the old ideas and findings that religions and even science supported, may go for a toss. In fact, one view is that the machines that man has been creating may one day go beyond his brain or in other words, may overtake his intelligence. These super intelligent devices may then start creating more advanced entities of their own and even human brain may become redundant.

Anyway, the intricacies of what lies within us are no less wondrous than the mysteries of the cosmos. If and when our scientists are able to solve the question of consciousness— they hope to do so by the end of this century— it would certainly be a big leap forward towards understanding some of the ways of God. In that case, the religions shall also have to vacate quite some space that has been their preserve for a long time. This, in fact, has been the case all through. The advancement of human knowledge has been an unending embarrassment for those who have chosen to regard religion a business venture and have been feeding on faith. The positive elements of religions should, however, be prepared to welcome light from whatever source it shoots. After all, both seers and scientists are on the voyage of discovery. There do not have to be any violent ripples in the world of faith, as and when some truth gets discovered. After all, both are on the same page and after nothing but the truth. Science, in fact, can provide periodic logical support as well as course correction for spirituality. In any case, the religions would always be left with a vast turf to play with. Many other puzzles like, who or what God is, what lies beyond space, when the cosmic clock started ticking, what exactly 'nothingness' is and how it transmuted in to such a colossal mass of matter bubbling with energy; shall still be churning in human mind.

Consciousness is something what the Upanishads refer to as 'atamn' or soul. This is what makes a man feel that he is he— absolutely a unique being. Nobody else can be 'he'. Besides, we are human because we think— 'cogito, ergo sum'. Deciphering of consciousness would therefore lay bare a good part of the mystery surrounding life. After all, this is the quintessence of our being— the seat of self-awareness, social-sense, emotion, memory, reasoning ability and even personality. In fact, the religions are also lodged somewhere in our consciousness only. Body is just a casing for consciousness and mind really is the place where man lives. If the contents the brain could be preserved and taken care of separately, body would go disposable.

Our first curiosity with regard to consciousness would naturally be to know exactly where in our body it is lodged. Our heart is just a pump and liver, a purification facility— though we are often made to feel, as if these organs have something to do with the pulsations of our inner self, particularly the sensation of love. In the 17th century, a French philosopher, Reni Descartes thought that this life-force lay in the pineal gland of the brain. However, the view now is that it lies somewhere in the complex circuitry of the neurons called the spindle cells. Whatever be the truth about these findings, one thing is quite clear that consciousness has its home in brain. It is a kind of software that gets processed in our brain which itself could be construed as hardware. The two are thus integral to each other.

If science is to proceed further from here it would have to first locate the exact spot in brain which deals with this mystical phenomenon. The next stage would be to decode the information on these nerve cells and download this on some super capacity computers. The whole thing could be viewed this way: A baby is born with a blank memory (His memory disc may well be carrying baggage from his past life also, but that is not retrievable in the ordinary course. Anyhow, we shall come to this a little later.) Right from the first breath, the child begins receiving messages from his surroundings through his sensory organs. Thus, a plethora of sights, smells, sounds, flavours and feelings make their way to his memory and start getting accumulated there. In course of time, the processing power of the brain also comes in to play and he starts reacting to events in line with what lies embedded in his brain i.e. his experiences.

Consciousness can thus be considered as just another sensory organ or the sixth sense. Anything perceived through this sixth sense means that the brain has already worked on the issue in the light of the data stored therein and arrived at a solution, but the necessary calculations done by it have completely faded from its memory screen. This leaves us with a feeling that things are going to happen in a certain way, but we really do not know why.

Similarly, a computer mimics the human brain. It has a C.P.U. corresponding to the processing power of the brain and RAM for memory. Computer gets inputs through its keyboard, imaging and voice modulations, while brain gets these through the sensory organs. Computer displays the results on its monitor, whereas brain does it through bodily expressions and actions. The computing ability of the supercomputers has already touched around 1% that of brain.

The scientists from various disciplines are currently on the job of networking computer with human brain, so as to be able to download and upload data from one to the other. The effort is thus at digitizing the brain and replicating consciousness. At the moment science has very little purchase on the idea. Yet, the pace at which the computers are evolving and the tremendous progress made in the intricate areas like the genetics gives the hope that, sooner or later, consciousness would also get decoded.

We are told that the Cole Polytechnique Federale de Lusanne of Switzerland (EPFL) has already started making efforts to replicate a neocortical column of brain on an IBM computer. If this works, a number of such simulated cylindrical columns would be linked together to understand the working of what is known as the 'grey matter' in the brain. Once this is successfully done, the mysteries of consciousness would get unraveled.

Aubrey de Gray is of the view that a person who is to live 150 years may have already been born and the one who may live for 1000 years is in the coming in the next twenty years. In his lecture before the British Royal Academy of Science, he said that all this would be brought about through 'gene therapies, stem cell therapies, immune stimulation and a range of other medical techniques'. (*The Times of India*, July 6, 2011.)

Ian Pearson, the head of the futurology unit of the British Telecommunications, is hopeful that by 2050, computer technology would have advanced to a stage where it would be possible to download the contents in a person's cranium on to a supercomputer. Once this happens, it would also be possible to upload this digital copy in another brain. Initially these simulations may be crude and hazy, but these would get satisfactorily refined with time. The process would also get less laborious and may eventually come within the reach of common man. It is not difficult to understand the staggering implications of this development, related as it is to the overall 'beingness' or personality of a person. It would also open the doors to immortality for humanity.

Ray Kutzwell, in fact, goes to the length of asserting in his book, 'The Age of Spiritual Machines' that the current generation could be the last one to experience terminal death. The biological puzzle of death is thus waiting to be solved. Our mortality is presently tied to the durability of our hardware i.e. brain. Death occurs when this system crashes, just because it is not yet possible to save its contents (consciousness). If, sometimes in the future, it becomes possible to port the mind-file on to some back-up device, the human battle against mortality would end in a decisive victory to man. The prospect is, undoubtedly, fraught both with promises and perils that are impossible to predict immediately. Just imagine, finding yourself in another body and seeing your own body laid in front of you!

Science is also separately trying to push the bounds of biology to create artificial life from a scratch. In fact, this exercise has already begun in right earnest and some success has also been claimed. Life sprouts as the cells start splitting. This is precisely what happens when a male sperm comes in contact with the female ovum and fertilizes it. It is the spark of life that energizes the cells to multiply continuously till a being is born. Rather, this chain reaction lasts almost a life time and its stoppage is the signal of a life-cycle nearing its end. Several biologists are working in many parts of the world to create a synthetic cell i.e. a cell without an ancestor and have it activated somehow to get in a mode to multiply. What has been achieved till now is the injection of a computer generated artificial DNA into a bacterial cell by an American biologist, Craig Ventor. This energised cell was then seen splitting in a life-mimicking manner. What remains to be done next is the creation of a purely synthetic cell, capable of being fertilised artificially, followed by a control mechanism and refinement procedures. Once man is through with all this, he would reach a lot nearer God.

There is yet another interesting area, PLRT (past life regression therapy) where hypnotic science is active. This is based on the belief, as we noted earlier, that a life is born with the signature of its past on its memory disc. This information mostly goes unread and unnoticed. However, Brian Weiss in his best seller 'Many Lives , Many Masters' has opined, "The human soul is eternal and only keeps changing the body it inhabits". This is quite in line with the philosophy enunciated in these two verses from the Hindu scriptures:

वासांसि जीर्णानि यथा विहाय
नवानि गृह्णाति नरोऽपराणि।
तथा शरीराणि विहाय जीर्णा-
न्यन्यानि संयाति नवानि देही।।

— *Bhagavad Gita* Chapter-II, Verse-22.

(A person switches over to new clothes when the old ones get worn out. In a like manner, his soul finds a new body to lodge into after he discards the old one on death.)

न जायते म्रियते वा कदाचि-
न्नायं भूत्वा भविता वा न भूयः।
अजो नित्य। शाश्वतोऽयं पुराणो-
न हन्यते हन्यमाने शरीरे।।

—*Bhagavad Gita* Chapter II, Verse-20

(Soul neither takes birth nor it dies; nor was there any time when it was not there. It is unborn, immortal and primeval. Body may get slain, but soul always stays alive)

The thing in doubt is whether the data carried over from earlier lives can be recalled. Wiess and many other psychiatrists and hypnotic-therapists insist that this is possible and the information thus obtained can be used to deal with many neural disorders of the patient in this life. Similarly an idea about the psychic computers that can read minds has also been muted. In fact, researchers have already been able to prepare crude video footages of brain activity by stimulating it with visuals and even by inducing it through other means to recall the past occurrences.

All this is, of course, creating a lot of misgivings in the world of faith. It is true that as the human learning expands its sweep (lately, this seems to be happening almost at the speed of light), a vast swathe of religious turf will pass on to science. Religions, however, will still be left with lot of space to operate from. Even when the human brain is ultimately able to uncover some of the closely held secrets of life and nature, God is not going to lose even a bit of His greatness. After all, even brain is not our own creation— it is also a gift from God.

# 17

# Balance-sheet of Religions

Religions cast a sort of mystic spell on man and have thus been rightly referred to as the opium of the masses. Their brainwashing power is, indeed, enormous. No community or country can afford to ignore their magnetism. They are dear to man in a big way, as they are seen to stream from his soul and to be able to secure his next life. In some cases, nothing really matters to man before his religion. We are told that Prophet Abraham readied himself to sacrifice his son in response to a divine command. Once when the Sikh Guru Govind Singh decided to test the religious involvement of the gathering before him by his sword, the Faithful Five (Panj Pyaras) readily came forward to offer their heads. Every religion, in fact, expects its devotees to remain ever prepared for supreme sacrifice at the altar of their faith.

Religions have been formally around for about four thousand years, though faith in some form must have sprouted in man's mind as soon as he got blessed with intelligence. As discussed earlier, the religions are the dealers in future, rather than the present. They talk more about the next life, rather than the present one. Impermanence being the destiny of us all in this universe, man has always been fearful of his future, especially about what awaits him in the next life. The religions draw a good chunk of their sustenance from this fear. They make out that those who believe in what they say shall enjoy the bliss and comforts of heaven and the others shall end up in hell. Going by their word, since all religions are in minority in relation to the rest of the world, majority of us are destined to burn in hell, however pious and virtuous we may otherwise be. They seem to say that what really matters is not the piety but the affinity.

Religions generally believe in status quo and are allergic to change. They try to make us believe that whatever was worth knowing has already been revealed and man does not have to rack his brain any further. He could simply follow what he has been told. The religions are thus attributed with sameness and dryness of outlook. They do not admit alternatives or change or any scope for variety. Yet, there is also something colourful about them. The world would have certainly been a drier place to live, if not totally unlivable, had they not been around. The religions do have a shiny side to them also. There are, undoubtedly, a lot many entries on the asset side of their balance-sheet.

We may begin with these positives first. The most valued gift that we have got from religions is God. Science or any other rational apparatus would have been absolutely incapable of doing so. It is true that God would have walked into our consciousness otherwise also. In fact, as per the Hindu belief, divinity already lies buried somewhere within in all the living beings. Yet, confirmation from the religious community about the presence of God has its own significance. The entry of highest value on the balance-sheet of the religions is thus God. Religions truthfully confess that they do not exactly know who or what God is. However, His presence is manifest in matter, motion, energy, space, vastness and in fact, in all things infinite and eternal. Scientists, however, have always been suspicious about the 'proofs advanced for the existence of God by the religions and theologians'. They would have none of this unless He is uncovered before their eyes. This is something which may not happen ever, whereas man had a need for God in the past, has it now and shall always have it in the future.

The discovery of God is thus the best thing that has ever happened to mankind. At least man has some straws to clutch on to in his life beset with uncertainties. Belief in His eternal presence by his side has been a source of immense comfort to man. This has sustained him through many situations of humanly unbearable pain and misery. God has really proved to be the last flicker of hope for the faithful in hopeless situations.

Not just this, religions also give meaning to our mundane lives. Without Him man would have definitely felt lonely on this planet. Many individuals, after achieving everything material that they wished for (the Beatles, for instance) still found themselves restless, because everything in this universe suffers from impermanence. They finally felt the urge to turn soul-ward for solace. The soul-soothing property of faith, in fact, has never been in doubt.

Fear of future is deeply ingrained in human mind and keeps him perpetually uneasy. In this situation, one can easily understand what comfort philosophies regarding indestructibility of soul can bring to him. Another rejuvenating verse from the sacred Gita readily comes to mind in this context:

> नैनं छिन्दन्ति शस्त्राणि नैनं दहति पावकः।
> न चैनं क्लेदयन्त्यापो न शोषयति मारूतः।।
>
> —Bhagavad Gita Chapter II, Verse-23.

> (Neither weapon can pierce it (soul) nor can fire burn it; nor can water render it soggy; nor can wind dry it out of existence.)

Islam and Christianity also believe that human beings just pass on into a state of deep slumber on death. They are then raised to life on the Day of Judgement and dispatched to heaven or hell as per their deeds in life. Death is not thus the end of existence. Buddhism and Jainism believe in salvation for those who earn it on the strength of their noble deeds and rebirth for others. Religions are thus a message of hope for the minds worried over the looming uncertainties of future.

Man loves to hear about the secrets of cosmos hidden from his view. There is a vast area in the universe not accessible to science as yet and most of it may not come within its reach ever. Besides, the numerous things that still remain beyond our comprehension in this very universe, the view now is that there are numerous other universes that man does not have any idea about. A new word 'multiverse' has been recently coined to describe this phenomenon. Science has always been shy of stepping into such eerie areas. If religions also refuse to delve into this mystic domain, a vast expanse of the cosmos would stop flickering on the human radar. They are at least giving us a glimpse into what the multiverse might possibly be like, before the science is able to say something more definite about it.

As a moral force, the religions are an excellent teaching tool for man. They help to suppress his base instincts and push him towards good deeds, assuring him that these would not only bring him joy in this life, but would also smoothen the things for him in the next life. Religions thus promote appropriateness and orderliness in societies. As the penal laws are meant to be a deterrent against crime in social life, the fear of God has been invented to keep man away from the morally malignant practices in his private life. State and religion thus complement each other in this important area of repose in life. Religions lead to laws, some of which get codified and the others are just habitually obeyed. A state cannot legislate on all aspects of life. It cannot, for instance, start enacting laws for subjects like flying of kites. The enforcement ability of the state is all the more limited. A vast area of human activity has to be left to the good sense of man. Some legislation has to come from within us and lot many things have to move through self-discipline. Religions come handy here to tell man what is appropriate in day to day living of life. If the religions had not taught us to manage our private life smoothly at our own level, policemen would be sitting in our bedrooms to supervise our morality. Religions thus lend a big helping hand to the state in running the societies.

There is yet another area where the religions have made a stellar contribution— the preservation of man's history. Religions, in a way, are the mystified version of history itself. You demystify the religions by staining out the fuzzy philosophies and the stories that you know could not be true, you would find fair amount of genuine history peeping out of them. A lot of historical information can be gleaned out of the religious literature, architecture, paintings, sculptures and seals etc. Histories, as we are told, 'make men wise'. So, religions could be viewed as a vast repository of human wisdom and values. Though it has not been possible to decipher the ancient Indus Valley script so far, some of the religious symbols of the period in the form of seals and artifacts yield some valuable information about the ethos obtaining in the era. The indication is that Shiva cult, Phallic worship; Yoga and Jainism are rooted in this age. Vedic literature gives a clue that Indus Valley establishment was militarily weak and suffered reverses in their skirmishes with the hardy Aryans. The epics and scriptures like Iliad, Ramayana, Mahabharata, One Thousand and One Nights, Bible and Koran etc. contain a wealth of historical data in their folds. The temples, churches, mosques, monasteries, synagogues, statues and paintings left behind by the religions of the period are also an invaluable source of historical information. They speak the mind of our past.

The religions have done a singular service to the societies in the field of education also. In the earliest times, the starting point of all learning was the scriptural knowledge and creedal practices. The subjects like statecraft, legal codes, ethics, astronomy, health and medicine etc. got added later. Religions continue to sponsor and support a large number of schools and institutions of learning all over the world. The Gurukul schools of the Hindus, the Muslim 'madarsas' and the Christian seminaries have a definite and direct connection with their sponsors. The Buddhist University at Nalanda in India was a great institution of higher learning with a faculty of two thousand professors. It catered to advanced studies in subjects like mathematics, astronomy, history, political science, fine arts, medicine and military science etc. Sadly, it met a barbarous end at the hands of Bakhtiar Khalji in the $12^{th}$ century. The modern systems of education have, of course, largely got secularised.

The ancient Egyptian priests took the trouble of chronicling the eclipses with great diligence. That eventually made it possible to predict them. Religions must also be given credit for fixing our calendar, the high importance of which often gets overlooked. Had this facility not been there, our life would have been in confusion on many counts. The religious orders have also done some scientific work and have made their own contribution towards pushing the frontiers of human knowledge and civilisation forward. Faith, after all, is intuition-based and intuition is the starting point of all scientific curiosity and the urge for inquiry.

The religions seem to have a health angle to them also. According to a recent research led by Dr. Michael McCullough, the religious-minded people live considerably longer. He observes, "The odds of survival for people who rated higher on measures of public and private religious involvement were 29% higher than those who scored lower on such measures." The rationale behind this finding could be explained this way:-

(a) The religions are generally against the consumption of alcohol, abuse of drugs, smoking and excessive sex etc. These addictions are certainly life shortening.

(b) The Hindu scriptures have made a direct contribution towards physical as well as mental well-being of man by inventing the yoga system of exercise, which is now universally recognised. The Vedic literature also talks about many herbs, metals, minerals and procedures that heal. Ayurvedic and Sidha streams of treatment based on 'vata', 'pita', 'kapha' and the 'panch bhutas' (earth, water, fire, air and space) make absolute sense and have scientific basis. The other religions of the world have also earnestly applied themselves to this important area of human welfare.

(c) Religions teach you to respect life that comes directly from God. The Hindu scriptures enjoin that a person should wish to live for one hundred years, while keeping himself engaged in his 'karma' (duty) all through.

(d) Frequent attending of religious services, discourses, functions and festivals etc. means lively interest in social intercourse which translates in to a healthy attitude towards life, besides of course some physical activity too.

(e) The religions rule minds. When they assure you that there would be another life after the present one, it homes in as a highly invigorating impulse.

(f) Another feel-good vibe that religions transmit is that justice may be delayed, but it would never be denied. This gives mental strength to man to face adverse situations with fortitude and drive away any sort of depressions that might be quietly building up inside. There is a Hindu saying that 'chinta' (depression) is just another word for 'chita' (pyre).

The religions provide a better medicine for minds than any ever invented by the pharmaceutical systems of the world. Healthy minds translate in to physical wellbeing. Religions thus play a positive role in the sphere of public health, both directly and indirectly. The faith-healing power attributed to Jesus may also have something to do with the psychological impact of faith.

Religions, in fact, pervade the human life in totality. There is something for everybody in the religions. For the intelligent, there are stimulating philosophies; for others there are stories with morals. The holy days of a religion have been the holidays for its faithful. Mythological stories, plays, pilgrimages, fairs and festivals like Passover, Christmas, Eid, Dipavali and Guruparv etc. have been a major source of recreation for the communities concerned for ages. Religions rejuvenate and light up lives in many other ways also.

This, however, does not mean that they are all sweetness and light. In fact, grey is the pervading colour of life and hence that of the religions also. They certainly are not lily-white, as they try to make out to their faithful. The religions are a vast compendium of ideas about God, man, nature and the interaction among the three. The difficulty about their thinkers is that, after acquiring some clout, they start attributing conclusiveness to their ideas. They try to tag on divinity to their writings to lend infallibility and permanence to their word, so that they are able to rule minds even from their graves. These stale philosophies keep churning in societal psyches from generation to generation. The communities thus get in to the mode of moving in grooves. Religions have a tendency to close door on freshness of outlook and thus often prove a roadblock to the forward movement of the societies. Proper progress is possible only when they are firmly shown their place in the shrines and asked to stay there.

As already discussed, religions definitely have a communal dimension to them also that has kept the cauldrons boiling ever since the organised religions came in to being. While talking of one God on one hand, they also claim that He is in special relationship with them. It is often lost sight of that the universal God could not be a private God too. All this leaves one confused if there is really only one God of this universe. What about the numerous others created by various religions? Millions have been massacred over the millennia in the name of these man-made Gods. Even today this illusion is claiming thousands of victims every year. God, who has created man and all else, is remembered only when wisdom flashes occasionally in man's mind.

Dr. Sarvapalli Radhakrishnan has pointed out, "Nothing is so hostile to religion as other religions". Religions feel awfully threatened by one another and that is why they insist that the adherents of other faiths shall burn in hell, while their own faithful would end up in embrace with beautiful virgins in heaven. This perception is, in fact, the primary reason behind bulk of the violence that has been perpetrated on this planet in the name of God. It is not God, but the religions that are so paranoid about rivalries. This also erodes some of the moral authority of religions.

God is a cosmic truth, but it is also true that nobody has any idea who or what He is. Man prefers to see God in his own image and seems to have fitted his own brain on to Him. The religions, no doubt, admit Him to be an all-powerful, all-pervasive and all-knowing Being, but simultaneously they think nothing of projecting Him as a biased and vengeful Being who loses His shirt at the slightest show of disregard and has His gas chambers working overtime to deal with dissent. One really wonders that, after having blessed man with brain, why He would insist that he should not use it and just go by the word of the prophets. Let me put the weight of Albert Einstein, a spiritually inclined scientific genius, behind this argument. This is what he writes:-

> "I cannot imagine a God who rewards and punishes the objects of His creation, whose purposes are modeled after our own— a God, in short, who is but a reflection of human frailty".

Elsewhere he says, "Gott wurfelt nichet." (God does not play dice with His universe.) God is, in fact, far above what the religions often think of Him. One would rather prefer to believe that He is perpetually benign towards His entire creation.

Religions feed on fear of the faithful. They convert people in to the spiritually frightened beings. Bhagat Singh, a great martyr of the Indian freedom movement, who also happened to be intellectually inclined, is of the view that the religions are a disease born out of fear and these have been a source of great misery to mankind. It is precisely because of the fear complex that all sorts of superstitions get hardwired in human brain. Even the educated and the highly placed are not free from this delusion.

Not only man, but even societies and states are, in many ways, the prisoners of priests. On the other hand, the religions are also often too willing to get hijacked. They come handy for communal mobilisations. For this reason, political leaderships rarely miss the opportunity to involve religions in their machinations. The experience shows that priest and politician often join hands happily to exploit the people. Politics and religions ('Meeri and 'Peeri' in the Sikh parlance), indeed, make for a heady cocktail. It is another matter that the compound proves to be highly toxic for everyone in the end. It was the unholy alliance among the king, clergy and nobility against the common man that eventually jettisoned that political earthquake in the European continent in the eighteenth century which goes by the name of the French Revolution.

Religions, as the so called custodians of the divine will, project enormous power and power, for sure, corrupts. Religions are considered just next to God and their prophets as some sort of Second's-in-command of God. Since God has chosen to stay out of sight, the prophets and priests start legislating in the name of God. Those habituated to power and privileges do not let these go easily. Politicians often feel impelled to use religions both as shield and sword. This struggle to keep the turf often results in mortal intra-religion rivalries and atrocities on the common man. John Bowker sums up the situation this way:

> "The history of religious traditions has its full share of lunacy, shameless charlatans, and unspeakable crimes of intolerance, cruelty, bigotry, social oppression and self-opinionated nastiness."[1]

The worst thing about the religions is that they have been unfair to woman. Some of them have gone to the ridiculous length of suspecting whether she has been really provided with a soul inside. As already noted, St. Paul was of the view that the only purpose that woman serves is that of coition. How they have remained degraded and deprived for ages has already been narrated in an earlier chapter. The point, therefore, need not be rubbed here any further.

Religions are thus loaded with entries on both sides of their balance-sheet. They are an area of light and darkness at the same time; they bond people with the Divine, but also divide them in to communities; they are the fountainhead of both love and hatred, piety and pettiness; they are a source of comfort, but also of conflict as well; they emancipate but also enslave man— one could go on recounting like this endlessly. However, on balance, the religions have a positive purpose to serve. They, in their simplest and spiritual form, are essentially benign. Both their philosophers and the faithful are important and a source of sustenance and strength for them. It is only the elements having vested interests in status quo and stagnancy that periodically spoil the show for them.

## Note

1. 'The ways of Religion', Ed. Roger Eastman, Oxford University Press, 1999, p. XV.

# 18

# Future of Religions

Pope Benedict XVI lamented during his recent visit to Germany, "We are witnessing a growing indifference to religion in societies——". This notwithstanding, one could be sure that religions shall remain perpetually relevant. Religions are an indestructible phenomenon, as they have God and morality at their core. As confided by a cardinal before Napoleon, even the religions themselves do not have the capacity to destroy themselves. Thus, without going deeper into the matter, it could be safely said right at this stage that religions have a safe future and they are in the world for ever. The reasons for this are the following:

First, they deal with things infinite, eternal and unknown. Man has an inborn interest and curiosity in such eerie areas. Blaise Pascal describes this phenomenon like this: "Engulfed in the infinite immensity of spaces whereof I know nothing and which know nothing of me, I am terrified". However weak be the observations and assertions of the religions, they would always meet acceptance, because science is not in a position to present a comprehensive view of the cosmic mysteries. If religions also withdraw from the mystic domain, many aspects and areas of the universe would stop blipping on our mental radar. After all, man has been blessed with a vast capacity to imagine. There is no harm if he feels impelled to look into the regions beyond brain. In fact, nothing can really stop him from doing so.

Secondly, life is not logic alone. Rather, if we limit ourselves to bare logic, life would lose much of its lustre and go insipid.

There is place for both fact and faith in man's thinking. Human mind is quite accommodative of even the things that lie beyond the realm of reality. Yes, once reality shows up, it should be readily accepted. Religions should not refuse to see what gets placed before their eyes and progressively keep on vacating the territories that get lighted up by science.

Thirdly, fear of the unknown is a fact of life. Man would thus always remain fearful about his next life and would not like to take chances in this area. Concerns of future are more important to him than that of the present. Religions deal with future and would thus remain relevant to man.

Fourthly, the spiritual ingredient of religions is truly soul-soothing. It works to provide man comfort in pain and paucity. It takes the sting out of our disconcerting feeling of impermanence and having to leave this world finally in abject loneliness.

Fifthly, it is true that religions are generally not happy with enquiry (nobody, in fact, is). They encourage believing rather than thinking. In fact, they make out that believing blindly is something virtuous and suspecting is a sin. They seem to say that all the necessary thinking has already been done by the prophets and theologians and everything worth-knowing stands revealed. Brains and eyes are now relevant just to facilitate compliance of what has been long laid down. Otherwise also, thinking is something much more strenuous than believing and bulk of the humankind prefers to take the easier course of moving in a herd.

Sixthly, vast differences in the intellectual levels of the people would continue to provide sustenance to religions for all time to come. If all become equally intelligent, religions would find it difficult to survive. But this is something that would never happen.

Seventhly, it is impossible to unlearn what the humanity has already learnt. Religious doctrines, dogmas, traditions, practices, rites and rituals, with small evolutionary modifications in line with the changing needs of life, shall keep company with us for all time to come.

Eighthly, but not finally of course, the balance of advantage also lies in believing, rather than disbelieving.

Religions have risen out of intelligence and they would last till the last intelligent being is around on earth or elsewhere. However, in the most unlikely event of the mass intelligence rising out of their control or just dying out on the other hand, all religions would also die.

It is a fact that the religions have been constantly losing importance as man is getting more and more knowledgeable about his surroundings. Thus, the vast turf that they are still holding would be slipping through their fingers inch by inch. If science is able to create life artificially and solve the question of consciousness, religions shall have to vacate quite some area that they presently occupy. But the domain that they prevail over is really boundless. They may have to contend with constant clipping of their wings, but they would still end up holding a lot of space to flail their arms. Religions have been repeatedly proved wrong with regard to their cosmogonic conceptions. Yet, no Darwin, no Newton, no Copernicus has been able to upturn their applecart. Pope may not be enjoying the clout of the Holy Roman Empire days, but the institution is still immensely important to the Christendom and counts to the rest of the world also. The same is true of the other religious institutions.

Before proceeding further, let us run through the observations that readily appeal to our mind:-

(a) God is not a being of history— He is a timeless phenomenon beyond all history.

(b) He is in control of all terrestrial, atmospheric and celestial zones of the universe. Only He knows what lies beyond the farthest star and the space thereafter. Religions have a tendency to regionalize and to appropriate Him.

(c) 'The universe is He Himself incarnate'. In other words, universe itself is the evidence of His existence. After all, as St. Thomas Aquinas (AD 1224-74) puts it, mere nothingness could not have led to something or all that we see.

(d) Though He permeates all space and time, He is yet undiscovered and would remain so. We do not know who or what He is— a male, a female, a hermaphrodite, a bird, an animal, a light, a gust of breeze or just a formless eternal. He may well be a being or a phenomenon that we are just not familiar with. We, however, see Him in our own image, capable of being pleased with praise and getting infuriated at disregard. Man thus has a tendency to tag on human attributes to God. This is nothing but downgrading the Divine to our own low level. We would also prefer Him to be a male, as we perceive males to be superior to females.

(e) All life comes directly from Him. So, if religions are sacred, life is many times more sacred.

(f) The fact of quantum physics that elementary particles, such as electrons, are absolutely identical everywhere in terms of their mass, electric charge and spin, suggests that everything in the universe has originated from a single source.

(g) We do not understand His ways. Nevertheless, as our body is the outer covering of our soul, nature is the outer manifestation of the Divine reality. It is possible to know what lies around us in nature and also within our bodies. Our intelligence has already succeeded in demystifying some of the processes related to nature and our physical being and the frontiers of our knowledge in these areas are rapidly expanding. However, there is something more than just matter and mind. There is a vast unknowable area that would remain perpetually beyond the reach of our brain.

(h) One God, for sure, is everybody's God.

(i) From His height all would look equal—the Prophets and priests, the kings and, commons and the prosperous and poor.

(j) All religions are in minority with those of the rest of the world. Against one Christian there are at least two who do not subscribe to his faith. Against every Muslim, there are four non-Muslims. The Hindus constitute just around one sixth of the humanity. So, all have to understand and appreciate that their views are by no means universal. They have to be thus accommodative of the viewpoint of others.

(k) The religions have resulted in both emancipation as well as enslavement of man.

(l) The religions deal with the Eternal alright, but there is nothing eternal about them. No formal religions existed four thousand years back, whereas the earth itself (not to speak of the multiverse) is billions of years old.

(m) Should our earth get sucked in some black-hole some day, all our earth-related Gods, gods, prophets etc. would disappear without a trace. However, the One who has made man and all else—whoever, whatever, wherever He might be—shall always be around. His existence does not depend on man or anything else.

(n) Coming to our own times, there could perhaps be no greater gods than Mahatma Gandhi and Mother Teresa. They have been truthful and benign beings, a source of solace and comfort to the world. Miracles would also get tagged on to them with time. After all, what else do we expect from our gods? Undoubtedly, they shall have to wait for a good while for antiquity to put formal haloes around them.

But for the 'revelation' factor, bulk of the humanity would subscribe to the above views. However, there are some religions like Buddhism, Jainism, the Chinese indigenous faiths and a few others, who do not believe in God. Most of them, however, believe in divinity in some form or the other. The 'high heaven' element in the Chinese consciousness is quite an equivalent of God. Buddhism and Jainism at least believe in spirituality, if not God. Among the rest, the majority comprises of Agnostics rather than the outright atheists. So, the real contentious element is the belief in 'revelation' and the related question is, if it would survive.

It is true that the revelatory claims do violence to our rationality. If nobody is in physical touch with God today, it could be safely concluded that nobody ever was. The Hindu doctrine that truth prevails, presupposes that whatever humanity comes to believe is true. Faith is a fact in itself. Man has been walking this way all through the last three to four millennia i.e. ever since the religions were formally born. Nonetheless, though revelation is revolting to reason and is involved only to reinforce the theological message, it has to be respected, as it commands the habitual acceptance of the billions. Moreover, it may have something to do with the inner experiences of the thinkers. Man in deep meditation may sometimes really believe himself to be in communication with the divine. In any case, revelatory claims do not deserve to be viewed as a fraud on the humanity. So, even these would subsist.

There is no danger of the religions going extinct. Faith has already filled this earth with numerous gateways to God—churches, mosques, temples and synagogues etc. These are the man's response to the glory of God and His creation. These would always remain in place till man and earth are around. However, if they are to exist in radiant health, they would have to take care of some aspects. First, religions must stand on the bedrock of truth. The truth is that they are about God alright, but not from God. The illusions of eternity about the faiths are not in order. Religions should be happy enough over the fact that they have streamed from the best and noblest of brains, that too when they were thinking of the Creator. However, all religions that believe in God also claim contact with Him. In heart of hearts, one knows that revelation is in the realm of faith and not fact. It has to be appreciated that untruth is ungodly.

Secondly, excessive rigidity is the foremost weakness of religions. Freezing in the time frame can lead to both intellectual and spiritual suicide. Religions must have some stomach for change. After all, change is the law or rather the life of nature, the very beating of its heart. Nature, as one perceives, is a sort of front office of God. Nothing against the grain of nature is ever going to succeed. Movement is a sign of life and stillness symbolizes death. That is how the running waters remain pure. Life just cannot be lived according to the maxims and mandates fixed ages earlier. Lot of churning goes on in the societies as the times tick. Life cannot stick to what our ancestors thought was proper in their time. God was involved in the religious concepts only to check unbridled flexibility and appreciating the need for some discipline in life. Otherwise, there is nothing all that sacrosanct about what was written centuries back to regulate life on the patterns, deemed desirable then. If the old laws cannot be rewritten, these can at least be liberally interpreted, choosing to go by the spirit rather than the letter of laws.

Prophets have always appreciated the need for change in the existing orders and have displayed courage to live up to their convictions. Abraham and Moses brought about the shift from gods to God. Jesus had the daring to declare that the private God of the Jews was in fact everybody's God. If he had to hang on the cross for upholding this truth, the cross itself now hangs by the neck of one-third of the humanity. Prophet Mohammad had the guts to take on the well-entrenched pagan order in Arabia and thus set the sands alive.

Thirdly, nobody has been entrusted with the task of making all humans to think alike. Most of the religions carry the ambition of universalisation of their faith, in the mistaken belief that this was their bounden duty. Had this been the case, God would have just sent one person in the world with brain and the others could just go by his thinking. Rather, brain is the most mysterious organ of our being and the greatest gift of God. Nature, thus, wants everybody to think. 'Whatever is forced is never forceful'. Spirituality is something much bigger and broader than the religions. It should, therefore, never be allowed to be subverted. No religion should have an illusion that only its own devout are moral. Similarly, the concept of 'believers' and 'non-believers' has never been properly understood. It has always led to misunderstandings. If the religions really wish to universalize their appeal, they must welcome light from whatever corner it comes and should not feel shy of borrowing good features from one another.

All means, fair and foul, have been used by some religions to secure conversions to their faith. This has caused avoidable turmoil and bloodshed in the communities and countries. Religions, no doubt, should have the right to propagate their views, but shifting of faith should take place only when there is genuine change of heart. On the other hand, it is time for religions like Hinduism to throw their doors open for those who wish to be part of their communities out of some inner urge. Islam should not follow the policy of keeping their flock together on pain of death. The carefully selective policy that

Judaism follows in the matter of conversions seems to be the correct course. All should be free to follow their heart without any hindrance.

Fifthly, they would do well to withdraw from the legislative area and leave it to the will and wisdom of the state. God must be kept out of politics.

Sixthly, as Paramhansa Yogananda says, "You have to individually make love to God". The job of the thinkers is not to create institutions, but to help us to look within ourselves. The future of religions, therefore, lies in promoting self realisation.

There are other smaller things that religions shall have to take care of like emphasis on piety rather than ritual practices; realistic attitude towards celibacy and birth control; orientation towards conciliation rather than conflict and ensuring that their faith does not fracture communities and so on. They are meant for the spiritual welfare of the societies and their attention should be mainly riveted on this aspect.

All said, the spiritual content of all the religions is basically benign. They have the good of humankind at heart. A lot of thinking has gone in to the philosophies and codes that various religions have produced over the ages. These just need to be kept in tune with the times. Christianity teaches us to steer clear of sinful propensities; Islam advocates equality; Hinduism asks man to look within; Buddhism and Jainism plead for piety and nonviolence. Confucianism stresses the need for some discipline, orderliness and respect for the elders. Taoism wants life to flow serenely in harmony with nature. All thus simply believe in living the life well.

Aryans and Jews were the first to discover the concept of God and His oneness. One really needs to build further on these ideologies in line with the changing contours of life. Religions are like the banyan trees providing shade and solace to the communities. However, they do collect lot of weed at their base which needs periodic plucking. If the founders of various religions were to suddenly rise from their graves, they would be aghast to find what their followers have made of their ideas. Still, the view of some that world would be better off without religions sounds to be a rather casually drawn conclusion. They would, in fact, prove to be a great gift of God to man, if ways and means could be found to push their spiritual content to the fore—well ahead of their communal propensities. All open-eyed intellectuals would like the faiths to fuse, because they have the same belief at their core. Is there any religion which says that there are two or more Gods of this universe?

# Bibliography


Amir Khusrao, Nuh Sipihr, Ed. Mohd. Wahid Mirza, Islamic Research Series No. 12 (London).

Anthony West, *All about the Crusades*, W.H. Allen, London, 1967.

Anwar Sheikh 1998, *Islam—The Arab Imperialism*, The Principality Publishers, Cardiff (U.K.).

Arvind Sharma Ed., *Our Religions*, Amazon.com (Dis.), 1994.

Beckerlegge, *World Religious Reader*, Routledge, 1998.

Clarence Burton Day, *The Philosophers of China*, Peter Owen Ltd., London, 1962.

Charles Bell, *The Religion of Tibet,* Oxford University Press, 1931.

Sir Charles Iliot, *Japanese Buddhism,* Edward Arnold, 1935.

David Barret, *World Christian Encyclopedia*— Available with the Amazons, 2001.

George T. Kurian, Todd M. Johnson, *A Comparative Survey of Churches and Religions in the Modern World.*

George Foot Moore, *History of Religions*, Charles Scribbler's Son, New York, 1948.

Gorden Stowell Ed., *Book of Knowledge*, The Waverly Book Co. Ltd., Farrington Street, London.

G. Buhler Tr., *The Laws of Manu,* Clarendon Press, Oxford.

H.A.R. Gibb, *Modern Trends in Islam*, University of Chicago Press, 1949.

H.H. Wilson Tr., *Rig Veda Sanhita*, Cosmo Publications, New Delhi, W.F. Webster Ed. 1977 (Reprint).

James Legge, *The Four Books,* Henry F. Fay, Seoul, Sout Korea.

Jawahar Lal Nehru, *Glimpses of World History*, Lindsay Drummond Ltd.

J. Jaini, *Outlines of Jainism*, Cambridge University Press, 1916.

John B. Noss, *Man's Religions*, The MacMillan Co., New York, 1949.

J. Takakusu, *Essentials of Buddhist Philosophy,* University of Hawii Press, 1949.

Judith Miller, *Sacred Imagery*, World Publications (MA), 1998.

Mohammad Iqbal, *Reconstruction of Religious, Thought in Islam*, Oxford University Press, 1934.

O.A.Wall, *Eroticism in the Religions of the World*, Mayur Publications, Delhi, 1986 (Reprint).

Pandit Shri Ram, Sharma Acharya, *Rig Veda Sanskriti Sansthan*, Barelly, 1993.

Patwant Singh, *The Sikhs*, Harper Collins Publisher India, Pvt. Ltd., 1999.

Paul Radin, *Primitive Region,* Dover Publications Inc., New York, 1957.

Robert Ellwood, *Words of the World Religions,* 1977.

Roger Eastman Ed., *The Ways of Religions*, Oxford University Press, 1999.

Prof. Satyavrata Sidhanalankar, *Glimpses of Vedas*, Millind Publications Pvt. Ltd., New Delhi, 1980.

Stevenson Sinclair, *The Heart of Jainism*, Oxford University Press, 1915.

Swami Madhavanda Tr., *Brhadaranyaka Upanisad Swami Yogeshwarnanda Advaita*, Ashrama, Almora (India), 1950.

V.P. Mehta, *Crusades—Cross vs Crescent : Longest War in History*, Arun Publishing House Pvt Ltd, 2004.

W.S. Urguhart, *Pantheism and Value of Life in Indian Philosophy*, Ajay Book Service, New Delhi, 1982. (Reprint)

Wendy Doniger, *The Hindus—An Alternative History*, Penguin, 2009.

Wing-tsit Chan, *Religious Trends in Modern China*, Columbia University Press, 1913.

# Index